Some Luck

Some Luck

JOHN BIRD

HAMISH HAMILTON
an imprint of
PENGUIN BOOKS

HAMISH HAMILTON

Published by the Penguin Group
Penguin Books Ltd, 80 Strand, London WC2R ORL, England
Penguin Putnam Inc., 375 Hudson Street, New York, New York 10014, USA
Penguin Books Australia Ltd, 250 Camberwell Road,
Camberwell, Victoria 3124, Australia
Penguin Books Canada Ltd, 10 Alcorn Avenue, Toronto, Ontario, Canada M4V 3B2
Penguin Books India (P) Ltd, 11 Community Centre,
Panchsheel Park, New Delhi – 110 017, India
Penguin Books (NZ) Ltd, Cnr Rosedale and Airborne Roads,
Albany, Auckland, New Zealand
Penguin Books (South Africa) (Pty) Ltd, 24 Sturdee Avenue,
Rosebank 2196, South Africa

Penguin Books Ltd, Registered Offices: 80 Strand, London WC2R ORL, England

www.penguin.com

First published 2002
1

Copyright © John Bird, 2002

The moral right of the author has been asserted

Set in 12/14.75pt Monotype Dante
Phototypeset by Intype London Ltd
Printed in Great Britain by Clays Ltd, St Ives plc

A CIP catalogue record for this book is available from the British Library

ISBN 0–241–14158–3

To Tessa, Theresa, Eileen, Linda, Pip and Lucie;
and to Kate de Pulford, who didn't get the chance
to be a mother.

Acknowledgements

I would like to thank my agent, Barny Allan, for all his support and friendship; Simon Prosser, who commissioned me and encouraged me throughout the writing; Tessa Swithinbank, Sinead O'Keeffe and Sarah Brown, who helped me meet my deadline; Fabrice, Felix, Phillippe, Dana and Diana from the city of Lille, who made me welcome. My friends Barbara Carter, Anthony Clarke Granville Grenfell, Danny and Wendy Keen, Maureen and Finbarr Martin, Terry Monaghan, Jack Plant, Cara Solomon and Brian Taylor for their patience and endurance. Phil Ryan, for all the hard work he did. My wonderful children, Emily Jane, Paddy Jack and Eileen Diana, and my son-in-law, Anthony Epes, for their inspiration and humour. My godchildren, Hannah Kate and Charlie Jake Russell Teare, for being their beautiful little selves. Fay and Phil Russell for their warmth and friendship. And Anita and Gordon Roddick, who gave me the chance.

Contents

PART ONE

Bad Name for Dogs

I

On the steps of the church the old man spoke to his dog: 'Bite him, boy. Bite him.'

The dog growled, but stayed put.

'Bugger you, dog.'

He hit the dog's nose. The dog whined.

'Bastard dog. A year ago he'd have had your arm.'

I was pleased that the mangy-looking Alsatian hadn't responded, but I didn't understand what the man's problem was – I'd only asked if he wanted to sell a street paper called the *Big Issue*. I asked him again.

He erupted. 'Bloody *Big Issue*, I've been out of work for twenty-five years. I don't need any of that.'

'Suit yourself.'

Later, 100 people assembled in the crypt of St Martin-in-the-Fields in Trafalgar Square. I saw the old man among them, sitting and waiting for the meeting to begin. His dog lay quietly beside him.

The speeches started. Anita Roddick described the importance of the founding of a street paper. Fearfully I sat beside her, dreading the moment when I had to stand. I looked around the room and noted the cameramen and the reporters with their notebooks. I tried to look calm. I smiled at a few people I knew. I stood and began to speak. I spoke loudly about the need for a street paper that provided work for homeless people. I looked down into the audience and saw a friend. He looked at me quizzically and his face unnerved me, so I looked away and ploughed on.

It was the first day, 11 September 1991. The crypt of a church in the centre of London. We'd wanted to launch in a place that befitted the image of a street paper; somewhere with the right feel.

And St Martin-in-the-Fields was often awash with homeless people.

We were exhausted by it all. Tired of the contempt of many homeless charities, of many homeless people. Tired of the specialist publicists who gave us advice as though we were starting a society magazine. The endless advice from people who knew better but had never done it themselves. No one had done what we were doing, yet the advice came thick and fast. You just had to smile at these people. Smile and think 'Arsehole'.

When the meeting was over, my friend came up to me, still with his quizzical face. He said he didn't know what I'd said, but whatever it was I'd said it with power.

'You know what they say: "It's not what you say, it's how you say it."'

I smiled at this.

We climbed the stairs into the bright sunlight. Everyone talked to me at the same time. Gordon Roddick shook my hand.

'Now the work begins.'

'Thanks for reminding me.'

I saw the old man with the dog. He had a scowl on his face. I pushed my way forward to talk to him, asked him if he'd signed up.

'I need the money. My "Big Issue" is that I ain't got a pot to piss in.'

'That's why we started it up.'

He flared up again. 'Yeah? I fucking hate you do-gooders. You middle-class arseholes. What d'you know about hunger and homelessness? Eh? Public-school tossers.'

'You've got it wrong, brother.'

'Don't fucking "brother" me.'

His dog, for the first time, leapt around. Strained at the end of its string leash. It opened its old mouth and showed its old teeth. I had a strong feeling of hatred for both the dog and the old man.

A publicist took my arm and led me towards a car. I was pushed into the back seat. A woman sat beside me, started talking about my speech. I couldn't listen. I still felt angry about what the old man had said. I was not a do-gooder. But he'd pulled rank on me, suggested that I knew nothing of poverty. In earlier times, I probably would have hit him.

The woman continued to talk as we made our way to a radio station. I continued to ignore her, trying to forget the words of the old man that had made me so angry.

2

It was a speck in the sky, floating high above me against the clouds. The speck circled and dropped level with the rooftops. Now I could see that it was a bird, an eagle. I could make out its wings as it corkscrewed down towards the street. It circled once again before landing on the handlebar of the big pram I was sitting in.

The eagle turned its head and looked at me in a wild way. Then it took off, causing the pram to rock. I watched the eagle climb and corkscrew again above the houses. Away from the people who would wonder what an eagle was doing in Notting Hill. In the summer of 1947, visiting a child of eighteen months.

My mother said I was always too quiet in the street, daydreaming to my heart's content. She said no one was that quiet unless they were wrong in the head. Perhaps this was my first invention, an eagle visiting the slum streets of West London. Maybe I'd really seen a pigeon, but that's not how I remembered it. In later life I was always mocked when I talked about this, my first memory. I must have made it up, to suggest some sign of later greatness. Yes: at best, it was a pigeon.

I was born in Notting Hill in January 1946, not long after the end of the Second World War. I was premature, my parents' third child. Thomas Henry was born in 1943, Patrick Finbarr in 1944, and then me, John Anthony. My father was a Protestant and my mother an Irish Catholic. He signed the necessary papers for us children to be brought up Catholic.

My mother, Eileen Mary Dunne, was born in Mallow in County Cork and in 1939, as a girl of eighteen, she left Ireland to escape farm life. She'd hoped to work as a nurse at the London Hospital in Whitechapel. Instead she became a barmaid in the Golden Cross pub on Portobello Road, Notting Hill.

As war began to look certain, her mother sent her money to return home. But Eileen stayed put, preferring the crowds, the boys and the pubs of London to the life she'd had in backwater Ireland.

One Monday night, days before war was declared, she went on a pub-crawl with a girlfriend. They walked Portobello to Notting Hill Gate, then turned off the main road. Slightly drunk and with fun in mind they ended up at the Princess Alexandra, just round the corner from where Eileen lived with her elder sister, Kathleen.

In the Princess Alexandra my mother sat with her friend at the bar and listened to the pianist play popular songs. She liked the look of him – she thought he looked like Humphrey Bogart, with his high forehead and intense eyes. He noticed her, too, and when she requested 'Danny Boy' he played it softly. And then he played 'When Irish Eyes are smiling'. Later, Eileen said it brought tears to her eyes.

Alfred Ernest Bird played most nights, for beer money. He liked a drink and being paid in pints suited him because he had a day job as well, in a bakery. He was twenty-one, shy and short but powerfully built. He lived at home with his widowed mother and young sister. Alfred's family were local working people; they'd lived in Notting Hill since before the First World War. Alfred had five brothers and a sister. When he was a boy they'd lived with their parents in a small flat above a stable in a mews, crammed into two bedrooms. His father was gassed in the trenches and died seven years after the war was over, leaving Alfred's mother alone to bring up seven children. But the father had been useless after the gas attack – he would sit in the street near the Princess Alexandra and sip beer.

Alfred had little experience with girls and Eileen had to do most of the running. He was too fearful to visit her in the Golden Cross, but he would hang about outside on the corner. Eileen found his shyness endearing but said it was almost crippling. He was a man of few words; she was a girl of many words. It was she who suggested they should go for walks in the park or visits to the cinema on her free Sunday afternoons. She said that if she'd left the courting to him it would have taken a month of Sundays. So she pushed on, and they soon became a couple.

When war was declared Alfred was called to attend an army medical but was never conscripted. The reason for his exemption is not clear. Perhaps it was thought that as the youngest boy of a widowed mother he should stay at home to care for her and his sister. Or perhaps he was considered unfit for service because of his voice impediment: he had a deep voice, rough and difficult to understand; at times it would disappear completely and he could only whisper. It may have been that he was saved from army life because all his brothers were signed up; the Birds were already doing their bit for King and Country.

Alfred and Eileen married in 1941 and moved into two ground-floor rooms in a house in St Stephen's Gardens, close to the Princess Alexandra where Alfred continued to play the piano. They had the main front room and one at the back which had been converted into a kitchen. Both rooms had fine features. Decorative plasterwork edged the ceilings and ornate rose patterns held the central light-fittings. There were solid skirting-boards and big windows. From the kitchen a balcony led out to the communal gardens.

By the time I was born, dirt and poverty were everywhere. The gardens were a mass of black earth and the trees and flowers had long gone, replaced by dumped bedsteads and old prams. Street children played in mud and filth among broken bottles and the like, and were always cutting themselves on the glass.

When they started a family the kitchen became my parents' bedroom. Tommy, Pat and I slept in the front room. My bed was two small, pushed-together armchairs that separated as the night wore on. A naked light hung from the ceiling rose directly above me. My parents entertained visitors at a large table in the corner. They sat smoking, drinking beer and listening to sport on the wireless.

Tom, my mother's young brother, spoke the loudest. He had a hard, piercing Irish voice that cut through the nights he sat at the table in the front room. He worked on the railways and went out drinking with my father. Tom spoke out about Ireland and what the English did to his mother country. My mother made comments about Adolf Hitler. She didn't see the bad in Hitler because he never did anything against the Irish. Tom would join in. My father would never argue but he'd just sit silently, drawing on his hand-rolled cigarettes.

My Uncle Ted's wife was called Alma. She was dark-skinned with a gentle, beautiful face. She came from Egypt and had met Ted in Alexandria when he was on leave with the Eighth Army during the war. Ted was my father's brother, a regimental sergeant-major. Alma spoke softly in flowery English. Listening to her I would almost fall asleep. Her voice was like a lullaby and her gentle hands would stroke my face. She called me an angel and said she hoped I would never grow up. When my mother complained about my quietness, Alma would protest. She said that not all boys had to roar and be noisy.

My mother's concern was that I might have been damaged at birth. That the hospital hadn't looked after me properly. She thought that because I was born premature I should have been cared for better. That, she said, accounted for my silence. But she loved telling everyone that she could put me in the street in the big old pram and completely forget about me. I'd happily sit and watch the world of dogs and strolling policemen pass me by while girls stuck their faces in mine. As though I was a fixture of the street, like a lamppost or a post box.

Tommy and Pat and I made the best of the noise and tried to sleep through the night. I would lie looking at the plasterwork patterns repeated round the edges of the ceiling. Tommy and I would stir; Pat would sit up in bed. We would be soothed back to sleep. The naked lightbulb hanging above me gave me the most problems. I longed for it to be turned off. As we slept through the

9

voices beneath the thick cigarette smoke, the naked lightbulb would feature in my dreams.

In the street the houses were black. Blackness was everywhere. We were surrounded by the dirt of the slums. My mother fought a war against the dirt. Tommy and Pat were boys of the street, forever needing to be washed and cleaned up.

From the pram it was a street of horses and carts, of children playing hopscotch and hide-and-seek. Old ladies sat out on the steps in their dark clothes, smoking and talking. Sometimes they'd come and fuss over me, check if I was all right in my great big pram. We were part of some big family that stretched the length of St Stephen's Gardens. We were the young Birds, Tommy, Pat and I, among this big family who spent most of their time outside on their doorsteps.

The eagle story might sound unlikely, but it's there among my first memories. I also remember music, the strains of American big bands, played so loud it shook the windows of our flat. My mother was wild about America. She mused that when she left the farm she could have gone to New York or Chicago to stay with cousins. But Notting Hill was where she landed and where she reared her family of boys. At times she regretted her decision and I think American big-band music was her consolation.

You could hear the rag-and-bone man from far off. As he pushed his barrow up the street he shouted his loud call to bring out your junk. People would flock to give him their cast-offs and he'd swap gifts for pieces of old or broken furniture – a surprise for a child, perhaps, a balloon, or a cloth to cover a worn-out table.

The tallyman would sell you ornaments and cutlery and dish towels. You didn't have to pay him there and then; he'd pick up the money later. He was a kindly man, and would run his hand through your hair and marvel with your mother at the wonder of you.

Sitting quietly, I'd watch the dogs chasing each other or trying to catch the cats that were wiser and cleverer than them. The cats would climb on to walls and arch their backs, hissing and spitting at the stupid dogs that could never catch them.

Soon I got too big for the pram and was allowed to stagger my way round by our front door. My mother would sit, smoking a cigarette and reading a magazine, her hair rolled up in a scarf. She'd be observant but lost in her read – until I tried to go too far or she had to call down the street for one of my brothers to come back because they'd strayed too far towards the main road.

As I grew older I was allowed to wander up and down the street. There was a mews I'd sometimes go down, where big carthorses lived in stables. The smell of horses was in the air we breathed. The smell of horses and manure. The big carts they pulled were loaded with goods and a driver would be sat on top with his whip. The horses slobbered, streaks of spit hanging from their mouths. They always looked tired and worn, as though they could only just move their big loads.

One time I was about to go into the mews when a horse came running out of the entrance, its reins swinging as it rushed into the street and down towards the main road. It got to the corner and turned again, back into the mews. I stood looking down the street for a moment, feeling frightened, then I carried on walking and entered the mews. There, lying on the cobblestones, was the horse. It was struggling to get up and men had come out of the stable and were trying to control it. I stood and watched until the men shooed me away. I went straight home to my mother but I couldn't tell her what had frightened me.

Another time, I saw a more fearful sight. As I walked to Aunt Alma's place I noticed an old woman climbing the few steps in front of a house. She stumbled and fell backwards on to the pavement in front of me. I heard the sound of her head hitting the ground and then saw a gush of red-black blood spilling out around her. I stood watching in horror as she lay there groaning on the ground before me. People came out to help her and then a van arrived and took her away. But now the blood had flowed across the pavement and was dripping into the gutter. I stood looking at the red-black blood, watching it as it made a small puddle in the gutter. Again I ran back to my mother, but again I couldn't tell her what I had seen. I tried, but I couldn't find the words.

My father got a job as a milkman, so he would leave the house early in the morning before we awoke and not come back till the afternoon. As I was the youngest, he would make a fuss of me and would sometimes bring back little gifts. I used to sit and wait for him on a piece of waste ground where a pub had been bombed in the war, watching the corner and hoping he'd come soon. Then he'd arrive, and would smile and pick me up and show me the toy he'd brought me.

One day he brought home a pack of balloons for me. We stood in front of the house and he blew them up, all different colours. My brothers came up and begged for a balloon, but they were mine and I cried at the thought of them having one. And I cried more when a balloon got free of my hand and drifted off into the sky. I stamped and ran around in circles until my father soothed me and carried me into the house.

I knew my father loved me the most. I was the special boy; Tommy and Pat weren't loved like me. Tommy and Pat could play with other boys in the street. But I had my father – and that was all I needed.

3

It was 1949 and I was three years old. There was great excitement in the house. My mother stood on the steps with a letter in one hand and a cigarette in the other, her hair tied in a scarf. She laughed. 'For the love of God, Tony, we're going to Ireland!'

In the envelope there were big pieces of paper that I recognised as money. She read the letter again and counted the money again. Then she looked at me and smothered me with kisses.

'We're getting out of this fecking place.'

That night, Uncle Tom came round and sat with my parents drinking beer from brown bottles. My mother kept leaping up and down, pouring herself another glass of beer. My father sat as he always sat: sipping beer and rolling himself cigarettes. Tom was going on about Ireland. Tommy, Pat and I sat and watched the three of them till we were told to go to sleep. I asked my parents to turn out the light but they didn't. The room filled with cigarette smoke and the clink of glasses kept us awake.

The big fuss carried on for days. Then instead of being put to bed one night we were taken to the bus stop on the main road. As we stood waiting for the bus, my parents and Uncle Tom talked about the fun we were all going to have.

At Paddington we boarded the train for Ireland. We sat among other people and were told to sleep on the seats, given pop and biscuits to keep us quiet. I soon fell asleep and the next thing I knew we were on a boat. It was rocking and I felt sick. We were sitting in a bar on the boat and my father and Uncle Tom were drinking from big glasses. The place seemed full of people singing and drinking. I became sicker and my mother took me up to the deck. She got me to lean over the rail and I vomited. The black of the sea rising and falling below us frightened me. I thought my mother was going to drop me. I cried and was sick again, then she took me back down to sleep in the bar with the others.

We arrived an age later and I was put to bed. My brothers seemed no worse for the journey. I woke in a strange room and I walked downstairs in the dark house. In the kitchen I saw only strangers; a dark-dressed old lady sat with two men in caps. They smiled and laughed as I came into the room. A big fire roared in the grate. The old lady grabbed me and I screamed – she frightened me with her strange look. And the two men came up and kissed me. I had never seen them before in my life.

My mother came in with flowers in her hand. She told me that the old grey lady was her mother, but I couldn't see how such a thing was possible. And these were her brothers, the two men in flat caps. I clung to my mother as the old lady tried to get me from her.

We went out into the farmyard. There were chickens everywhere, and dogs that sniffed me and offered me their paws. Through a gate was a pink-looking pig. Everything was different from Notting Hill. My father was off somewhere with my Uncle Tom and I couldn't see my brothers anywhere. I clung fast to my mother and she laughed at me. She was home, but I was not.

In the dark house that night we all sat in the kitchen. The men in the flat caps and the old lady smoked from pipes. Another man came in, big and old; he ran his rough hand over my face.

'This is my father, Tony', my mother said as she stood by the big old man. He looked like the kind of man who might live in one of the basements back in Notting Hill – the kind of old man who had no family. I looked at him but could not understand that he was the father of my mother. My own father looked so different, sitting making a cigarette by the fire, talking to the other two men. The big old man put out his hand again and ran it through my hair. It was like being touched by sandpaper.

I was sharing a big bed with my mother and father. There was a candle in the room that they blew out when they got in. I slept between them all night, and when I woke I soon closed my eyes again.

This was Ireland. Green fields, and pigs and chickens, and people who wanted to hold me as though I were their own. People dressed in old torn shirts, like they were going to work on building sites. My grandmother had an old broom that she used as a walking stick and my grandfather used a piece of tree – it even had green leaves growing from it.

In the morning it was raining. After breakfast my mother stood me at the big window and pointed out the hills and the rain. She said you could watch the rain coming down from the hills, a long way away.

There were cows in the field, her father's cows. And the dogs and the pigs behind the gate, as well as the chickens. And she was so pleased at everything.

They gave me Wellington boots to wear. The boots were too big for me, so to stop them slipping off they stuffed paper in the toes. Then when the rain had stopped my mother took me out to walk down the lane. She showed me the big hole in the ground where they got water from. There was a bucket that she filled by dropping it down the hole on a piece of rope. She told me I had to keep away from the hole. When we got back to the house she emptied the water into a big barrel.

The house was lit by lamps and when you went upstairs to bed you took a candle. The house was big and there was darkness everywhere, except where there was a lamp.

After a while it didn't seem so strange. I got used to the darkness of the house and to the old grey-haired lady who talked to herself. She talked to the cat and the dogs, and even to the chickens. One time in the farmyard she leant down and grabbed a chicken, then swung it in the air as I stood watching beside her. Round and round she swung it until it stopped making a noise. Then she went inside and started pulling off its feathers. I couldn't believe what I had just seen. How could the old lady be so nasty to a chicken?

In a field behind the house there was a railway line. We were told to watch out if we crossed through the gates to the next field. Every now and then a train would pass and there'd be people hanging out of its windows. Everyone waved at the people on the trains.

When we were settled I slept in a bed with one of the men, Uncle John. He'd get up early in the morning and I would wake and go downstairs with him. He would make me a cup of sweet tea and then I'd be sent back to bed while my grandmother made breakfast. The old man, my grandfather, would be sitting looking into the fire. He said very little, and when he spoke to me I never understood him. I couldn't understand anyone unless they spoke slowly. My grandmother would laugh because I didn't understand her. Then she'd call me a 'little Cockney' and laugh even more.

Uncle John was the best of them. He was fun to be with. He would carry me on his shoulders, and chase me in the farmyard. At night I would always sit on his lap by the fire and I would sit beside him when we ate at the big table in the middle of the room. He made a fuss of me, saying that I was his little John – though everyone called me Tony.

My father and Uncle Tom had to go back to London. They left on the back of a cart to go down to the station. Later my mother rushed into the kitchen and pulled me out into the field near the railway line. Everyone lined up to watch the train go by. And there were Uncle Tom and my father, waving from the windows of the train. It was bad seeing them leave but soon I forgot about their going. There was so much to do on the farm.

Tommy and Pat spent all their time out in the fields with my grandfather. I would always be near the farmyard. My mother kept telling me not to wander off, but I would go down to look at the big hole with the water. One time I was in the lane when sheep came down over the hill towards me. I was frightened of them and ran back into the farmyard. But John took hold of me and as the sheep passed the house he put me on the back of one: there was nothing to fear from the sheep.

I loved John like I loved my father. But one day I hurt him. We were standing in front of the house and I picked up a stone and threw it at his head. He got mad and chased me. Then he shook me again and again. I cried; I loved him so much that I wanted to hurt him.

My mother and my grandmother were crying. We had to pack. I started to cry and John took hold of me and squeezed me. My brothers cried too. Soon we were on the back of the horse and cart and being taken to the station. Later the train went by the farm, and we waved as everyone waved back at us.

It turned cold. Now we didn't play out in the street; there were no adventures outdoors. Tommy and Pat were at school and it seemed to rain most of the time. The streets and houses were blacker than ever. No green fields, no chasing chickens and poking the pig with a stick through the wooden gate. No riding on the back of horses. I asked my mother why we hadn't stayed in Ireland. Why couldn't we live there forever? Away from the black houses and the naked light bulb. Weren't we happy in Ireland?

'Your father has to work,' she said, looking as sad as me.

Sometimes after my brothers finished school we would wander down to Portobello. I was not allowed there on my own because there were too many people in the market. We would walk among the stalls and pick up orange and vegetable boxes, and we'd have to plead with the men who ran the stalls. When we got boxes, we'd tie string to them and drag them off up the streets that led away from the market. We'd knock on doors and try to sell the boxes as kindling for starting coal fires.

One time I had three boxes in tow and my brothers were further up the street. I knocked at a house and an old lady came out.

'Kindling, missus.' She bought the boxes and gave me two pence, but I had to help her carry them into the kitchen where I helped her break them up. She was nice and asked me about my family. I told her I was Alfred Bird's son.

She smiled. 'I know your grandmother, sonny. The widow Bird. And I used to know your grandfather, God bless his soul.'

She made me a cup of sweet tea and a sandwich of jam and butter and I sat with her while she talked to me about my family.

Out in the street again my brothers went mad. They thought I had been kidnapped. Tommy grabbed me and shook me. The old lady stood on the doorstep and told them to leave me alone. They were happier when I showed them the two big brown pennies she'd given me.

I knew nothing about my father's mother. She lived round the corner from us, in the same small flat that my father had grown up in, but we never saw her. It was strange, hearing from someone else about my grandmother and my dead grandfather. What else was there to know about my Notting Hill family? I now knew my mother's family in Ireland better than I knew the people close by.

We sold lots of wood as the days and nights got colder. Towards Christmas we spent more and more time down at the market getting boxes. It got more difficult because there were always other boys doing the same thing. Pat would fight with them; he was very brave. Tommy would watch with me as Pat beat off the other boys. Pat was the bravest of us and didn't mind if he got hit. Tommy and I were useless.

On Christmas Eve I was unable to sleep properly, and I woke early on Christmas Day. Tommy and Pat were already up, opening presents, pulling crackers and eating oranges and chocolate. Beside me was a strange-looking metal horse. It had the same look as the crazy horse that had fallen down in the mews. I sat and looked at it for a long time. It seemed so mad, with its staring eyes. I told my mother it frightened me and she said not to be so silly.

I rode the horse madly. I had to push down on the pedals to make it move forward. Tommy and Pat tried to push me off so that they could have a go. I fought with them, biting and scratching. My mother had to tell them to leave me alone.

Uncle Tom came round for Christmas dinner and brought a woman with him. He was drunk and fell asleep at the table. The woman walked out and left him snoring. My mother shook Tom awake and he played games with us, but he kept falling over – he nearly fell into the fire.

Ted and Aunty Alma came. They brought more presents with them. Ted brought a big box of crackers and we went mad pulling them. Then we had to leave the room while Ted hid money for us to find; what we found we could keep. Tommy and Pat were better at finding the money than me, but because I cried my father gave me some of his own money. Tommy called me a cry-baby, though, which just made me cry even more.

I thought the news was good, but it wasn't. It was bad news. No one seemed happy about my mother having a baby. My parents argued about money as they sat at the table at night. And Uncle Tom didn't think it was a good thing. It might be a girl, my mother said. But my father still looked annoyed. Another mouth, he kept saying, another mouth to feed. I didn't understand what he meant about another mouth. If it was just a mouth it wouldn't be much of a baby. Real babies have everything; legs and arms and heads. I asked my father about this and it made him laugh. But he didn't laugh much; he was angry at the idea of a new baby, even if it was just a mouth.

My mother got bigger. She stopped picking me up. I would have to climb out of the sink myself from now on – she told me it would be bad for the baby, that it might hurt the baby if she picked me up. She said she had to be careful or the baby might be born wrong. Like I was born wrong: brought into the world too early.

Most Friday nights Aunty Alma would look after us so my parents could go round to the Princess Alexandra. But as she got bigger my mother gave up going to the pub and my father would go round on his own. And come back drunk and angry. They would fight in the kitchen. We would hear them, and it was all about money and how useless my mother was with it.

The baby was born in the hospital and my father looked after us for a few days. And then Richard Alfred was brought home. I was worried, not knowing what to expect. But he was beautiful and smelt so clean and new. He had lots of blond hair. He was perfect, with fine hands and feet. And he wasn't just a mouth. He was like all other babies but more perfect than any one of them. Now *he* was placed in the old pram. I spent a lot of time looking at him. He would scratch my face and I wouldn't move away. My mother said I was stupid, because his little nails cut me. I looked like I'd had a dog fight, she said. But if she pulled me away I would always go back. And Richard would scratch me again. Even Aunty Alma found it strange that I would just stay and allow myself to be scratched.

Now Richard was my father's favourite. My father would come in from work and fuss over Richard like he used to fuss over me. My mother said I had had my nose put out of joint, whatever that meant. I watched my father as he played and cuddled Richard and I didn't understand. I was his favourite, wasn't I? But I knew it wasn't Richard's fault; Richard was the most perfect thing in the world.

4

My mother's eyes looked strange. She held my hand as we walked towards the school and she kept looking at me.

'Are you all right, Tony?'

'Yes, Mum.'

'Are you sure, Tony?'

'Yes, Mum.'

We walked past St Michael of the Angels church. Some nuns stood on the corner with a priest and blessed us as we blessed ourselves. At the corner you could hear the noise from the playground. Boys and girls screaming, shouting and playing games. It was a great noise. The sun was out and I felt happy. I pulled my mother's hand, trying to get her to walk quickly.

We stopped by the gate into the playground. Her eyes still looked strange. They were red and sore-looking. At home she had cried about me going to school. She said I had to be brave and it was all right to be upset. Tommy and Pat had been upset – they'd cried and she had to stay at the school on their first day. But I kept telling her that I wanted to go to school more than anything in the world. I was five. Five-year-olds went to school.

As we stood there I just wanted to kiss her and run into the playground. School was going to be fun. Even if Tommy and Pat didn't like school, I was going to like it.

'But Tony, you'll be upset.'

'I won't be upset. I promise.'

She kissed me and said that I was a strange boy and she didn't understand me. In the playground one of the nuns came up to us and took my hand. She said to my mother that everything would be all right – just as I had said.

When my mother left I walked round the playground and looked for boys or girls I knew. I hardly knew anyone; there was no one from my street. It must have been a Protestant street and all the children in the playground came from Catholic parts of Notting Hill. Nuns walked among us and told us to talk to each other.

I didn't want to talk; I wanted to just look at everyone. I had nothing to say to anyone. Maybe later I would play games.

The class was full. The teacher was a tall woman with blonde hair. She was friendly and gave us each a place to sit in. But there were too many children in the class so some of us had to share a chair. I had to share with a boy, half a chair each. The teacher talked about Jesus. We were Jesus's children and he looked after us. We had nothing to worry about if we had Jesus in our hearts. Now we were at school we had lots to learn. We would read, and learn to tell the time, and draw and count. It sounded good.

At playtime we had milk. A small bottle each and we had to drink it all. They gave us capsules to swallow so that we would be strong. I hated the milk but I drank it. When we'd finished we had to take our bottles to a nun who checked that they were empty.

Later the teacher told us a story about rabbits. She took out a big picture of a wood full of trees and rabbits. She came round and showed us all the big picture so we could see the rabbits hiding under trees and rolling on the grass. Then she told us about the fox that always wanted to chase and catch the rabbits. Like the dogs in the street wanting to catch the cats.

The teacher told us more stories. And on the board she wrote small words that she wanted us to learn. Then she gave us paper and crayons and we drew flowers or trees or clouds like she asked us to. She walked around and helped us do the drawings.

When my mother came to collect me her eyes didn't look strange any more. She seemed happy.

'Did you like school, Tony?'

I told her I loved it, and told her about all the things we'd done that day. I told her I didn't like the milk and that I preferred water. And I didn't like swallowing the capsules. She said that the capsules would make me strong and big, like Tommy and Pat.

She had Richard with her, sitting there in the pram smiling and looking beautiful. Tommy and Pat ran off ahead because they liked walking home by themselves. They were playing on the steps when we got back. I felt like I'd not been in the house for a long while; I'd only been away for the day but it seemed strange. Even the street seemed strange.

I told Alma what I'd learnt and she said I should be pleased with myself. But my father was too busy to listen – he was picking up Richard and throwing him in the air. I looked at him and thought maybe he wasn't my father after all. Maybe none of them were anything to do with me. Sometimes Tommy and Pat didn't seem like brothers. And when I looked at them tonight I could see that they were nothing to do with me at all; they were just boys.

Uncle Ted gave me two shillings for being good at school. He said he would get me some books and Alma said she would buy me a globe. My mother said I shouldn't be spoilt.

School was good, even though I couldn't always understand what the teacher said. We learnt songs, and hymns to sing in the church. And we learnt more sums and more words. And then we had games in the playground. We would do exercises to make us strong. Hoops and hopscotch and playing with balls. And at the end of the day there was always a story. About Jesus and rabbits and farmyards. The stories reminded me of Ireland. They reminded me of playing with the dogs and chickens in the yard out the back of my grandmother's house.

I came home from school with Tommy and Pat. I had to run after them and didn't catch up with them until I got to our street. Outside our house was our furniture and everything that we had in our rooms. My mother was standing with a policeman and two men.

She held Richard in her arms and she was shouting. We walked up and stood looking at them. Tommy asked my mother what was going on.

'These feckers are throwing us out.'

She told my brothers to stay and then she took my arm and pulled me off down the street. She carried Richard and pulled me along behind her. We turned the corner at the end and crossed the road. Then she knocked on a big black door. An old lady came out.

'Mrs – ' That's all my mother got to say before our landlady slammed the door. My mother kicked and banged on the door and shouted but the door wasn't opened again.

Back at our house, my mother was mad. Like one of the people we'd see walking the streets talking to themselves. One minute angry and the next minute crying. The next minute shouting at the policeman and the men. And then my father turned up. He also looked mad. I'd seen that angry mad face before. I'd seen him like that with my mother and one time with Uncle Ted. But now he looked like a pan about to boil over. He pushed one of the men and the policeman pushed him. Then they were all pushing each other and my mother was pulling my father. Richard started to cry. My brothers and I stood watching.

They stopped and one of the men went into the flat. Everyone else was standing around. It was bad, and my father paced around. Richard stopped crying and my father took him. And then he walked off down the street. I tried to walk along with him but he told me to go back. Then he changed his mind and told me to come with him.

We walked round to my grandmother's house and he pushed open the door.

'Mum? Mum?' he shouted up the stairs. She was standing in the kitchen when we went up there. He told her that we didn't have a flat any more. She started shouting and banging saucepans and wagging her finger at him.

'Stupid, stupid, stupid,' she kept saying to him. He didn't say much, just stood holding Richard. Nobody spoke to me; but Aunty Lilly, my father's sister, came out of a room and stood looking worried, then put her arm round me as my grandmother shouted even more. My grandmother was telling my father that she had a hard life and he should get used to having a hard life. Lilly tried to say something but my grandmother told her to keep quiet.

Lilly took me down into the mews. She thought I was frightened, but I wasn't. I didn't like my grandmother shouting at my father, but I wasn't frightened. Then my father came back down and we walked back round to the house with all the furniture outside.

It was a room at the top of my grandmother's mews house. There was no window, but there was a big bed and a table. My mother and father slept in one end of the bed and Tommy, Pat and I slept in the other. Richard was in a drawer on the floor. Each night we would go to bed at different times. I would go first. My mother would bring me upstairs and tell me to say my prayers. Most nights I couldn't sleep, so I'd lie in bed listening to the traffic or to the talking in the room below.

I hated being the first in bed. I would listen to them enjoying themselves downstairs and it would come back to me, the feeling that they were nothing to do with me. The rain pattered on the roof. I could hear it talking to me, talking about those people downstairs. I was not part of their family and maybe they were planning to do things to me. Maybe I'd wake up in the morning and they'd be gone. I'd be on my own. What would I do? Who could I go to? My Aunt Alma? Maybe she would be gone too. Maybe I wouldn't even know the streets and the mews any more; maybe I'd be lost and there would be no one to talk to.

Tommy or Pat would piss the bed. I would wake up with their piss on me. My father would roll over complaining, trying to sleep but now the bed was wet. We were all wet because of my brothers. And in the night one of my parents always got up to piss in the big bucket they brought upstairs with them. In the morning we would be cold. The smell of piss everywhere. The bad faces of everyone in this small room under the roof of my grandmother's house.

My grandmother said nothing to us. She spent most of the time in her room. When she did sit in the front room it was by herself. We'd sit in the kitchen being quiet; we had to be quiet at all times. Lilly would be nice, but my grandmother would not. Lilly would wash me and dry me carefully. I thought she would be a good mother. Sometimes she would take me to bed and read me a story. She wanted to be a mother, you could tell.

There was a factory in the mews, where dolls were made. The smell was awful. Bits of dolls would be left outside, arms and legs and little bodies. We'd play football with the heads. Pat was always in goal. We would make goal posts with piles of doll parts and Pat would dive for every doll's head that we kicked at him. He would throw himself at the heads, trying to stop every one. When he grew up, he said, he wanted to be a goalkeeper. He would cut himself when he fell but he didn't care. Pat was the toughest of us.

Tommy was a good kicker. He scored the most. Tommy said that when he grew up he wanted to be a centre forward. What could I be? Nothing. I was no good at kicking dolls' heads. Pat would tell me to try harder, but I never scored against him because he was so good in goal. Other boys would come into the mews and then they'd have a proper game. But I was too small and would be pushed aside, so I'd just watch as Pat threw himself about and Tommy and the other boys tried to score against him.

If we made too much noise my grandmother would come out and tell us off. She would curse at us and we would stop playing. Then we'd wander off. We'd go to Portobello Road and try to get orange boxes or pick up damaged apples.

My grandmother was a rough woman who rocked as she walked. You could see her coming a mile off. She was like all the other old ladies in Notting Hill but with this walk, swinging from side to side. If I saw her coming I'd hide behind a rubbish bin beside the doll-factory gates, then, as she came into the mews, I'd peep out at her slowly walking. She always had a big black bag and wore little glasses. And she always looked angry. I would stay out in the mews for as long as I could after I'd watched her go inside the house. I didn't want to see her. I tried to like her, but I couldn't. She was always telling people what to do. She'd tell my mother how to look after her money. And she'd complain that we used too much gas; the gaslight in the kitchen and the front room would run out, and my grandmother would shout at my mother.

When there was no money for gaslight my mother would hammer down brown pennies to put in the gas meter. She said that the meter thought the beaten pennies were half-crowns and would give us more gas – and most of the time it did. She always had her tongue sticking out as she hammered. She was very clever. She had to make the pennies bigger but keep them round, because if they were square they wouldn't go in. So she kept turning them; a hit here and a hit there. She was so clever because she always did it right.

When the meter man came round he would make my mother pay for the gas she had got from the flattened pennies. She always asked for the pennies back but he wouldn't give them to her. Sometimes there was no money to give him, so if my mother looked out the window and saw him coming we had to be quiet. She wouldn't open the door to the meter man when we had no money. He would knock and knock and we would be sitting upstairs as quiet as mice. He played games sometimes; he would go away and then come back. Sometimes he tried light taps on the door. He'd shout through the letterbox – he knew we were there and he was going to report us to the gas board.

One day he came and we were playing in the mews. The door was open and when he knocked my mother had to let him in. But we had no money. My mother gave me a note and sent me round to see her sister, Aunty Kathleen. When I knocked for her she opened the window and threw down her keys. Upstairs she kissed me, then I gave her the note and she cursed.

'Your mother is a fool.'

Aunty Kathleen was clever. She knew how to look after her money. Her husband was a postman and she had one son, called Paddy. She didn't have loads of children.

She gave me the money and said that I was a golden boy and I wasn't to grow up like my mother. I didn't say anything because I loved my mother; I didn't like to hear my aunt saying my mother was a fool. Kathleen was lovely, but she shouldn't have called my mother a fool.

When my mother had paid the meter man and he'd gone, my grandmother came out of her room and shouted at my mother. My mother cried, told the old lady to leave her alone, but my grandmother went on at her. And then she went into her room, slamming the door behind her. My mother looked like a little girl. Her eyes were red and there were tears on her cheeks.

There was an argument that night. My grandmother had told my father about the meter man. She said it made her house look bad; she never did things like that, however poor she was. My father turned on my mother and called her stupid, useless. Tommy and Pat watched. They were frightened and I was too. I took my father's hand. I wanted to push my grandmother down her stairs.

Friday nights were the worst. Lilly would look after us while my parents went to the Princess Alexandra. They would come back drunk and argue in the mews. One night we were in the front room and we could hear the shouting and screaming. Tommy and Pat started crying. I put my arms around them. I told them that it would be all right. Tommy and Pat were like babies to me; I had to look after them, even though they were older.

My grandmother wouldn't stop my father fighting and arguing. Lilly would try, but my father would push her away and carry on arguing. Telling my mother that she was destroying us. Telling her that she was useless. My grandmother didn't seem to care. But Lilly cared and she would cuddle us, to stop us feeling bad. Tommy and

Pat would cry. But I didn't cry; didn't know how to cry. I could only watch.

We had become ill. Tommy, Pat and I were sitting in the room at the top of the house. Sheets were hanging up everywhere and it was raining. The pitter-patter of the rain talking to me again. All of us were coughing. We had a paraffin heater and the room was hot, but we were all coughing. Even my mother was coughing. And we were all hot, our heads wet with sweat.

The doctor came to see us. He put a cold thing on our chests and gave us medicine to drink. He didn't look happy. He told my mother to keep us hot: we had to sweat. We all had a fever and we had to be careful. We couldn't play out in the street. But we would be all right. He smiled at my mother as he went down the stairs. I heard him talking to my grandmother and then I heard her shout at the doctor. When the doctor left, my grandmother slammed the front door.

Aunty Kathleen came to see us. She sat on the chair and told my mother that she had to be careful with her money.

'What fecking money?'

'You can't spend money you don't have, Eileen.'

It was strange, hearing my mother called Eileen. Eileen sounded like a girl's name. Once upon a time my mother had been a girl and it was strange to think of her like that. The younger sister of another girl, Kathleen. But it was true that sometimes my mother looked like a washed-out girl; troubled, like a child. But everyone seemed to tell my mother off, saying she was a fool, she was stupid, no good for anything. But she was the best mother in the world, and we knew that.

They sat smoking Kathleen's cigarettes. They talked about Ireland, about my Irish grandmother. Perhaps we should all go and live in Ireland. Kathleen said she should ask my grandmother to pay for us to go back. Kathleen said that she would say a decade of the rosary so that we could go back to Ireland. England was not a place for us. Our family was too big – only small families could live in England. Living on a farm was the best thing for all of us.

When Kathleen left, we asked my mother if we could go and live in Ireland. She said she would think about it. But there was no work in the whole of Ireland; that's why the Irish were over here.

When we got better we didn't go back to school for a few days. My brothers and I went walking round Notting Hill, up to Notting Hill Gate then into Kensington Gardens. It was sunny and we walked down to the Round Pond where boys played with their boats. The boats had sails and cabins, and flags of red, white and blue. Nannies pushed big prams. Everyone looked so happy and healthy, so well dressed. We never played with the well-dressed children, but we watched them play. And they watched us watching them. Like we were in different zoos.

A man and woman came to see us. The man smoked a pipe that made a bad smell in the house. My grandmother told him not to smoke in the house and he put the pipe out angrily. The woman said nothing but looked around. She looked at things as though she'd never seen them before. She had a funny hat that made the back of her head look like a football.

The man and woman had come to talk to my mother just after we had been ill. My mother showed them where we all lived, in the room under the roof. The man and woman wrote on pieces of paper and mumbled to each other. The woman tousled my hair, but they said nothing to me. When they had gone I asked about them.

'Council.' That's all she said. When I asked what she meant she told me to lay off her.

We went back to school the next week. The teacher was very nice and told everyone to be kind to me. Children were always off school ill, so I was surprised she made a fuss of me. But she got me to come up to the front of the class and tell the class what I'd missed about school. I told them it was the stories and the life of Jesus. That pleased the teacher, but I still couldn't understand why she was fussing over me. Later she told me that she had missed me. That I was bright and interested in everything. That was why she'd made a fuss of me: she was glad to see me back. I was happy about that.

I felt weak, though, and I couldn't run around like I had before. Tommy and Pat were weak as well, so we just sat and watched the other children play. But I was so glad to be back at school.

That night my father had a wide smile. He had a letter from the council saying they were going to give us a new place to live. We would be moving to a flat – out of that room, away from my grandmother's house and all the bad faces she made. My mother wasn't stupid: now we were going to have our own place.

They went down the pub that night and when they came back they were singing. They were happy because we'd be saying goodbye to my grandmother's and all her moaning, all the bad things we had to put up with because we were living in her house. They brought back pop and crisps and we sat in the front room enjoying ourselves. My father couldn't stop smiling.

5

Our ground-floor flat had a condemned room that we weren't allowed in; the floor had a hole in it. But it was a good flat. Tommy, Pat and I slept in the front room; it had a fireplace and a mantelpiece. On the mantelpiece was an electric clock that my father had bought in a pub. It had sat in a box for years, but now that we had a house again we could use it.

And we had a garden. The garden had rubbish in, but it also had a lilac tree, buried among the old mattresses, broken furniture and bits of iron. My father said that one day he'd clear up the garden – he'd pull out all the rubbish and make space for us to play in. He said he would get a bench and place it under the lilac tree. It would be like having our own park; maybe he'd put in a swing.

And I had my own bed. I wasn't pissed on any more. There were three mattresses that were laid out on the floor of the front room. It was good waking up dry in the morning. Even though there were wet sheets hung out to dry and everywhere smelt of piss, it was much better than at my grandmother's. We had a kitchen that we sat in listening to the radio and my parents had their own room, at the back of the flat. Richard was in their room with them. He was now walking and he was happy. We were all happy.

Trees lined the pavement of our new street. A short walk from the end of the road there were shops, selling groceries, clothes, books and newspapers. This was unlike Notting Hill, with its dark mews and dirty streets. Here there were crowded streets with cafes and restaurants. It was as if we had moved to another city not just a mile away. Nearby was a library and a swimming pool, and there were big squares with trees and grass. We had come out of the shadows and into the open.

There was a gang in the street. It didn't have a proper name, just 'the gang', and it was made up of just one family: Jesse, Sonny, Billy and Johnny. They lived a few doors from us. When we first met them they came over and looked at us.

The leader, Sonny, came up close. 'You'll be in our gang.' He pointed at Tommy and Pat. And then pointed at me. 'But not you.'

Pat put his hand in the air, as if he was talking to a teacher. 'He's our brother.'

'So what?'

'He's six.'

'I don't give a fuck how old he is.'

He then went up even closer to Tommy and Pat, looked at them as though he was the toughest boy ever. 'I give the orders.'

That was it. Tommy and Pat joined the gang. I told them that we should start our own gang, but Tommy said if we did we'd always be at war with the other gang. And the other gang was stronger than us. And anyway, soon they'd let me join.

They played football and cricket and hide-and-seek in the street. Sonny always made the rules. If he was batting and was out, he'd say he was still in. So playing cricket meant letting Sonny hit all the balls he wanted. When he got tired of that he would bowl. And when he said that he'd got someone out, they were out. He did what he wanted to do. When he played football he scored all the goals; that was the way he played. And even if all I was doing was watching them from the steps outside our house, it was better than playing their stupid games.

It was summer and there was no school. It was good being out of my grandmother's house. It was good not being pissed on by my brothers. Having no one to play with was definitely better than being at my grandmother's.

My father stopped being a milkman and became a builder's labourer. Building houses and garages. He built a school, he told us, and offices and a police station. He came home from work tired and dirty, covered in dust and muck. He would sit in the kitchen, saying nothing, doing nothing except reading the evening paper. My mother would rub cream into his hands because they were so sore and dry. He was always tired, and would fall asleep in the chair. We had to be quiet. My mother would whisper to us to keep quiet so my father could rest.

At times Sonny would say that I could join the gang. I was included when the gang went wandering around the bombsites of Bayswater, full of broken houses and bushes. But when they played in the street I didn't exist; I was invisible to them.

They let me go with them to the Lost Jungle because there was another gang that went on to the bombsite. Though the fence was 'easy' Pat would help me over. Then Sonny would laugh at me, call me a baby. But they wanted me in the Lost Jungle because of the other gang; they wanted me to be the spy. They'd send me out to 'scout' after them, like the scouts in the film called *The Lost Jungle* that we'd watch on Saturday mornings at the cinema. I'd pretend to scout the other gang but whenever I saw them I ran off. I never really scouted them, but I'd tell Sonny I had.

Sonny was always planning to ambush the other gang. His plan was that one of us would throw a stone at them so that they'd chase the stone-thrower and then run into the ambush. We never did ambush them. But Sonny talked about it, planned it all the time.

We would sneak after the other gang but we never attacked them and they never attacked us. When we met, they would always run off one way and we would run another. It was like a game. Pat always wanted to throw bottles and stones at them. If Pat had been in charge we would have stoned the gang and driven them out of the Lost Jungle. But Sonny was in charge, and he said he was waiting for the best time.

There was a bank on the corner where our street met the main road. A girl lived with her parents in the flat above the bank. She would sit on the small wall by the side of the bank with other children, mostly girls. I would watch them playing, but they would never ask me to join in; they never even spoke to me. I was invisible to them as well. One time the girl looked at me and smiled and then went back to playing. Her friends didn't even look at me. I could tell they were posh – they dressed well and had good hats and coats – and I knew they didn't talk to me because I wasn't like them. But it didn't matter. I didn't want to play with anyone who didn't want to play with me.

One day the girl by the bank spoke to me. The gang had gone off to the Lost Jungle. This time Sonny said I couldn't come because I always slowed them down. They had to fight the other gang and they didn't need me; I wouldn't be useful. Pat said I would be useful but Sonny said no. Today was the day when they would drive the other gang out of the Lost Jungle and they would never return.

'Where are your friends, boy?'

She was playing with her long hair. It was very black and curly. Her skin was very white and she had big brown freckles. She was taller than me and very skinny. But nice to look at.

'I don't have any friends.'

'But you have brothers.'

'They're not friends.'

She walked away and sat on her steps. 'Do you want to play with my teaset?'

She had it laid out on the steps. She was pouring water from one pot to another and then pouring it into teacups. I laughed. 'Boys don't play with teasets.'

She made a face at me, pointing her tongue. 'They do. My friends play with my teaset.'

'But they're girls.'

She looked angry. 'Some are boys.'

She had a scar on her forehead. 'Where did you get the scar from?' She didn't answer me, so I walked off.

She ran after me. 'You don't have to sulk.'

We stood on the corner looking at cars. Her name was Jacqueline. She said her father worked in the bank. But another bank, not the one below them. I told her that my father built police stations and schools. She said she didn't believe me. I didn't care if she believed me. She talked to me as if she didn't want to talk to me. Like she was doing me a favour by talking to me. I knew it was her game, that she did want to talk to me and probably wanted to hold my hand. And get me to chase her so that she could scream – girls liked screaming and being chased and caught, and I knew that because I'd seen them in the playground.

We walked towards Westbourne Grove. At the junction of two big roads Jacqueline took my hand. It was nice holding her hand, even if it was hot and sticky.

'I can't cross the road,' she said. 'I'm only seven.'

'I'm only six and I can cross the road.'

I crossed on my own, very carefully. Then I crossed again, very carefully.

I didn't run. I waited for the lights to change. When I went back I stood in front of her, smiling. At least I knew how to cross the road.

'See how easy. And my mum doesn't mind.'

She looked hurt. 'But your family doesn't care for you. Mummy says poor people don't care for their children.'

She was a funny girl. She said funny things. I liked her because she said funny things. I told her so: 'You talk in a funny way. I like it.'

'I'm not funny – you're funny. You talk funny. You dress funny.'

She started to cry. Grown-ups looked at us as she cried.

When we got back to our street her mother was walking up and down looking very angry. She didn't say anything but took Jacqueline's hand and walked away. I heard her ask Jacqueline what she was doing with 'that boy', and what she was doing holding my hand. She would have to tell 'Daddy' all about this. Jacqueline cried again, said she was 'sorry, sorry'.

Pat and Tommy were standing on the corner doing nothing. They didn't look too happy. I asked them where the gang was and Pat said that Sonny had sent them away, for no reason at all. They'd seen the other gang, Pat said, but Sonny said they couldn't attack them; they had to wait for the best time. Pat had asked when the best time was.

Pat had met one of the gang by himself and had asked him what they were called. The 'Irish Gang', the boy had said. When Pat said this I was very excited. 'We should be in their gang. We're Irish. Sonny's gang isn't Irish.'

Tommy told me to shut up. I said that I was going to join the Irish gang: we were Irish, and I loved Ireland and wanted to be with Irish boys. Tommy grabbed me, said if I so much as talked to the Irish gang then I'd be hit.

I saw Jacqueline in the street a few days later. She looked at me sadly. Her mother had told her not to speak to me.

Jacqueline went into her house and I felt sorry that we couldn't play together. It was the end of the summer and soon we'd be going back to school. There would be stories about winter and autumn, stories like the one about the grasshopper that spent the summer playing the fiddle and was cold and hungry in the winter. I might not see Jacqueline for a long time.

Tommy and Pat were supposed to walk with me to school. But they never did; they'd run off and say I was a 'slow coach'. It didn't bother me. I could walk slowly and go into the shops, ask if they had any damaged apples or broken biscuits.

At school we were told that we would be preparing for our First Holy Communion. Next Easter we would be taking Communion and we had lots of things to learn. It was exciting to look forward to and the teacher said that we should be proud of ourselves. We were going to enter the Church and we would no longer just be children. We would be Jesus's little supporters. We would have minds of our own because we would be seven and on the way to being grown-ups.

My father sat reading the paper in the kitchen, stroking his chin as he read. He looked happy, even though we had just had 'goody':

bread put into a cup with tea and milk and sugar. We ate it only when there was nothing else to eat, when the money had gone. I loved goody, but I didn't like the tealeaves that were left in your mouth when you finished the cup. I had tried to talk to my mother about the tealeaves, but she was busy drying sheets. She'd told me to talk to my father.

When he smiled he had the best smile in the world.

'Dad, I've got an idea.'

He looked up with that smile of his. 'You have?' He put down the paper and looked at me as if he was listening. Grown-ups often didn't listen, but you could tell when they were.

'You know when you put tea in a cup, Dad – you get all the leaves, don't you?'

'The leaves make the tea. If you don't have the leaves then you don't have the tea.'

So I told him about my idea that would be useful, very useful: 'If you have something with holes in it, Dad, you can pour the tea over the holes. The tea goes through the holes and the leaves get left.'

He laughed. He had a laugh like a car with a cold engine; a huff-and-a-puff laugh. He called my mother over. 'Tell your mother, son.'

I told my mother and they both laughed at me. She said I was simple in the head. He said I had just invented the tea-strainer. I didn't know what that was.

'It's for keeping the leaves out of the tea, son.' He laughed again. Like the engine that mixed the cement when they laid new paving stones by the library.

'Are they a lot of money, Dad?'

'No, son, not a lot of money.'

'So why can't we have one?'

He laughed again, bubbling, stopping, starting. 'Because, son, we are piss-poor. That's why.'

★

Jacqueline didn't often come out into the streets. It was getting colder and the leaves all fell from the trees. The lamp-lighter came round earlier and earlier. He pushed his long pole up, pulling the little ring that let the gas come. He looked happy, perhaps because he could get home earlier.

When I saw her she would always take my hand. Unless her mother or father were with her. Her mother always smiled as though she was trying hard to look friendly. The smile didn't come from inside her; it was there because she'd told her face to smile. And I knew it. Her father always looked the other way, as if he hadn't seen me. I didn't mind. I could understand that I wasn't like them. They were probably frightened of me. Maybe people like me made too much noise in the streets.

One time, Jacqueline took my hand and pulled me up the street away from her house. She looked up at the windows of her flat above the bank. She tried to whisper something in my ear but a lorry went by and I couldn't hear her. She had to tell me again: 'Don't tell anyone, but I'm going to invite you to my party.'

I looked at her. I didn't know what she meant by 'invite'.

'You get "invited" to parties, silly. You can only go if you get invited.'

She said an invitation was like a ticket, and that she'd get me one for her party.

I wanted to pull her round in a circle, but she kept looking at the windows. I was happy that Jacqueline was my friend, but she kept looking at the windows.

I asked her when the party was.

'At Christmas. But you mustn't tell anyone.'

I was disappointed. 'But we haven't had Bonfire Night yet.'

She pushed me away and went off in a huff. She said she didn't like me any more because I was too selfish and I wasn't kind; her mum was right about me. Then she stuck her tongue out and ran inside. She was crying. I wished I hadn't said what I had said. Jacqueline was a good girl but I had a stupid mouth.

39

When Bonfire Night came the fire was bigger than any I'd seen before. All day people were bringing old wood and furniture, old clothes and rubbish out to the corner of the street. After school we stood and watched them building the pile for the fire. The gang all stood together. I didn't stand with them. I tried to help the men, but they kept telling me to go off. They said I'd get a splinter in my hand, or a cut from the nails that stuck out of the old wood. I kept trying, though, and in the end they let me help. But the gang were told to stand back. Tommy had a look on his face as I helped build the pile, as if I had stolen something from him.

The guy looked like a real man. He had clothes and a hat, and a pipe was stuck where his mouth would be. An overcoat kept him all together, though you could see the straw sticking out from his neck. He sat on the top of the pile and I looked up at him, knowing that soon he'd be burning.

Only after people had their tea did the man with the big torch of fire hold it over the guy's head. We all stood as close as we could. It was a cold night and you could see everyone's breath. Everyone was waiting for the man to light the pile. Then he put out his hand to me. 'Come on, sonny.'

He gave the burning torch to me, though he still held it too. We lit the fire together. The man was very careful, making sure I didn't burn myself. Soon the sides of the pile were roaring with flames, and people were jumping in the air. As I moved away from the fire I looked at the gang. They looked annoyed, especially Tommy.

'Think you're so fucking great,' he said.

But I danced round the fire with the others, holding hands in a ring. Even the old people tried dancing, laughing all the time as the fire grew fiercer and stronger. And people brought more things to put on the fire. When new things were put on, we'd cheer as the flames licked them. Like a dog licking a new bone, or a cat licking one of its legs.

Because part of a tree caught light, the police came. It was only some hanging branches but an old woman had complained that the fire was killing the tree. People shouted at the police and they went away, but they said they were going to get the fire brigade. An engine came and squirted water at the tree, then the firemen went away and everyone cheered.

We stayed out until the fire fell back. We were almost the last to go and by the time we did the fire was looking sad, becoming more and more burnt out. I took a last look at it as we went into the house. It was the best Bonfire Night we'd ever had.

Jacqueline came out on to the street one Saturday even though it was cold. I was sitting on her wall. She whispered in my ear. 'Mummy says you can come to my party.'

She had forgotten that she hated me. Her breath was hot in my ear. Her hair touched my ear and it felt good.

She was pretending to smoke a cigarette. She put her fingers to her mouth and pulled on the imaginary cigarette. I pretended to smoke as well. We laughed.

'How did you get the scar on your head?'

She touched the scar, then she took my hand and made me touch it too. 'Feel it. It used to be very deep. It was a bomb that dropped out of the sky when I was a baby.'

'Bombs always drop out of the sky.'

She ran into her house and slammed the door after her. But then she came out again. 'I get sad when I talk about my scar. Everybody was killed except me.'

I was puzzled. 'Everyone? Not your mum and dad?'

She laughed. 'How could they? You can't die and then be alive.'

You could if you were Jesus Christ. But I didn't argue.

'No. They were away fighting the Germans. I was with my granny and my grandfather.'

'So they're dead?'

'No, of course not. They're coming to the party.'

'You said everyone got killed.'

She pulled my arm. 'You don't understand anything. The firemen, and the soldiers. And the milkman.'

She was like everyone else. Jacqueline told stories; she made things up. 'Sure you're not lying, Jacqueline?'

She slapped my arm. 'Don't you ever call me a liar.'

She turned to go back into the house, but stopped. I knew we were still friends. She smiled at me, stroked my face. 'When a boy is lonely you have to be kind to him.'

The sun brought no warmth, only light. You'd be freezing in the bright light, standing around in the playground, hoping the bell would ring. The big hot pipes were the best thing to sit on when it was cold. They ran along the corridor into the classroom. It was cold in the toilet in the yard; you'd run into the toilet and then run back into the warm corridor. The fog was worst. It followed you everywhere, even into the house. It only went away when you became warm. Then the grey air of the fog disappeared like a steamy mist.

My mother was in trouble: she was having another baby. My father was angry. He said to her that we were stupid, we should just take his wages and pour them straight down the fucking drain. He couldn't keep up with all the fucking mouths. Mouths coming out the fucking ground. He was so angry he took his coat off the back of the door and went out, slamming two doors behind him. My mother looked unhappy. She shouted after him that he should have thought about that when he was having fun. He came back and waved his fist at her. 'We're fucking broke!'

Then he went out again and my mother sat and cried. I put my arm round her. Tommy and Pat asked her if she was all right. She sat for a while and then made us all a cup of tea. She told us not to mind our father – he was working so hard and another baby wasn't good for us. She sent us into our bedroom to play snakes and ladders. Pat usually won; Tommy sometimes – although I once won three games in a row. But Pat nearly always got the good numbers.

The gang didn't play very often. We would go to Saturday-morning pictures, or to Whiteleys to look at all the toys and the

Christmas decorations. Sonny didn't seem to mind me tagging along. Every now and then he'd say I had to go home, but I wouldn't, I'd just hang around. And he would forget and leave me alone. The shop people would tell us to leave – they didn't like the look of us. We looked too rough and we might steal things. But we didn't, we weren't thieves. We were just kids with nothing to do now that it was too cold to play in the streets.

There was no money in the house for any of us.

'We ain't got a thing for Christmas.'

My father was sitting in his chair, rubbing his rough hands. My mother was looking at him with a serious face. She was getting big in the belly. My mother said she would write to her mother in Ireland. Maybe she would send us some money for Christmas. My father said nothing. He rolled himself a cigarette, closed his eyes and lay back in the chair. Richard stood beside the chair and my father ran his hand through Richard's long blond hair, then he smiled with his eyes shut and pulled on his cigarette.

There was a knock on the door and Tommy answered it. He came running in with a stupid grin on his face. 'There's Tony's girl for Tony at the door.'

Tommy and Pat laughed at me because I played with a girl. My mother told them to shut up. I felt angry with them when they laughed at me. As though I was a sissy, a girl myself. But at least I didn't follow Sonny around like a pair of dogs. At least Jacqueline was a real friend, not someone who made me feel I was just a stray. That's what Sonny did to them, making the pair of them do what he wanted. Sonny was an arsehole. Jacqueline wasn't. Did I laugh at them because they pissed their beds? Did I laugh because every day there were wet sheets hanging up to dry? And the gang smelt of piss as well. They all smelt of piss, the whole lot of them. Maybe they even smelt of shit. But I never said anything to them. I didn't laugh at them. But they laughed at me because I played with a girl.

I went out to Jacqueline at the door. She had such a big smile it made me want to kiss and squeeze her hard. She gave me an envelope – inside was the invitation to her party.

She stood looking through the doorway and into the house. The hall was dark and dirty. The wallpaper hung off the wall and you could smell cat and dog from the people who lived upstairs. There was no light in the hall, which was a good thing as Jacqueline stood in the doorway. At least she couldn't see in to all the dirt and the paper hanging off.

Jacqueline turned and waved. I watched her cross the road. Even though there was no traffic she was careful. It was dark and I watched her go into her house door at the back of the bank. I could see the bright lights of her flat; they looked so warm. I bet there were no arguments in their house about babies coming along all the time. There was only Jacqueline, and Jacqueline was probably enough for her mother and father. All they needed was one girl.

On Saturday when it was dark I crossed the road to the party. My mother had got me a card and a small bear. She'd wrapped it in coloured paper and told me not to scrunch it up. So I had a present for Jacqueline. My mother had said that she didn't want me to look like a 'fecking pauper'.

I knocked on the door but no one came and I had to knock again and again, each time louder. Then I heard the sound of clumping shoes coming down the stairs. The door was opened by Jacqueline, wearing a red dress and with her hair held back by a band. 'Tony, Tony, you're late.' She kissed me, then took my hand and pulled me upstairs.

There was music in the big room, and mirrors and flowers and decorations. A large Christmas tree stood in the middle, next to a piano. Jacqueline took my present and card and put it on a mountain of others by the tree. She told everyone that I was Tony and I lived across the road. Everyone smiled at me. Most of the children there were girls – there were some boys but they were playing by themselves. The girls were dancing and jumping around while the boys played with games on the floor. Grown-ups sat in chairs by the wall, all smiling and happy as well. And they waved at me when Jacqueline told them I was Tony.

A big woman sat at the piano and played nursery rhymes. She was smiling. Jacqueline's mother was smiling and holding my hand. I sat on the floor with Jacqueline and girls came and sat with us. Jacqueline's mother knelt down to speak to me, and as she did I could see up her dress. I could see her stockings and her knickers and I kept looking at them. Then she stood up and wandered away. Jacqueline's mother was very beautiful, with a big flowery dress on. And she smiled and talked to the grown-ups sitting by the wall.

I was given a piece of cake on a paper plate, and I ate it while Jacqueline and her friends sat around me and talked, all at the same time. Then Jacqueline's mother clapped her hands and shouted out loud: 'Let's play musical chairs now, children.'

I'd never played musical chairs before, but I soon understood it and I was very good at it. I won the second game, and then the third. It was great fun. When we'd finished, Jacqueline took my hand and pulled me over into the corner.

'Very good, Tony. But you are a bit rough – it's only a game.'

We had songs, and pass the parcel. I had never played that before, either, and it was great. One boy took two lots of paper off and was told to leave the game, then a girl won and everyone clapped and shouted.

After that we sat down to eat. I sat next to Jacqueline. She asked me if I liked the party and I said it was the best party in all the world. She asked me if I had been to all the parties in all the world, and then she laughed at me and pulled my ear. There were bananas and apples, cake, biscuits and jelly, and pop and orange juice. There were crackers and pieces of chocolate wrapped in silver. Then the grown-ups gave us jelly and ice cream.

After the food we all sat on the floor and Jacqueline's mother told us the Christmas story about Good King Wenceslas and got us to sing the song.

After that, she said she was going to turn the light off and while it was dark we all had to lie on the floor or hide in the corner. I saw Jacqueline go to hide under the piano, and I got under there with her. I was so happy, I kissed her on the lips.

She screamed and her mother turned on the light. 'What's the matter?' She looked angry.

Jacqueline got out from under the piano and I came out after her. 'He kissed me, Mummy, when the light was out.'

Her mother took my hand and walked me to the door. She gave me my coat and three tangerines, then she led me downstairs. She told me that I had been very naughty. I went out the door and she slammed it after me. I stood in the street with the three tangerines. I didn't understand what was wrong with kissing your friend under the piano. But I didn't cry, even though I felt like crying.

My father asked me why I was home so early. I didn't want to tell him that I had got thrown out. 'The girl got a headache, Dad. So we had to leave.'

He laughed. I gave the tangerines to my mother, who gave one each to Tommy and Pat and just a piece to Richard. I wasn't happy; when I went to bed I felt bad about the party and lay there thinking about the wrong I'd done.

When Christmas Day came we were still without money. We had a few things, but it wasn't like the Christmases we'd had in St Stephen's Gardens. My father looked sad. No money had come from Ireland, and my mother said my grandmother could be a tight bitch. But it didn't matter; at least we were in our own place. At least we had some chicken for dinner.

We played around with the crackers and the Plasticine, making models. I didn't mind that we had no money if we were all together.

After dinner the sky was very dark and I sat out on the step in front of the house. I wanted to see the street on Christmas Day, to see if it looked different. But the only difference was that there was no one around. Not a car or a horse or a person in sight. The dark sky and the empty street made me happy that at least we were warm in our house. I did see a stray dog walking down the street, and a few cats sitting on walls. I thought to myself that the dog and the cats knew nothing about Christmas; it was like any other day for them. Cats and dogs had no parties.

Then, down the street by the railway bridge, I saw a man walking. He moved slowly, as though he was tired and worn out or old. As he got nearer I could see that he was very tall and very skinny-looking. He was a black man. He had a hat on his head and he was hidden in a big overcoat. When he reached our house he stopped and smiled at me.

'Happy Christmas, child.'

'Happy Christmas, mister.'

I was still sitting on the step. He came over to me and put his hand in his pocket. He took out some money and put a half-crown piece in my hand. 'Here, child. Happy Christmas.'

The half-crown felt big in my hand. The big black man smiled again and lifted his hat to me. Then he turned and walked away.

I ran inside. 'Look, Mum. A big black man gave it to me.'

She was shocked when she saw the money. She couldn't believe it. My father looked shocked as well, and went out to the street with Tommy and Pat to look for the man. When they came in they said they'd seen no one. My father asked me if I was making it all up – maybe I'd just found the half-crown in the road and had made up a story about it.

6

The teacher told us that this was going to be one of the most important times of our life. We were seven and old enough to take our first Holy Communion. My mother said that I would make a good Catholic because I was so good about most things. She said she never had to worry about my soul; I would be the best Catholic in the family and I should thank God that I had no badness in me.

'Tommy and Pat are good, Mum.'

'They can be little feckers at times.'

She was peeling potatoes as she said this to me. She was big in the belly and she moved slowly.

'Do you remember your first Holy Communion, Mum?'

You could ask her questions some times. Other times she would get mad. But tonight, as we talked about Communion, she was in a good mood. 'I cried my eyes out. In Ireland everyone makes a big fuss of you. Not like here, in this God-forsaken country.'

She often called England a 'God-forsaken country'.

The teacher kept telling us the same things, in case we forgot that this was to be an important day. 'You are to be soldiers of the Lord. After Communion you will have to be good Catholics. You cannot commit sin without having to confess.'

She told us all the things we would have to do. She told us about Mortal and Venial sin and the need to go to confession. We would not be innocent like children; we were in charge of our own souls. From being simple children, all pure from our Baptism, we'd become sinners.

We had to learn to say the Catechism, and each morning and afternoon we had to repeat it out loud. We had to learn the Latin Mass. We had to learn what to say after the priest in church had spoken, even though we didn't understand the Latin words we were learning.

It was just before Easter and the sun was shining. The trees in the street were green and we were allowed to play out. We played in the evening until it grew dark. The gang came out to play football. My mother had a boy, named Edward William. He was beautiful, but different from Richard; he had light-brown hair. We called him Eddy.

Jacqueline ignored me in the street, as if I didn't exist. She might as well have joined the gang, because the gang didn't think I existed either. I didn't exist for anyone in the street. Except for my mother and father – and Richard, of course. Now I would sit out in front of the house and look after Richard. He was getting bigger, and was walking well with me holding on to his reins. He smiled a lot and was interested in everything.

I was upset that Jacqueline ignored me. I didn't understand why she was doing it – I hadn't done her any harm. She'd kissed me many times; sometimes till she made my face wet. So why had she now got so angry about that one kiss under the piano at her party?

It was the Saturday before the Holy Communion. We had to go to the church next to the school to practise for the next day. My mother was supposed to come but she had too much to do, so Tommy came instead. He moaned his arse off. He kept stopping me and pulling me because I was so slow.

When we got there the teacher, the nuns and the priest showed us what to do. It was all very simple. We had to walk in all together, sit down at the pews and then walk up to take the Divine Host. The statues in the church were covered with black and purple cloths. But in the morning, when Jesus had arisen from the dead, they would take off the black cloths. And we would be given our first Holy Communion.

Walking back with Tommy, I was very excited. But Tommy only wanted to get home so he could go off with the gang. I hated Tommy. He was mean; he was only helping his mother, not me.

In the morning I was sick. My mother told me it was nerves. I couldn't have breakfast because of going to Communion. Instead I had a cup of water. She dressed me in a white silk shirt and new black short trousers. I had new socks and new shoes. She said I looked a picture. And then all of us except my father went off to church.

It was a very bright morning. I was frightened and happy at the same time, and my mother kept telling me not to be so nervous. But I couldn't help it; my stomach was rattling and I was shivering even though the sun was hot. When we arrived, everyone else went into the church but those of us taking our Communion had to wait outside. Each of us was given a sash to wear and a small prayer book that had been blessed by the priest.

We walked into church in a line of twos. The organ played and people sang, and everyone turned and looked at us. I was still shaking. When we walked forward to kneel at the altar, my mother and brothers were looking at me and my mother smiled and waved. But I turned and looked ahead. The priest placed the body of Christ in my mouth. You had to swallow it; you couldn't chew on the body of Christ. You also had to stop it getting stuck to the roof of your mouth.

Later, the adults and other children went up, hymns were sung and prayers spoken. It was all over and we were members of Jesus's church. We had become like grown-ups. As we left the church people cheered and threw rose petals over us. It was wonderful. I picked up some of the petals and put them between the pages of my prayer book.

I cried in bed that night because I didn't want the day to end. As I lay there unable to sleep I promised that in the morning I would turn over a new leaf. I would be as good a Catholic as I could be, all the things that Jesus wanted me to be. He would be expecting me to be a good boy, so I would be.

I got up and looked out of the window into the garden. I was hoping to see a cat but there were none around. I could hear the sound of the train whistles and there was a moon in the sky; a little moon, only a bit of one. There was silver light on the wall at the back of the garden. But no cats. Nothing except the moonlight and the darkness. I got back into bed and knew that in the morning I was going to be the best Catholic ever.

They were not happy. It was the money. They argued in the kitchen at night about what they could do. My father couldn't earn any more and my mother couldn't work because she had to look after us. I would lie in bed wishing I had money to give them. Maybe Tommy and Pat and I could work. Maybe we could get some jobs after school that would help. Maybe my mother had a rich cousin in America who could send us money. If only they had money, then everything would be all right.

Sometimes Ted and Alma came round and brought nice things to eat – crisps and bars of chocolate – and a crate of beer. Then they'd sit in the kitchen with my parents after we went to bed. Ted would give us a shilling each and he'd be happy and cheer everyone up. But he said he didn't like Bayswater: it was strange, not as friendly as Notting Hill.

Uncle Tom would also come. He would drink a lot with my father; they'd go to the pub together. But hardly anyone else came any more. It was as though we had moved a hundred miles, instead of a mile down the road.

The good times, when we had visitors, didn't last. Soon there'd be arguing and shouting about money again. My father saying he was working his fingers to the bone. One evening my father was sitting in his chair and my mother said she had something to tell us.

She was smoking and her eyes were red. 'You may have to go away for a while, kids.'

I wasn't really listening. I was pretending to play a piano, on the table.

Tommy was listening. 'I don't want to go away, Mum. I like it here.'

Pat agreed with him. But my mother said it was just for a short while. Tommy started to moan and my father told him to shut up. He did.

Then I listened properly to what my mother was saying.

'We don't have any money. And you may have to go and stay with the nuns for a while.'

I couldn't understand why we would go and stay with nuns.

'In a convent. It's a kind of school. It's in the country. It'll be very nice.'

I was excited about it being in the country. 'In Ireland, Mum?'

But no, it wasn't in Ireland. It was near London, so that they could come and see us.

'Your dad and I will come to see you all the time.'

She talked a bit more about it. I was still very pleased that we might be going to live in the country, but Tommy and Pat were sad about it all and when we went to bed that night they told me off. Tommy said I wouldn't like it when I got there.

'Yes I will. I will.'

In the morning I asked my mother if it was true, that we might go and live in the country. She told me to shut up and get ready for school. She didn't look happy so I said no more. She didn't want us to go away, and that was what was making her so sad.

It was June and there was a big party in the street for the Queen's coronation. Tables were put out on the street, with lots of food and soda and party hats. People were singing and dancing. Even my mother looked happy, though she said she didn't think much of the royal family; she said they did nothing for Ireland. But she still had a good time. Jacqueline came out to the party, with her mother, but they didn't talk to me. I wished that we were still friends. When her mother wasn't looking, I spoke to Jacqueline. 'You won't be seeing me soon, Jacqueline.'

'Why?'

'Because I'm going away to live in a convent.'

She screwed up her face. 'Boys don't live in convents.'

'They do if they're living with nuns.'

Planes flew through the sky. They were so loud that people had to cover their ears. And everyone shouted and sang 'God Save the Queen', even my mother. We all sang and enjoyed the crowning of the Queen.

My mother didn't tell us when we were leaving until the night before. Tommy, Pat, Richard and I were going to one place. Eddy would have to go to somewhere else because he was too young to go where we were going.

That night when we got into bed Tommy and Pat told me off again. Tommy said it was my fault that we were going away. 'If we'd all said we didn't want to go they might have changed their minds.'

I called him stupid. 'We're going because we're poor. Poor people have to do what they're told.'

I couldn't sleep. I was too excited about the morning. Soon we would be living in fields and hills. I couldn't understand why Tommy and Pat weren't excited.

In the morning they were unhappy. My mother got us ready. My father had already gone to work, so we couldn't say goodbye. We took the bus to Notting Hill Gate and then got on another. I was in a fever. I kept asking my mother when we'd get to the country. I complained that I couldn't see the fields or the cows. Where was the countryside?

She got annoyed. 'Shut up. Shut *up!*'

I watched her angry face and was surprised at how bad-tempered she seemed.

After a long while we came to fields. I shouted and my mother hit me. Tommy and Pat sat quietly; Richard didn't seem to notice anything. He was two and the countryside meant nothing to him.

From the bus we walked along a road with grass beside it. There was a pond, with white ducks, and big trees beside it. It looked beautiful. But my mother was still angry and she kept telling me to shut up.

St Vincent's convent had gardens with flowers and grass. I ran ahead and she called me back. There was a big black door. My mother knocked and soon a nun came out and smiled at us. My mother had a worried look, but now I noticed that she was sad. The nun led us in and soon another nun came along. She was old, with glasses, and she smiled but her face looked unfriendly. Now my mother started to cry. The nuns were kind to her.

She hugged us. 'I'll come and see you, kids.'

Tommy and Pat clung to her. Richard was picked up by one of the nuns. My mother pulled away and stood wiping her eyes and nose with a handkerchief. I felt so sorry for her, but I was still excited. And then she turned and walked out the big black door. Tommy and Pat cried and Richard still didn't notice anything. I stood and watched her go. I called after her, told her not to cry, but she was gone.

A nurse came and took Richard away; he didn't seem to mind. Then a nun led us down corridors to a big room where lots of other boys and girls sat at long tables. The nun told us to sit down, and told the other children that we were the three Birds. We were the three Birds and we were going to live there for as long as we had to.

There were so many children, all staring at us. And all dressed the same: the girls in skirts and blouses and the boys in shorts and shirts. Grey shirts and white blouses and everyone had short-sleeved pullovers. Whenever I looked up from eating, these children were watching us. I was beginning to feel strange; maybe this wasn't going to be as much fun as I thought.

The nuns stood round or walked among the tables. They told the children to eat – we must eat everything because elsewhere there were children starving and it was wrong to waste a thing.

After we'd finished eating, Pat and Tommy and I were taken to the clothing room and given the same kind of clothes as the other children. We were given a toothbrush, a flannel and a hair comb, too, then shown our bedrooms. Tommy and Pat were in one, with the older children, and I was in another. A nun then said we should meet the other children and we were taken to the playground.

In the playground, no one talked to us at first – they just looked. We stood by a shed. Girls came up to look at us, but nobody spoke.

Then one girl came up to me. 'Where you from?'

I told her Notting Hill and her eyes lit up. 'I'm from Notting Hill too.'

She thought it was stupid that we were at the convent just because we were poor.

'My dad killed my mum – that's why I'm in here.' She just said it, just like that. 'My dad killed my mum because she was seeing someone else.'

'Why would your dad kill your mum for seeing someone else?'

She laughed. 'You don't know nothing.'

I couldn't believe it. Was she lying, like Jacqueline? 'Why aren't you with your dad, then, if your mother's killed?'

She laughed again. 'Stupid. He's killed as well, for killing my mum.'

Tommy and Pat stood there watching – they were shy now. The girl pointed at them. 'They don't talk?'

'It's only our first day.'

She said she was eight. I told her she looked six to me.

'I'm seven.'

'You said you was eight.'

'I'll soon be eight.'

'So you're seven.'

'OK, smarty, so I'm seven. And you?'

'I'm almost eight.'

'So you're seven.'

We were both laughing now.

'My name's Josephine.'

'I'm Tony.'

Then she walked away. I watched her play with other girls, running around. I was forgotten.

Later, at bedtime, Pat came into my room. 'If they ask if Tommy and me wet the bed, you're to say no.'

I laughed. 'But they'll find out in the morning.'

Pat put a fist in my face. 'Don't you tell 'em.'

He walked away. I knew when Pat had made up his mind, so I didn't call after him.

They did ask. A nun with a kindly face came up to me. 'Do you wet the bed, Tony?'

'No, miss.'

'Do your brothers?'

'No, miss.'

She tapped me on the head when I said my prayers. I asked God to forgive me. I didn't want to lie, but I had to – I couldn't tell tales on Tommy and Pat.

Boys whispered to each other that night. Now my bravery was gone; I knew that this was going to be a bad place for me. Tommy and Pat were right, they'd understood what I hadn't understood: this was going to be another prison, just like my grandmother's house.

On that first night, I even wished I was back at my grandmother's. That prison would be better than this prison, with its clean sheets and big beds and the silence. A clean, tidy prison.

I cried in the night – I couldn't stop myself. The big room with all the beds made me feel bad. I wanted to be home again with my mother. I kept closing my eyes and opening them, hoping that it was all a bad dream. And that the room with all the beds would turn into our little room with the mattresses on the floor.

A woman wearing a headscarf came into the bedroom and I thought it was my mother. I jumped out of bed and ran to her.

The woman hugged me. 'Now, now, boy. Get back into bed and go to sleep.'

She put me back into bed and stroked my face. I looked at her face and her headscarf and I wished she was my mother. I stopped crying and tried to sleep. She went away and I got right down under the covers. I could still hear the trains whistling in the distance. Like Notting Hill. Like Ireland.

In the morning while I was getting dressed with all the other boys to go down for breakfast, the woman with the headscarf came up to me. I recognised her but now she looked different, angry. She came up close and smacked me hard in the face, then again.

'You liar, you little liar.'

I kept trying to pull away, to cover my face, but she held me by the arms, shouting: 'May you burn in Hell, you liar.'

Then she stopped hitting me and pulled me close to her. 'You liar. Why did you lie about your brothers?'

I could say nothing. I stood, and said nothing.

We went down to breakfast all in a line. I was sobbing and my face still hurt. Boys looked at me but didn't say anything. I felt frightened by the woman who had been nice in the night and then had hit me. In the big place they called the refectory, Tommy and Pat were already at the table. They didn't look happy.

I had to tell Pat. 'You got me hit.'

'I didn't.'

'You did. The woman hit me for lying. Did you get hit?' Neither of them had, and that made me angry – I'd been hit and they hadn't.

I cried, I was so mad, and Tommy told me to shut up. 'You're the one who wanted to come here.'

But not any more. If they could hit you when they liked, they were worse than our grandmother. At least she only made you feel bad; she didn't hit you.

Her name was Miss Philips. I would watch her. Whenever she was around, I would watch her. I was hoping that one time she'd get caught in a net, like the lion. She'd be stuck in the net and I would be like the mouse. She would ask me to rescue her before the hunter came. And I'd tell her how bad she'd been to me. I wouldn't help her; I would just watch her crying.

Other boys and girls on the long table just stared at us. I looked around to see if I could see Josephine, but most of the girls looked the same. Some had blonde hair, some had black hair, but their clothes were all the same; everyone looked like everyone else. Even the nuns looked like each other.

In the playground we stood together and some boys came up and started talking to us. I went looking for Josephine and found her playing in the corner with some other children. She was like a leader, strong. You could tell that she was stronger than other people. She wasn't like Sonny, pretending he was strong; there was no strength in Sonny, but there was strength in this girl, Josephine.

Josephine started wrestling with me. The girls and boys pushed us and we wrestled in a silly way, then Josephine was 'he' and we had to run off. She had to catch us. She counted to one hundred in fives and we went off to all parts of the playground. But Josephine only came after me – she only wanted to catch me.

When the bell was rung for the end of playtime we were sent to our classes. I was seven and in a younger class than Tommy and Pat, who were in with the over-nines. They were together. My classroom was bigger than any at the school in Notting Hill, maybe twice as big. Pictures of Jesus from the Bible and prayers were stuck on the walls. There were some pictures of nature, but not many. And it wasn't crowded like the classes in St Michael of the Angels.

The teacher was a nun. She welcomed me and made me stand up at a desk she'd given me at the back of the room. I had to put my hand up to show where I was. She told everyone that they had to be nice to me. That I was going to be at the school for a long time.

We had prayers and a word lesson. It was like my other school except that the teacher was a nun. Josephine was in my class. She was sitting at the other end of the room from me, but I could see her sometimes when people moved their heads. Sometimes I could see her making faces at me, poking her tongue out and rolling her eyes, but never when the teacher could see.

At dinnertime, Tommy, Pat and I were taken to a room where the nuns asked us questions. Then they told me to go outside and play. When Tommy and Pat came out, Pat was excited. 'We got jobs – we're helping the nuns. They like us.'

'Helping the nuns do what?'

'This and that.'

Tommy and Pat looked happy now. They had their new gang: the nuns' gang.

One Sunday, my mother came for the first time. We were told by the nuns that we had to behave ourselves; we couldn't cry because our poor mother would be upset. I went to the nursery to get Richard. The nurses in there were very nice. They'd often allow me to take Richard out, to the big field out the back of the nursery or along the path that ran down to a farm. I'd taken him into the farmyard and into the hay barn. But today I was going to see my mother and I felt upset before she arrived. Sister Veronica, the nun with the smiling but hard face, told us again: no crying. She said it without a smile – she smiled only when there were parents around. She didn't fool anyone. She didn't fool me.

I took Richard to the room where the visitors went and where Tommy and Pat were already waiting. When my mother arrived she looked upset and I cried. Then she cried, and Sister Veronica smiled; she grabbed me and squeezed me and told me not to cry. Richard screeched loudly and Tommy and Pat said nothing, but we were all glad to see my mother.

We walked in the gardens. I asked my mother if I could go home with her. 'Tommy and Pat are happy and Richard's happy, but I'm not happy.'

She said she was sorry, but she and my father were living in a little room by Paddington Station. 'You're better off here.'

However much I disagreed, she wouldn't take me back with her.

We walked round the garden again and then she said she had to go home, there was a lot to do.

I cried, but I was the only one who did. When she left she looked so sad. I think it made me sadder than I had ever felt. I had to try and be brave, but I couldn't.

In bed that night, I heard the rain outside. It reminded me of Notting Hill and Ireland. I thought my mother would be gone forever, and that I would never be out of the prison I was in.

Tommy and Pat had their nuns' gang; they were liked. But who liked me? Josephine, but that was all. I wasn't liked at all by most people. Whenever I saw Miss Philips I felt certain of that. The nuns said I was stubborn. Tommy and Pat told me off – they said I made it hard for them, that the nuns didn't think I behaved myself. I'd asked Tommy what I did wrong.

'You're stubborn and downright awkward.'

'About what?'

'You're just stubborn. The nuns keep having to tell you to hurry up.'

'What else?'

He couldn't tell me. Nobody could tell me. I was just stubborn.

Miss Philips wandered round the bedroom but she didn't notice me. She looked around with anger; she had no smiles for any of us. I would never cry out again, never. So that woman couldn't feel sorry for me and hit me.

7

When winter came we were cold in the playground and would huddle together, dozens of us, crushed into a mob. We'd wrap our arms in the fronts of our short-sleeved pullovers and the nuns would tell us to stop it, we'd ruin our pullovers and the orphanage would have to pay. But we carried on because it was so cold. It would have been better if we'd had jackets, but we didn't.

Sister Catherine sent for me in the sewing room. She was another nun with a hard face. She had glasses, like most of the nuns did, but she had good eyes, green and bright. She told me I had to do certain things for her – cleaning up and taking messages – the things she wanted. Pat also worked for Sister Catherine, but he said nothing to me when he came into the room. She said I should watch my brother, he was a good little worker. 'He works all the time. And see, he doesn't even talk to you. He's very serious. You should behave like your brother, little Bird.'

Music played in the sewing room while girls sat at sewing machines. They were older than me and they looked up whenever anyone came into the room. Pat had been packing stuff into bags and when he'd finished Sister Catherine thanked him. He said nothing; he didn't even look up at her. He was like a clockwork machine.

After an hour, Sister Catherine sent me back to the playground. She said I was useless, that I didn't care for the Lord. I couldn't understand her. I'd done nothing wrong – I never did.

Except the night I went with Josephine to her dormitory. She undressed for bed and I watched her. She laughed at me, said boys didn't like girls.

'I like girls.'

'D'ya like watching me?'

'I do.'

And then a nun came along the corridor and I ran off. The nun shouted after me and I thought that she'd chase me. But she didn't. I hid, waiting, frightened that I'd be discovered.

The next morning I asked Josephine if she'd told the nun who I was. 'Don't be stupid, I said I never saw you before. She was old.'

That was the worst thing I did, watching Josephine undressing in her dormitory. I didn't climb on the roof, like one boy did, or smash a window with a ball. I didn't beat up any other boys, or try to piss in the water fountain with the saint statue out front by the lawn. A boy had been found doing that and they'd punished him. But they said I had no respect. What did they mean? That I had no respect for Jesus, or for our Lord, his father? Or maybe for Miss Philips, who slapped me and frightened me. That was true: I didn't respect her.

Tommy and Pat were never in the playground. They were always working. They liked it. I asked Tommy why he liked working for the nuns and he said they did him and Pat favours.

'What about me, Tommy?'

He looked at me angrily and told me what he'd told me before: 'You're trouble. You give us trouble. The nuns don't like you.'

Pat said the same. I looked at them going round and they were not like my brothers. Richard was still the best boy in the world, though. He'd be three after Christmas. When I took him out I talked to him all the time. But Tommy and Pat never went anywhere near him. They said they were too busy.

The days got darker and we were in the playground less and less. My mother came to see us. I didn't cry. I asked about my father, when he was coming to see us.

'He's working, Tony, getting our house together. So that you have somewhere to come back to.'

She came in a new coat. She said she was working in Woolworths. She brought boxes of Wine Gums and chocolates and comics for us all. It was so cold we sat in the visitors' room. We didn't walk among the flowers and along the paths between the lawns. There was nothing to do but sit in the room with the dark-wood walls and chairs. It was like we were meeting in a railway station.

When my mother left I cried a bit. But, again, no one else did. I cried because I kind of felt I was losing her. That she was someone who one day would be like my brothers; she'd go off. And I didn't want to lose her. It wasn't the same with Tommy and Pat – I could lose them any time, winter or summer – because they were like themselves but not like me. But I didn't want to lose my mother. Or Richard. To me, Richard was perfectly made. Just looking at him was a joy.

My mother said she would come and see us at Christmas. As she walked away she was looking back at us. The nuns said nice things to us all, as though we were some big family. We were no family.

One afternoon, we sat in the big hall. Everyone was excited. American airmen arrived, carrying drums and trumpets and guitars. They brought toys, sweets and games. They laid out tables and we watched as they put together the best of all parties.

They gave out gum and crackers and then started their performance. The nuns watched with us as the airmen performed. We were all watching these strange people from somewhere else in the world. I knew about America because my mother was always talking about it. There were cousins and uncles of hers in America, families in cities like Chicago and New York – Irish cities. And there was her American music all the time, making my mother go misty-eyed.

The airmen were the best people. They played games with us, made jokes. One man tore up newspaper into small pieces and then threw it in the air – 'Merry Christmas, everyone' – as though paper was snow. The nuns laughed and clapped as much as we did. We sang the American national anthem to them; we'd been practising. Some of them cried and others picked up children and held them in the air.

After their party, we watched the airmen leave. The nuns were happy. We were happy. And Christmas was coming soon. There would be more parties. Catholic families from all over England gave us presents they had collected for us. People were good to us because they felt sorry for us.

Christmas came. My mother didn't visit. On Christmas morning there were no presents at the bottom of the bed. The boys in the dormitory ran around. It was a happy morning. Jesus's birthday was a happy morning.

Richard played in the snow. He threw snowballs at me and we built a snowman. Richard screamed, he was so happy. But the nuns walking by the big field at the back of the nursery didn't like it.

'Stop that, boys! You'll get soaked to the skin. Get out of there.'

We were told to go back to the nursery. We pretended to, but just turned a corner and went the other way, down the path to the farm. Richard was happy, asking me about everything. It didn't matter what it was about, he just asked me questions. He was three now, no longer a baby. He could run around, climb trees. He always seemed happy; he was the best fun to be with.

'Richard, shall we climb that tree?'

'Yes, Tony, and when I fall you'll catch me.'

'I'll catch you, Richard.'

Walking in the snow was cold but good. Richard wanted to see the cows, the horses and the sheep. But more nuns came along, told us to go indoors, so we just saw the cows in their shed, with the straw on the floor and the muck.

The nurses were happy to see us when we got back. They fussed over Richard. They told me I was a good boy, that I cared for my brother very much. A nurse asked me about Tommy and Pat.

'They're always too busy, miss. They work for the nuns.'

'Don't you work for the nuns, Tony?'

'No, miss. They don't want me to.'

★

The snow melted and turned to slush. It was no longer good for snowballs: you couldn't scoop it up; it was like broken glass. Sometimes the sun shone so red on the snow you could see the heat rising, like the heat of a bath. And you could slide on it. But if you fell you got badly wet.

The trees were bare, except for some by the saint with the green fountain. These were tall, pointed trees that swayed in the wind. Birds played round them. When the snow had gone, the colour of the grass looked brighter. Josephine held my hand on the green triangle by the main gate. She looked sad.

'When the snow goes, there's nothing to do in this place, nothing.'

Mother Superior came to see us after supper one night. She held her hands in front of her. I thought she was going to pray, but she told us we were going to a circus.

In the playground, everyone talked about the circus. I saw Tommy, asked him if he thought everyone was going. He said he thought they wouldn't let me go because I was a little cunt.

'And you're a big cunt.'

He chased me and caught me and hit me hard. I tried to hit him but he was too strong.

We left for the circus on coaches after lunch. We were given popcorn. The excitement was great. I sat next to Josephine and she told me stories about her mum and dad. About the killing of her mother and the police, and her going to her aunt's.

'I don't know where my little sister is.'

She was unhappy because we were in the streets again. There were old people crossing roads and standing on corners. Boys and girls walking and looking in shop windows.

I recognised the Edgware Road and the Kilburn State, where my father went to the cinema. Jo and I were sad and excited at the same time. It was strange being in the streets of London again.

We were sat in the front row. Clowns came up and talked to us. The nuns had their kindly faces on. Men built a cage and the lion-tamer came in with his whip. Lions jumped from one stand to another and the tamer cracked his whip again and again.

I was terrified by the lions. I'd never been to the circus, so I was surprised by everything – the horses, the clowns, the high-wire, the trampolines – everything looked exciting. Jo was so excited she jumped up and down.

A clown brought on a donkey and asked if anyone would like to ride it. A man went up from the front seats. He got on to the donkey and fell off. His trousers fell down and everyone screamed. I felt sorry for the man – he'd only got on the donkey to be helpful. He tried again and again but kept falling off, and his trousers fell down each time. I felt sorry for him because he was so foolish-looking.

We went back to the orphanage in the dark. The streets were full of cars and people walking along the pavements. You could see boys and girls. They weren't in the nuns' control; they were free. But we were in a kind of prison and we were going to be in it for a long time. There was nothing to look forward to, now that the snow had gone and the circus had gone. I could only look forward to the day when my mother came. Maybe my father. Or the day when I could get out of this place, with its nuns and their false faces – faces that pretended smiles when my mother came.

The boilerman was to be our sponsor. When the cardinal confirmed us in the church at Mill Hill, the boilerman would stand like a godfather.

It was spring. The clouds were white against a light-blue sky. A man jumped out of a plane. His parachute opened up and we watched him as he floated in the sky. He hung in the air, far off above us. We watched him for what seemed like hours as he floated, kept floating, high in the air. The plane he had been in circled, leaving a trail. A nun said it was a sky-writer, that the man in the plane could, if he wished, write his name with the trail of white smoke.

All the time we watched the man in the parachute, he never

seemed to leave the same spot in the sky. The nun said the man was travelling faster than a car, but he didn't seem to be going anywhere. He just hung around in the blue sky and white clouds.

The nuns were preparing us for our confirmation. We had to choose a confirmation name. I thought about this for a long while; I wanted a special name. I chose Joseph because Joseph was Jesus's human father, the husband of Mary. He looked after Jesus when he was a child. He was a carpenter and he knew that his wife had given birth to the Son of God.

When I went out into the playground again, the parachutist was no longer in the sky. I was surprised and disappointed – he'd hung around in the sky for so long that I'd thought he would still be there, stuck in the sky above the houses.

We walked in twos out of the school, a dozen nuns keeping us in line. We walked up the road past the pond and I remembered the day we'd arrived here. I'd seen the same trees, gates and houses, but they looked different now; now I didn't like the look of the pond and the trees.

Jo was holding my hand and her palm was sweating. She was happy and excited that we were out of the school again, away from the playground and the classroom where we were made to work so hard. And she was happy that Jesus was going to bless us again.

Her confirmation name was Mary. When the teacher asked her why, she said it was after the Virgin Mary. The nun had patted her head: the name Mary was the best, apart from Jesus. But you couldn't call yourself Jesus – that wasn't allowed. Joseph was probably the nearest you could get; Joseph, the man who had made a home for Jesus.

The church was packed, and gloomy even though it was sunny outside. The cardinal wore bright-golden vestments. As each of us came by, the boilerman put his hand on our shoulder. And minutes later we were Soldiers of Christ in the fight, the big fight for goodness and the Holy Roman Church.

★

Tommy and Pat stood by the nuns as they chose who was going. I was upset. My mother had given me a little Saint Anthony statue made of plastic. It had a little dome over it that protected the statue. It was only a few inches high, the size of an apple. But it was special because my middle name was Anthony. Now it was lost. Gone. First the dome had gone, then the statue itself. It troubled me that it was gone, considering that Saint Anthony was the saint you prayed to if you lost anything. When they lost things boys and girls would come to me and ask me to pray – just because my name was Anthony. I was unhappy, standing in the playground as the nuns chose who was going.

'Tony Bird.'

My name sounded strange coming from the nun. Sister Ursula had the best face of all the nuns. It shone. She was young and had freckles – she was kissed by the sun, as my mother said. She had the best voice. It was a kind, Irish voice.

Why would she be calling my name? This was about an outing and I never went on outings unless everyone was going too. Like the circus. But I was not usually allowed on the outings because they were for the good boys. Like my brothers or Dunleavy, who was always licking his buck-teeth that stuck out of his mouth. Dunleavy always went on the outings to the ice rink or the aerodrome. But I never did. I didn't run round the nuns as though they were special, as though they knew something about God that we didn't know.

We formed a queue. I was at the back. Sister Ursula told us to move off in line; Tommy and Pat were to lead the line and she would follow at the back. I soon forgot about my Saint Anthony statue.

We went to the cinema. Sister Ursula stood us before the big doors and told us we were going to see *Escape from Fort Bravo*. 'It's a Western film, children, so no banging and shooting and shouting afterwards.'

We filed into the cinema and sat silently, like we were told to, all quiet and well behaved. The film was in colour, about soldiers, cowboys and Indians and men fighting. When it was over we left the cinema firing guns and ducking bullets. That annoyed Sister Ursula, so we had to behave ourselves even more than before. Walking back, I looked at Tommy and Pat just in front of me. I watched them as they walked, whispering to each other. As they talked, silently.

My mother came and she took us to the cafe near the station. I always asked her the same question: 'Where's Dad, Mum? Is he coming?'

'He will, but he's always working.'

Through the cafe windows the sun came in on to the table. It was shining so hard that it melted Tommy's chocolate sweets. Tommy ate one sweet after the other. People talked about people chain-smoking; Tommy was chain-eating. I hated him even more as he sat and stuffed sweets into his mouth.

My mother wore new clothes. She looked smart.

'Is he ever going to come?'

Pat told me to shut up. 'Mum's got enough on her plate – don't you understand?'

'I wanna see Dad.'

Tommy leapt at me. 'We all wanna see Dad.'

'Shut up now. Just shut up.' She sat smoking. Richard sat on the floor. The wireless played behind the counter. Tommy sat back down, putting another chocolate toffee in his mouth. Richard was sucking a sticky lolly. Pat and I were having ice-cream sodas. Pat's nose had ice cream on it.

'He will come, boys. But he has to work so hard, so we can get a house again. So we can all be together.'

My mother lit another cigarette and blew the smoke against the hot window. She looked as though she was thinking of something else. I was thinking of the tea shop in Westbourne Grove, with the big windows that got hot in the summer. Everyone looked so small in that cafe, because the ceiling was so high. Even the adults looked small – even the tallest of men, like my uncle Tom Dunne, my mother's brother. Even he looked small with the ceilings so high.

She had another tea. She sipped the tea and smoked. The man behind the counter asked if the kids were happy.

'They're happy now. I had to get them out of that place for an afternoon.'

The man agreed; everyone needed a break from that place. Many people came from the orphanage down to the cafe by the station.

Pat told my mother how good he was at the place. They all liked him and Tommy. 'We're always working with the nuns.'

'Good, Pat. You should be useful.'

Tommy had to tell my mother how I was useless. And how the nuns didn't like me.

'Don't keep on at him.'

Tommy shut up and ate another chocolate toffee. The music from the radio was a big band. My mother tapped her feet. The cafe cat came up and sniffed Richard. He stroked it heavily.

So when were we going home? Tommy and Pat didn't like me asking. You could tell that it upset her because she didn't know how to answer. She brought us comics when she had another cup of tea and some more cigarettes. We looked at the comics and then we had to go.

'Goodbye, love, goodbye, kids. Behave yourselves.'

And we all said goodbye to the cafe man. As we began walking up the hill, I got sad. It had been nice to be out of the place, away from being ordered around.

One Saturday, we went for a walk, along the path through the fields. Jo and I were together. I hadn't wanted to go, because I'd told Richard that I would take him out – we were going to play in the field out the back. We were going to pull up the long grass and build walls; a house of walls of grass. But the nuns said we had to go for a walk. They let us pick blackberries, but they kept on walking and if we lagged behind they shouted. Jo and I were behind the others. I got stung by some nettles and Jo got a dock leaf and rubbed it on my leg. She knew about dock leaves and nettle stings. She was bright; she knew more than me.

We ran and caught up with the rest of the children. Dunleavy was talking to a nun. He was licking his teeth with his lips. They were talking about Jesus. Only people like Dunleavy talked to nuns about Jesus. I loved Jesus, but I wouldn't talk to a nun about him.

Summer came and went and we weren't allowed to play in the fields out back. A man came with a big cutter and chopped all the long grass so it was too short to hide in like you could before. Richard used to run off into the grass, and I would have to find him.

But now we couldn't even play in the short grass. And the nuns said that I couldn't go and see Richard so much. Sister Veronica said I had to stop going to the nursery even though the nurses didn't mind – they liked me taking Richard out. But the nuns got annoyed with me. Tommy and Pat got annoyed with me. But still I would go into the nursery and see Richard, even if I couldn't take him out. Until eventually the nurses said I couldn't come so much, because of what the nuns had said.

That winter Sister Ursula came to me one day and said, 'Your people are here, Tony.'

'My people, sister? My family?'

She took me along one of the corridors you weren't usually allowed in.

'Not your family. Your people are Catholics who want to be nice to you. You'll see.'

She took me to a room where a man and a girl sat waiting. They both had ginger hair and the girl was bigger than me. The man came over and took my hand.

'Hello, Tony, we're your people.'

Sister Ursula left me with them. I still didn't know who they were. 'Are you my family, mister?'

The girl stroked my hair. 'No, no, we're not your family, but we want to be kind to you.'

They told me everyone had 'people' – all the boys and the girls did. People adopted you, they said. They would be kind to you; they'd write to you and send you presents when it was your birthday. They gave me sweets and fruit and a prayer book and told me how they helped their church. And how they were going to be nice and friendly to me because I was in the orphanage. We had tea and cakes and sandwiches, and they said that I must write to them and they would write to me.

When they left, Sister Ursula took me back to the refectory and I asked her if Tommy and Pat would have people. She said they would and that their people would come and see them. When I saw Tommy and Pat, I told them all about it. Tommy laughed at me. 'We've already seen our people, stupid.'

I couldn't believe it. They hadn't told me.

'Did they have ginger hair?'

'Don't be stupid.'

Pat said his people had black hair. An old woman and an old man. But Tommy wouldn't tell me about his people; why should he?

Pat was playing with a ball, banging it off the wall and catching it again fast. He was quick. Then he threw it to me. And now we played the game together, banging the ball off the wall to each other.

Usually when there was nothing to do, I would look at the sky, at the clouds floating past, going somewhere with the birds and sometimes a plane. Or I'd just think about not being in the convent.

These days, though, Pat was better to me – Tommy was sometimes, too. They'd begun playing with me. And now the nuns didn't cause me so many problems; they didn't chase me round as though I was trouble.

So now I was playing this game with Pat. He always kept the ball right in the air, though I wasn't so good. Pat stopped playing with the ball, said he had something to tell me. He said it in a sad way.

'I don't think we're ever gonna leave here, Tony. I think we're always going to be here.'

'No, not always, Pat.'

'Tony, when did Mum last come and see us. You tell me?'

It was months and months and months ago. But she'd said she had to have an operation. Pat didn't believe that, though. Or that our parents were leaving the flat in Bayswater.

'I bet they're still there. I bet they could afford us.'

I had never seen Pat sad like this. He was always the one that went out helping the nuns. Not going to see Richard, but always behaving himself. The good boy, the nice boy, the right boy. Tommy behaved himself to keep in with people, but Pat was just well behaved and there was nothing you could do about it. As my mother said, he didn't have a bad bone in his body.

'Pat, don't say that.'

'That's what I think about in bed. And why we're in here. We shouldn't be here. We're not fucking orphans. Orphans don't have mums and dads; we have a mum and dad.'

At bedtime Pat walked off ahead of me, looking lost and beaten. As though now there was nothing left for him to do but drift around sadly. It worried me. My mother and father always said that you could get Pat up in the middle of the night and he would work. He was useful, always useful. Now he looked like a stray dog in the orphanage.

I lay in bed and thought of Pat, about how unhappy he must be. I may have been unhappy, Tommy as well, but it was simple unhappiness we felt. Pat, though, he was suffering, properly suffering. But who could I tell? Who would listen? Not the nuns; they would just tell you about children dying in other countries. What did it matter that Pat was stuck in an orphanage?

When my people came to see me with birthday presents, months after my birthday, I wanted to tell them about Pat; I wanted them to know that he needed to be got out of this place.

But I didn't. They couldn't help; they could just listen. And I didn't know how to explain that Patrick Bird was having a bad time.

And then, a week later, my mother came. It was unbelievable. Even Tommy was excited. Pat was beside himself and Richard chirped like a bird. There was nothing better than our mother coming to see us. This time I didn't ask about my father. I just wanted her to know we all loved her and that we weren't going to make her sad.

But there, for Pat and me to see, was the scar around her neck. A thin line, a half-circle that went round under her throat.

And she was smiling. I looked at the scar and looked at Pat. Pat looked at her and he looked at me. This was what she had said; she said she had to have an operation and there was no two ways about it. They'd taken out her thyroids, she said, but she didn't know why.

She took us down to the cafe and we'd never been so happy. Everyone just enjoyed it. Pat was happy again, like he always used to be. And then she told us: 'We might be getting a flat soon, kids. In Fulham.'

We looked at her with our mouths open.

'It may take a bit longer, but they are getting us one, kids. So we'll all be home together soon. Eddy's coming too.'

We jumped around. We went kind of mad. The man behind the counter seemed happy. We would be going home.

Pat asked, 'Where's Fulham, Mum?'

'It's near the river, Pat.'

It didn't matter where it was. I wanted to be home. I wanted to be with my mother and father.

As we walked back up the hill to the orphanage, I thought we'd never be sad again. Soon we'd be leaving. Pat jumped around, running ahead and coming back, chasing me. My mother told us not to feck around.

When my mother had gone, Pat and I played ball in the playground. He smiled all the time.

'You're happy, Pat.'

'I know I am.'

I told him I'd thought that he liked this place, and the nuns.

He stopped playing and looked at me. 'The nuns? The nuns are all right, but I want Mum and Dad.'

8

It was a Sunday. The wireless was playing loudly in the refectory. Tommy, Pat and I sat at the same table we'd sat at when we first arrived at the orphanage. Back then, we'd been frightened and worried, but now we were leaving.

A nun called to us: 'The three Birds.'

They always said 'the three Birds' when our mother came; all the time we were there, they called out 'the three Birds'. As though we were some kind of family. But we had not been a family at St Vincent's convent; we were just three boys who came together whenever our mother came to see us.

The nuns smiled and led us out. Some boys and girls said goodbye. Jo looked over at me. She waved, not looking happy, then turned the other way.

We walked down the forbidden corridors, towards the room where my mother was waiting for us. Going back the way we came all those years before, to the room we'd been left in on that first day.

She stood with two nuns. She looked happy, and laughed out loud when she saw us. We all ran forward to meet her. Sister Veronica tousled our hair. And then we were out the door and away, down the same paths that I had thought looked good. How stupid I had been, to think that being here was going to be some great adventure.

The adventure was going to start *now*, now that we'd left. My mother carried Richard to the bus stop, with Tommy, Pat and I crowding round her, hugging her for the fun of it.

On the bus, we sat looking out of the window. Everything looked different. People walked about but didn't seem to understand that this was a big day for us; it was our day, the day of the three Birds.

We had to take another bus. We tried to behave but we were excited. I felt like screaming, but I didn't. I just kept putting my hand over my mouth to stop myself.

Broxholme House was a block of council flats set among some small houses. It stood on a corner of a big square with a flower-bed in the middle. We ran into the square and looked up at the flats. On the top floor was my father, looking at us from a balcony. When we got upstairs, he stood smiling but we didn't run to him; it was so odd to see him. The flat was on the third floor of the block and felt small – the ceilings were low and everything seemed crowded in on us. Our new home could have fitted into one room at the orphanage.

My father was like a stranger, even though he didn't look any different. He was silent as he looked at us. Then he said, 'I've had peace and quiet. So behave yourselves.' So we behaved ourselves. We talked quietly because we were a bit frightened.

Fulham was nowhere near Notting Hill and it wasn't like Notting Hill. We had to get used to it. The houses were too small. The sky was bigger and there were more clouds. It looked cleaner, though; there were no slums in Fulham, or if there were we didn't see them.

My mother worried about us. We were nervous in the streets. Tommy went to a senior school and Pat and I went to St Thomas of Canterbury, near Fulham Broadway. My mother took us the first day. It was frightening; everybody stared at us and I didn't like the look of the place. Pat and I were used to the convent and didn't want to start again. Boys and girls rushed round, pushing and shoving; they weren't friendly. There was nothing to look forward to in this school.

At lunchtime, Pat and I stood together. We were two new boys, and we weren't ordinary. The convent had done something to us: we had become shy and frightened. And, of course, everyone could see that; they could see how we hid in the corners.

I realised that we were going to get into trouble here. Boys always took advantage of people who were frightened – I knew that because I'd seen it in the orphanage. As soon as you stopped being brave, they went against you and you were pushed and bullied. That was the way boys worked.

'Tony, let's get out.'

'Go home?'

'Just go. I don't like this at all.'

That was all right by me. We hurried away, running through the graveyard at the back of the school. There were nuns and priests outside the church, but we didn't stop; we just kept running.

We ran down side streets and came to a busy marketplace where stalls lined the road. Pat thought it might be Portobello, but it wasn't. As we walked around the market I asked Pat if he thought we'd ever get back to Notting Hill.

'I don't think so. We're stuck here.'

I almost wished we were back at St Vincent's – at least we knew everything about the place; there were no surprises there. But we'd have to settle in at our new school eventually. We'd have no choice.

Hayes and Coleman watched me. Coleman was quiet with blond hair. Hayes was fat with black hair. He was round; he had a big arse and he would try to sit on people and crush them. But he never tried sitting on me. At first, Hayes had tried to bully me, tried to push me around. But I'd lost my fear – even Pat had become stronger. We'd begun to go further, like we did when we lived in Notting Hill, down all those streets that we didn't know.

Hayes became annoyed when he realised he couldn't bully me, but I had no problem with him. If he came up against me, I would push against him. He'd get angry, but he'd do nothing.

Every now and then he'd get hit by a bigger boy. Then he would cry like a baby, but he'd still go off and pick on someone else. How could you feel sorry for this boy? He made me laugh because he wasn't even a good bully. Most people laughed at him, or they got someone else to take him on. Hayes said his father was a policeman, but that seemed to be a lie – he was always making things up. Coleman just hung around him. Without Coleman hanging around him, Hayes was nothing.

One day Hayes asked me if I wanted to go shoplifting with him. I didn't know what he meant.

'Nicking, you idiot.'

'Nicking what?'

'Anything. Whatever you want to nick. Coleman and me nick all the time.'

He showed me a bubble-gum game he'd stolen. I said I didn't want to nick anything. Hayes said I was a coward.

'What's so great about nicking?'

'It's fun.'

Hayes was always in trouble, getting told off by the teachers. The headmaster told him off and so did his parents. His parents came to the school once, to talk to the teachers. Hayes was proud of that, boasting about how tough he was. I didn't listen to him; I just looked at Coleman, following on behind.

I knew that Hayes would ask me again to go stealing with him, but I couldn't do it. Hayes wanted a gang. That's what he was after me for. He wanted to have boys who followed him.

He didn't care when Dominic's mother became ill. Dominic was an Irish boy in our class. And one day he said to me that his mother was very ill. He said he hadn't told anybody, but he was telling me because Jesus had said I was a good boy. I didn't understand. Had he been talking to Jesus? No one talked to Jesus – only the Pope, cardinals and priests, and maybe nuns. Jesus didn't speak to anyone.

Dominic said he'd had a dream, and in it his mother died. His mother was in heaven and Jesus said there was a boy who was good. He thought that boy was me, even though Jesus hadn't told him who the boy was.

'He said I would have to find the boy, Tony, and I think it's you.'

Hayes tried to bully Dominic. He still had the accent; he wasn't like us boys. We had grown up in London and were London-Irish boys. But Hayes said that Dominic was different: a poor Irish boy. Hayes pushed Dominic; he pushed him with his big fat stomach. And Coleman stood behind him, saying nothing. I pushed Hayes and said to leave him alone. I told him to fuck off.

Hayes pretended to be surprised at that, as though anyone who told him to fuck off didn't know how powerful he was. Later, in the playground, I told Dominic not to worry – Hayes was all wind – but Dominic was still frightened.

The next day, he didn't come to school and I thought it was because of Hayes. But it wasn't. The day after that, the headmaster called us into the assembly room and a lady teacher stood up and told us that Dominic's mother had died. I'd known that Dominic's mother had been ill, but I hadn't known she was *that* ill. She must have been very ill to die.

Hayes thought it was silly. He laughed in the playground; he laughed about Dominic's mother dying. I wanted to hit him. Dominic was a good boy who'd never harmed anyone.

Before Dominic came back to school, the class teacher spoke to us: 'I want you not to talk to Dominic about his mother. The poor boy has suffered; you must be kind to him.'

When Dominic walked into the playground the next day, everyone stopped talking and looked at him. He walked around on his own and no one talked to him. So I went over and spoke to him, but I didn't mention his mother.

We went for dinner together, and Dominic looked very white. He asked me: 'Tony, do they know about my mother?'

I told him that we all knew, but that we'd been told not to say anything.

He looked like he was in pain, about to cry. 'But my mother died. She's dead, Tony.'

I took his arm. I imagined that he was Tommy or Pat and our mother had died, that I had to tell them about her dying. That we had to be strong about our dead mother. I put my arm round Dominic and squeezed him as he cried.

'Dominic, your mother is with Jesus. She is happy with Jesus.'

I had never experienced the death of anyone in my family. But I thought about it now. I thought about all the bad things that happen when someone dies.

Dominic cried and cried as I stood with my arm round him. Other children walked by – a river of schoolchildren, all walking to the dinner hall. And in their midst was Dominic, crying.

I hadn't been his friend before, really – I'd just been all right with him in the playground. But now it seemed like I was his only friend. After dinner we walked down to Fulham Library. On the way, we saw two men digging a hole in the pavement and I stopped.

'Let's look in this hole, see if your mum's in it.'

He looked at me in a strange way, then he moved and stared down into the hole. He laughed. 'She's not in the hole, Tony; we had to take her on a boat to Ireland.'

He laughed again and I chased him down the street. I wanted him to laugh. I didn't want him to be sad about this. But I knew that if my mother died I could never look into a hole and joke about it.

The summer holidays came and Tommy and Pat bought a bike from a boy for two shillings. A bike was the best thing you could have. My father had said we could never afford one, but now Tommy and Pat had bought one – and because it was summer they could ride round all the time.

It was a two-wheeler. I'd never been on a two-wheeler before and I kept asking them to show me how to ride it. They told me to fuck off; they had paid a shilling each for it and I wasn't getting a ride. Eventually, though, Tommy told me they'd teach me how to do it. I would probably break my neck, but that was my fault. They could help me get on the bike, but then I had to learn how to balance myself: I had to be let go.

It was a hot day and the park was very green. I felt frightened as

I sat on the bike, but it didn't matter – if I fell off, I could always get back on again.

Tommy held me and I soon lost myself. I left the path and ended up on the grass, grazing my knees. But it didn't matter. Tommy put me back on the bike.

I fell off many times, but I kept getting back up. And then Tommy and Pat held me steady, screamed at me as I cycled down the path towards the fountain. Miraculously, I stayed on; I kept going and balanced myself as I got to the fountain in the middle of the park. And then I kept going, turned on to a path that ran to the left. And before I knew it I was at the end of the park – and again I turned, without stopping, and cycled back.

I went round the park two times. Tommy and Pat were clapping and screaming at me because I had learnt to balance myself on the bike: now I could ride.

They let me ride it for the rest of the afternoon, round and round the park, until we had to go home. They were very excited that they'd taught me how to cycle.

The next day I wanted to go back on the bike. But Tommy and Pat told me I'd learnt and that was the end of it; I wouldn't be allowed on it unless they were both too tired to ride. And then the bike was taken off them. The boy who'd sold it to Tommy and Pat didn't own it – it was stolen. The boy who really owned it came with his father and took it away. I was very unhappy. I now needed to ride a bike. A bike was the best of all things.

One afternoon, near the end of the summer holidays, I stood watching a girl and her friend riding a bike. It was a boy's bike, and they were taking turns to ride it round the park. I didn't talk to them but, after a long while, she noticed me watching them.

'D'ya want to have a go?' she said. 'You can, so long as you bring it back.'

I couldn't believe she was going to let me have a go. Bikes were something special; people didn't just let you have a go on them.

I rode off towards the fountain in the middle of the park. Then I turned and went up towards the cafe. I turned again and went back past the fountain, then rode to the far corner of the park. When I finally stopped in front of her she said, 'Do it again.'

She didn't think I would steal her bike. Later that afternoon, after I'd ridden round the park many times, she had to go. She asked me my name and laughed when I told her. Everyone laughed when I said 'Bird'.

Her name was Geraldine Osbourne. She said she lived in Parsons Green and went to school at St Thomas of Canterbury.

'That's where I go!'

I was so excited. I watched her leave on her bike, cycling down the little path and out of the park with her friend running along beside her. She'd said she'd see me at school. I looked at her, cycling down towards Parsons Green, and I loved her.

Geraldine was older than me – she was almost eleven. She had short brown hair. I thought about her all the next day. I went looking for her and couldn't find her. Then I tried to stop thinking about her. I hoped I would see her soon, though. We were going back to school in a week. I might have to wait, but at least I knew I'd see her again.

I was bored, that last week of the holidays. Pat was making friends, because he was going on to his new school in September, and Tommy was working at the butcher's below the flats. I was without company, and Fulham didn't offer much in the way of excitement.

At school I watched Geraldine in the playground, but I was too frightened to approach her. When she finally looked over and saw me, she smiled such a big smile that I blushed. There she was, the girl I'd been thinking about constantly since I met her. She came running over to me, clapping her hands and calling my name.

I thought she was going to kiss me. But she just threw her arms round me. She didn't care – she had no fear about looking stupid. She told me she was glad to see me, that she'd been thinking about

83

me all the time. I couldn't say the same, even though it was true; I
couldn't say a thing.

'Let's walk together to dinner, Tony.'

'All right.'

But I was shy and my face felt hot, burning.

The bell sounded the end of break and Hayes came over.

'Got a girlfriend, Birdy?'

'Shut your fucking mouth.'

He laughed. I'd said it so hard, he knew he'd got something right.
I realised that I hated Hayes; I hated that he knew something about
me.

At dinnertime I waited for Geraldine, my legs shaking. She came
out of her class with a few girls who walked off as soon as she saw
me. Geraldine smiled a lot at me but I could hardly say anything.
She asked me if I was shy, and I told her maybe.

It was OK: she had enough talk for both of us. So she spoke and
I listened. She told me that she lived with her sister, that she didn't
have a mother and father – she'd lost them. I didn't ask too many
questions. When she asked me about my family, I felt like lying. I
felt like telling her that my father ran a company and my mother
worked in a flower shop or something. When I told her I had four
brothers, she looked surprised.

'Are you poor, Tony?'

'All the time.'

I wanted to lie. I wanted to say all sorts of things – that my father
had a big red American car, and that we had a boat on the river. But
I didn't; I stopped myself lying.

In the afternoon, I nearly had a fight with a big boy. He was
pushing people over and when he pushed me over, I jumped at him.
He hit me. And then Hayes threatened him and I stood and watched
him back off, frightened. I was shaken by this incident; the boy was
big. I wished that Pat was still at the school.

After school I was supposed to go straight home, but I walked
with Geraldine to Parsons Green. We talked all the time now. I told

her some lies. I told her that we had a big house in Ireland, not just a farm. She listened but I wasn't sure if she believed me.

She took me inside her house and made me say hello to her almost-deaf grandmother, who was sitting in a chair, knitting. Geraldine had her own door key and I thought this was very grown-up. I wasn't allowed a key to our flat – no one was. At our house a key hung behind the door on a piece of string and we had to put our hand through the letterbox and pull it out.

Geraldine's was a big house, with a little garden in the front and a big one out back. The house looked old, and all the furniture was old, but it looked clean. Geraldine was very proud of her house. She showed me her clean kitchen and her room, full of books and dolls.

We went cycling down at the green, by the White Horse pub. We had an hour there before I had to go.

'I like you, Tony Bird.'

'I like you, Geraldine Osbourne.'

We cycled together as far as the park, me on the seat and her pedalling. I showed her the back of our flats and she looked at them for a moment then said, 'They look very nice.'

When I got home, my mother was mad. She grabbed hold of me and asked me where I'd been, said she'd thought I'd been run over. I was to come straight home from school in future.

'But, Mum, I have a friend now. She says . . .'

She cursed me and told me to get out of her hair. I went out and stood on the balcony, wondering how I could tell her about Geraldine.

As usual, the Red Hall was packed. I was sitting with Pat and we were waiting for the film. Saturday-morning pictures were always mad; kids jumped around and screamed. And then a man would come on to the stage and shout into the microphone that everyone should keep quiet.

He had to shout many times: 'No films, boys and girls, until you're all quiet.'

But the shouting always carried on. So he would stop and count to ten, then everyone would be silent. We had to sing a song first:

> We come along
> On a Saturday morning
> Greeting everyone with
> A smile, smile, smile . . .

It was the same every week. The cartoons, followed by the serial and then the main film.

When the show was over I rushed off to Parsons Green, as I always did now. I never went out with Pat; I'd go over to Geraldine's. And however much I liked Saturday-morning pictures, I loved going to see Geraldine more. She would be waiting for me outside her house, or sometimes on the corner. We were best friends now and were together as much as we could be, after school and on Saturdays. On Sundays she had to go to church and stay in, and I was never allowed to see her on Sundays anyway because it was the Lord's day of rest. But even then, after church, I would walk down to Parsons Green in the hope that she might be outside her house. She never was, though. I hated Sundays.

When I reached the fire station I could see Geraldine standing on the corner. She rushed over on her bike, breathless and talking ten to the dozen.

We sat in the dining room at Geraldine's house, just the two of us, and her sister made us lunch. Geraldine whispered to me that her sister thought I was very nice.

'Does she? I like her.' It was true – she was always kind to me.

'She likes you. She doesn't always like my friends.'

I had to eat carefully, slowly. Even though I liked having lunch and being in Geraldine's house, I felt better out on the street.

There were pictures of Jesus and Our Lady everywhere. Her family were Irish, but they were Holy Irish, as my mother called them: Irish people who took God very seriously. They were different to us.

After lunch we went and played in the park. I saw Pat with his friends but I kept away. I didn't want them taking the piss out of me like boys always did if you played with girls.

At the end of the park there was a metal bar to stop people from driving in. Geraldine was turning herself over and over on it while I watched her and cycled round in circles.

'You're looking at my knickers.'

I stopped cycling. 'No I'm not.'

'Yes you are; you're trying to see my knickers. Boys always want to see girls' knickers.'

I swore at her.

She ran over, took the bike from me and cycled away. I stood and watched her. I was really angry. And then she came back and screamed at me: 'I'm a good Catholic. And I only play with good Catholics!'

She cycled away again and I shouted after her: '*I'm* a good Catholic, a fucking good Catholic!'

I watched her cycle off and I felt like running after her. But she was upset and wouldn't have listened, I knew that.

I walked around feeling angry for the rest of the day. I loved Geraldine. She probably loved me.

At dinner on Monday she ignored me. I stayed with Hayes and Coleman, and after we'd eaten we went to some shops in Fulham Road. Hayes and Coleman went inside and I stayed on the pavement. They came out with sweets they'd stolen.

Hayes gave me a handful. 'See, it's fucking easy.'

I ate the sweets and felt that maybe Hayes wasn't such a bad boy after all.

I hung around for Geraldine after school. She came out with some other girls and together they walked down the street. I followed them, walking only a few feet behind, and every now and then Geraldine looked over her shoulder at me. Eventually she left the girls but she carried on walking ahead of me. We were almost at her corner when she stopped.

'I don't like you, Tony Bird.'

'I like you, Geraldine Osbourne.'

'What am I going to do with you? You've such a bad mouth.'

'I swear, but only when I'm angry.'

I knew she wanted to make up, but she didn't know how.

'I wasn't looking at your knickers; I was looking at you.'

'Maybe, but boys do look at girls' knickers.'

I could see she was breaking. 'Not me. I like *you*, not because you wear knickers.'

She laughed. 'Girls always wear knickers.'

I wanted to grab Geraldine and squeeze her. I wanted her to know that I loved her, that she was the best person in the world. But I couldn't. I could only look at beautiful, strong, big Geraldine.

I wanted to tell someone that I loved Geraldine. But who could I tell? My brothers would have laughed. My mother would have said I was stupid. My father would have laughed, but he would have been good about it if I'd caught him in one of his good moods.

We played out on her bike, and talked about being good Catholics. I told her that I thought Jesus was the greatest person in the world. I told her about my first Holy Communion and how good it had been. I told her about the orphanage and she listened very carefully.

Night was coming when I got home. My mother hit me, said she'd told me to come straight home.

'Wait until I tell your father.'

He was very tired when he came in from work. He sat in his chair, looking as though he was suffering. My mother rubbed cream into his hands and then she told him I wasn't coming home straight from school. He was getting old, you could tell; looking grey, tired.

He smiled when I told him about Geraldine, and he looked good, now, even though he was tired. 'You're a lad.'

He told my mother that at least I was keeping out of trouble.

She moaned, but he said there was nothing wrong with chasing girls.

'But he's only a child,' she said.

So Geraldine and I were friends again, like we'd been on the first day of school after the summer holidays. Sometimes we'd argue – every now and then – but we were good friends. I knew the arguments were silly and they didn't mean anything.

Hayes, meanwhile, was still trying to get me into his gang; it was still just him and Coleman. And one day Hayes told me he had a great plan for getting money. He was going to steal the money being collected for a dead priest.

The priest was Father Digby Best, from the church next door – the school's priest. I didn't know him, but he had died and each day the teachers were collecting money for him. It was locked in a cupboard in our classroom. What it was for, I didn't know.

Hayes said he was going to take a bit of money out each day. That way, they'd never realise it was gone. He wanted me to be the watch while he and Coleman went into the cupboard when no one was around.

'Three people is better than two.'

I couldn't see why they needed me, and I didn't care – I wasn't going to get involved. But Hayes wasn't bothered either; he was going to do it anyway. He said he could give me money and when I asked him why he'd do that he said, 'Because you have to join my gang.'

A few days later, Hayes stopped me in the corridor. He told me that money was being collected every day now, and that meant we could take more of it.

'What do I have to do?'

'Stand outside the classroom, and call out if anyone comes.'

I did it, two or three times, just stood in the corridor and kept a lookout. I didn't mind. Then Hayes would give me some of the money and we'd go and spend it in sweet shops.

It was a week when Geraldine and I weren't talking so I didn't mind spending time with Hayes and Coleman. We'd had a big argument because she'd said that anyone who swore couldn't be near to Christ. I said she was being silly, but she carried on: she said that I wasn't near to Christ because I swore, and that meant that everyone I knew – my mother included – was a bad Catholic. I told her she was talking through her arse.

One morning, my mother said she didn't want me to go to school. She didn't tell me why. She sent me out to buy her cigarettes and then I stayed at home all day, helping her round the house and looking after Richard and Eddy. My mother seemed unhappy about something – she didn't say anything, but I knew she was unhappy. I was pleased to stay home. In the evening, she had an argument with my father. He beat her. He beat her with his belt and I watched him do it. It was horrible; I couldn't do anything. Tommy and Pat sat watching too. My father shouted as he beat my mother, and then he went to bed. He had turned into a horrible man. My mother cried as she sat in the chair. I tried to comfort her, and so did Tommy and Pat, but she kept sobbing. She just sat in her chair, crying.

The next morning, at school, the headmaster called me into his office. He was a soft man. His name was Mr Angel – and in a way he was like an angel, so gentle and friendly.

'Tony, have you stolen money from Father Digby Best's collection?'

'No, sir.'

'Have you helped Hayes and Coleman steal?'

'No, sir.'

'I thought not.'

He told me to go to my class. Hayes and Coleman were not there.

I was later told that Hayes and Coleman had been caught the day before. The teacher had noticed that money was going missing, so they'd set a trap. Hayes had said I was involved, but no one believed him. The headmaster hadn't believed him, and that's why he'd asked me: Mr Angel thought I was innocent.

That was Hayes. He betrayed people, tried to spread the blame. In the playground he came up to me, angry that I'd got away with it.

'Fuck off, Hayes, you shouldn't have told on me.'

I hit him. I hit him again and again. He pulled back, tried to hit me, but I was too quick. He ran off. I hated him for telling on me; I would never do that.

Geraldine told me that she didn't want to see me any more. But I loved her, I told her. 'I love you, Geraldine. Please don't stop seeing me.'

But Geraldine had problems with me. I didn't know what to say to her.

One Saturday she was going to the hairdresser's. I walked down with her and waited outside. I waited for hours, standing on the corner. When she came out, her hair was different. It was cut very short; she looked like a boy. She asked me what I thought and I told her: 'You look like a boy.'

She looked at me with a sad face and I realised I'd said the wrong thing. We started off to her house, but when we got to her street she turned to me and said, 'I can't see you any more, Tony.'

I knew. I knew that I couldn't argue with her. She told me I was a very difficult boy, and I didn't know what she meant by that.

'Geraldine, Geraldine.'

'What?'

'Geraldine, I'll love you forever.'

She walked down her street and went into her house.

Hayes and I went out one dinnertime. He was showing off, nicking stuff he didn't need. We stopped at a shop near the market and he said he was going to show me something; he was going to nick a ball.

I stood outside and waited for him. Inside, he pushed a ball up his jumper. It was obvious what he had stuffed up there; he was just showing off. And then he tried to leave the shop. He almost got outside but then the shop-owner grabbed him. Hayes shouted at the man: 'It's not just me, mister. He's in on this.'

I was still standing on the pavement, in the street. I hadn't gone inside. And now Hayes was shouting and pointing at me. I turned and ran off, back to school. I went into my class, and acted as if nothing had happened.

The police came. I was asked to leave my classroom and then I was taken to Fulham Police Station. They told me that they were going to get my parents, that I was being charged with shoplifting. They brought Hayes in. He stood beside me and I had nothing to say to him. He had told them all sorts of things: he and I had been shoplifting; he had gone into the shop and I was watching out for him. I didn't know what to say. I just looked at him and knew he was the biggest sneak I had ever met. He was the worst kind of person. He had shopped me, even though I hadn't done anything.

Coleman wasn't involved this time; he hadn't been there. If he had, he would have been accused too. But it was me – Hayes was accusing me. And all I'd done was stand on the pavement.

A few weeks later, we went to Chelsea Juvenile Court. The magistrate sentenced us to a ten-shilling fine and three years' probation. I didn't understand what they meant by probation. My mother sat in court with me, and she asked what probation was. She was told that each week I had to go to an office in West Kensington and that if I didn't I would be brought before the court again.

We took our eleven-plus, the exam to determine whether we'd be going to the grammar school, or the secondary-modern school. I failed: I was to go to the secondary school. I went for an interview there with Mr Murphy, the headmaster. He was very polite, but I realised that however the interview went I would be going to his school.

My mother sat with me in Mr Murphy's office while he asked me questions.

'What have you been studying, Tony?'

'About the coalmines, sir.'

He smiled. 'Oh, yes. Now, where are the nearest coalmines to London?'

I didn't have to think. 'Kent, sir.'

He looked confused. 'Kent?'

'Yes, sir.'

He smiled again. 'No, no, boy. Derbyshire. Derbyshire. There are no mines in Kent.'

When we left, I told my mother he was wrong.

'For the love of God, he's a headmaster – he should know these things.'

'He's wrong, Mum.'

She told me to shut up, so I did.

9

In our classroom at St Thomas More Secondary Modern School, Miss Ferrier told us what she expected from us. She was a small, dark-haired teacher. She told us that this was the beginning of our education, that up until now we had been playing with words and numbers. Now we had to learn and there was a lot to learn. She talked a lot about learning. There was only a short time in which to learn everything, and if we wanted to learn she would help us. But if we didn't want to learn, well, that was our problem. But our lives would be affected by our education.

Miss Ferrier walked round the class. She stopped every now and then and looked at us, as if she was inspecting us. She talked all the time, about the things we could do with our education.

She was very interesting; she seemed tough but nice. She was one of those people you didn't mess around. She wouldn't let you.

I was sitting next to Jimmy. Jimmy was two days older than me and was the funniest boy ever. He was also the kindest. He didn't cause fights. I had known him for about a year, had first seen him over the park, playing on the swings. Everyone liked Jimmy, and now here I was sitting next to him.

At break time we gathered together. It was a large playground and we were the small people in it. We were the ones to be bullied and picked on.

The girls seemed very grown-up. The boys played games, but the girls stood round in groups talking about boys and hair.

Pat came up to me with a group of other boys. He looked pleased with himself.

'If anyone picks on you, you tell me.'

'What if they're bigger than you, Pat?'

'Never you mind, I'll have them.'

Who was he impressing? Not me. I knew he was just showing off and that I'd have to fight my own battles.

The maths teacher always wore a suit, as though he was going somewhere nice. Everyone else dressed for their work, but the maths teacher dressed as though his work was in a men's clothes shop. Each day he wore a different suit: he had five suits, one for each day of the week.

I ran into problems with him straight away. He accused me of not paying attention, but I couldn't understand what he was going on about. On our first day, he said that he was introducing us to what came after arithmetic. I couldn't see the point of anything after arithmetic.

But the music teacher, Mr Beswick, was the really bad one. He seemed to be angry all the time and he spoke to me as though I was the biggest fool. He pulled ears and grabbed hair and noses; he always seemed to be torturing people. And even during those first few days it was obvious that I was going to get into trouble with him.

Miss Ferrier thought I was going to be trouble. She told me so. She said that I would have to behave in her class, that I shouldn't even think about playing the fool. The teacher always won and, if she felt like it, she would send me to the headmaster for the cane.

I was eleven and I was on probation, so already they were expecting trouble from me. My father said I wasn't to get into any more trouble: any more trouble and he was going to thrash me to within an inch of my life. So of course the new school was going to be trouble; I could tell that much.

Early on Saturday mornings, I needed to get Beat the coke for her fire. She needed hers first because she went out with Len to the allotment. This morning was wintery, drizzling and grey. Beat was on the top floor, a few doors away from us. Mrs Roberts was on the second floor and Mrs Cleery on the ground floor. So, Beat first,

Mrs Roberts second, Mrs Cleery next and then us. And then Mrs Southgate at number 49 was asking if I could take her on as a regular.

The gasworks opened at eight o'clock and closed at twelve. I would have to make four journeys. Four journeys with the old pram I'd found out by the park. It still had four good wheels, though the handlebar had broken. I mended it with wood and string.

Beat was stood waiting on the balcony when I came out. It was eight already and really I was fifteen minutes late. But Beat didn't complain. She had a cigarette sticking out of her mouth and she was coughing. She got up at six every morning, and she'd still be coughing at eight. You could hear her along the balcony. Someone was always coughing. If it wasn't Beat, it was Mrs MacCarthy or my mother.

'Sorry to rush you, Tone.'

'No, Beat, I should've been up and out by now.'

Len came out, smiling. His mouth held a cigarette, hand-rolled and thin.

'Mornin', Tony. Do you want any help?'

I told him no, it was my job.

They gave me the five shillings and sixpence for the two bags of coke they wanted. Plus another sixpence for the top-up. The top-up almost doubled the amount of coke, probably bringing it up to fifty pounds a bag. I went and got my pram from the old disused washing rooms and quickly bumped it down the stairs. I would be late all day. It wasn't so much getting the coke that took time; it was queuing up and waiting around. The easy part was putting it in the pram, two bags each time, and pushing it down the length of Imperial Road. And it wasn't that difficult to get it to the flats and carry the bags one at a time upstairs. The carrying and the pram-pushing probably took twenty minutes. But at the gasworks I had to line up for half an hour behind old-age pensioners who made everything so slow.

Not many eleven-year-olds went for the coke. But I made nine shillings' profit each Saturday. It was dirty work: my hands got cut, I got wet and cold and it strained me – carrying fifty-pound bags up the stairs was no joke. But the money and joy of being left alone made me happy to do it.

So that morning, late, I rushed. The rain was thick. I had on my old clothes – an old overcoat that was too big for me, a shirt that was ripped at the collar, and a pair of trousers held up with string. I looked awful, going up to the North Thames Gas Board Coke Works. But it didn't matter: I'd get nine shillings and I could clean up afterwards.

The rain and the grey made the day very cold and it was still dark. I didn't mind the dark in the morning, though; it was good fun, getting up in the dark and going off to work. The street was full of people, pushing old prams and barrows. I knew I had to be quick, or Beat would be late for the allotment and they wouldn't be able to plant their carrots or whatever. Len and Beat wouldn't have a day of it like they usually did, with their sandwiches and their flask of tea, sitting in the small hut on the edge of their little allotment.

I'd been up there once, but not to help. My mother and I went up with Eddy and Richard, just to see what it was like. You could tell Beat and Len were very pleased with their hut. They had a little heater and an oil-lamp. Len said it was so cosy he sometimes felt like staying there all night.

Beat's husband was deaf and stayed at home. He'd been injured in the First World War. He had big ears and his face had a worried look. Len was Beat's brother. He was short – shorter than her – and had no teeth and a few fingers missing. When he shook your hand, it was all stumps. He loved shaking people's hands, just so he could give them a surprise.

Near the gasworks entrance I joined a long line of people. I reckoned it would be a half-hour wait, but then they laid on another man and it became a twenty-minute wait and soon I was standing in front of the big coke-shoot. He shot the coke into the bags and I pulled them aside and paid him. With the bags in the pram, I set off at a gallop.

I had to be careful as I ran down the road, because if I turned too fast I could easily topple the pram. Opposite the flats, I looked up at the third floor. Beat was looking out the window. I went upstairs with the first bag and at the top Len had already laid out newspaper in the hall so I didn't leave dust everywhere. I did the other bag very quickly, and Beat and Len were soon on their way.

I'd finished by eleven-thirty. I cleaned up, put on my ordinary clothes and gave my mother five of the nine shillings. The other four were mine to spend. I was meeting Robbie from my school. We were going across the river to Putney to see a film called *Trapeze*. It was always cheaper to go in Putney because they showed films two weeks after they'd been shown in Fulham.

Robbie was the quietest boy in all the school, but he never got pushed around. I wondered how he managed to keep himself out of trouble – I was always having to fight my corner. I'd get into fights while Robbie, small and quiet, remained free of trouble.

We walked by the river because we were early. Robbie told me about the fish he and his father caught, not in the Thames but out in some little canal or stream miles from London. He said they fished right out in the country, where there were no houses, just trees and fields. I told him that I loved the country, that I wanted to live there. I told him about Ireland and my grandmother's farm. He seemed excited for me, but he was really only interested in rivers and streams and canals.

Trapeze was the best film I ever saw. Burt Lancaster had broken his leg when he fell from a trapeze before the film had begun. Tony Curtis was the new man in the act and Gina Lollobrigida was the beautiful girl they both loved. Afterwards, Robbie and I decided that we might go off with a circus and learn to risk our lives on the high wire. We crossed the river and walked back to Fulham, and imagined this dangerous life. But Robbie then said that he'd rather be a fisherman and go off on a big boat out to sea. And stand on the end and cast his line into the water and catch fish as big as himself.

Miss Ferrier said to me one day that she didn't like my manner; I was surly. She wanted to know why I was surly. She'd asked me to stay back at breaktime when the class went out to the playground. She said I was getting bad reports for music and maths. I told her I didn't know why, but really I did: I knew why. I wasn't good at maths. I couldn't add up. I could do some of the stuff, but I had problems with the difficult stuff and that made the teacher angry with me. He said I was the troublesome one in the class. I couldn't understand why I had to learn the stuff he was teaching. I could see why I needed to know how to add up, but not the other stuff.

Miss Ferrier was my form teacher. She was in charge of me, so when I got bad reports she always heard about it. She said I was letting myself down. She said my PE teacher had told her I was the worst in his class. I never had any kit and I couldn't play football.

What did I want to play football for? I'd told the teacher that my parents had no money to pay for plimsoles and shorts, and he still said I had to play football.

Miss Ferrier looked at me in a hard way. 'You're bright,' she said. 'I can say that. But there's trouble all round you.'

I couldn't defend myself. What could I say? That my music teacher hated me and pushed me around? That my maths teacher was horrible and had a nasty way of talking to everyone?

Miss Ferrier looked at another piece of paper.

'And you're still on probation for shoplifting?'

'Yes, miss.'

She sighed. 'Pull yourself together, Bird.'

I'd been going to see my probation officer each week for about a year. Each Tuesday, after school, I would get the bus up to his office in West Kensington. He'd ask me how I was getting on; he'd ask about my family and about school. He was a very good man and he would talk to me kindly. He had my school reports and he always said I had to do better. I told him how some of the teachers didn't like me. He always listened, and then he'd smile and say I had to try harder. Then he'd tell me to come back at the same time next week. Nothing really happened at the probation office, but at least he listened to me. He didn't give me great advice, though, and he couldn't explain to me why I was picked on by some of the teachers. I was twelve, now, and I thought school was supposed to help people like me.

When I told my mother about Miss Ferrier keeping me back, she looked at me hard. 'Have you been fecking about, Tony? Tell me the truth.'

'Mum, I ain't. God's truth, I ain't.'

She had a wild look in her eye, her angry-eyed look. 'Give a dog a bad name.'

I knew what she meant: give a dog a bad name and it'll be bad. Her eyes were now on fire. She sat at the kitchen table and wrote a letter to Miss Ferrier.

'Give that to Miss Fecking Ferrier tomorrow. I'll be coming to see her.'

I didn't read the letter, but I didn't give it to my teacher. I tore it up and put it in the rubbish bin the next morning. Later, Miss Ferrier called me as I was walking down a corridor to class.

She smiled – not a real smile, but the kind of smile you give when you think you have to. Then she said what my mother said, about giving a dog a bad name. A bad name could make me bad.

And she smiled again and sent me on my way.

The hambone man had a smile like a mask. And he was bent, his shoulders hunched over, and his hands were strange: he held things as if he wasn't holding them. I noticed that he couldn't grab things. You'd ask for a pound of ham and he would hold it as if he wasn't really holding it.

With his made-up smile and his bent back and funny hands, he didn't look well. But he always served me politely. One day, though, my mother sent me to ask him for credit.

It was always me who had to ask for credit. If we were so desperate that she couldn't even give my father his fare to work, then I would have to go begging. I'd go to the post office on a Monday and beg the postmaster to give us our Family Allowance before time. Ten shillings a week, due on Tuesday mornings. The postmaster would always moan at me, but he'd do it in the end. He'd throw the money down on the counter and complain in front of the other customers. They would look at me, but I didn't care what they thought. We were poor; we had to do things that poor people did. Like beg.

Pleading, begging, was my thing. Tommy and Pat were the workers; they had jobs in the evenings and at the weekends. My job was to beg and plead for the family. When the rent was due, I'd go to the rent office to tell them we were broke, they'd have to wait for the money. I'd always give them some elaborate story – we'd lost the money, or one of the kids had eaten it or thrown it away. They didn't believe me, but they'd let us off.

Then there was begging from Aunty Kathleen. I'd have to get the bus to Notting Hill. There, I'd walk past the school I used to go to, past the church I was baptised in and where I had my first Holy Communion. It was strange, going back to Notting Hill; it didn't seem like the same place. The streets looked small and the people looked different. There were black people everywhere, standing on corners and sitting on cars.

Aunty Kathleen would always welcome me, tell me I was her favourite, even though she knew I was coming to beg from her.

'Why do I only see you when your mother's broke, Tony? I'd like to see you when she has money in her pocket.'

She would always feed me and give me cups of tea. Usually it was just her and me. Her son was in the army and her husband would be working on the trains.

My mother never had any money in her pocket for long. But

Tommy would be working soon, and Patrick a year after that and me two years after him. She'd have money when we were all working.

Aunty Kathleen said that was a lifetime away. 'And it'll only be for a while. She'll soon be separated from her money.'

My mother was always being separated from her money. When she got my father's pay on Thursdays we were rich. We'd eat a good dinner and have sweets and chocolate after. Friday was a good day and Saturday too. My mother would do the shopping on Saturdays. Sundays, we'd have roast. But every week, Monday through to Thursday, before my father came home with his pay, were the worst of times.

On this particular afternoon, I was in the hambone man's shop, below our flats, waiting to ask him for credit. I'd never asked him before.

'What can I do for you, Tony?'

His face was smiling and he was rubbing his hands. His head was like Mr Punch's.

'Mr Williams, my mother says can she have some things and pay you on Friday?'

His face changed, and he kind of straightened up. Then he looked at me with his smile again. 'So long as she pays on Friday, Tony, I don't mind.'

My mother was leaning over the balcony when I went outside. I held up the stuff so she could see it. And when I got upstairs she kissed me.

But we were always broke. After that day, the hambone man gave us his goods for a while. Then, sometimes, she didn't pay him. He got annoyed and in the end he stopped giving us credit. One day I went into his shop and he grabbed hold of me, or tried to.

'Tell your bloody mother she can't have another thing before she pays for last week.'

And that was the end of the hambone man. We never went in there again. He came up to see my mother and she told him to feck off. He fecked off, angrily shouting at her as he left, calling her a criminal, saying the Irish were the scum of the earth.

My mother was crying in the kitchen. I tried to put my arm round her but she pushed me away.

'That'll do no good. Feck off out into the square.'

'Mum, what's the problem?'

'No problem you can solve.'

She stood up, made herself tea and lit a cigarette. I watched her, tears running down her face.

I sat beside her, said she had to tell me what was wrong.

She looked up, red-eyed, red-faced, her nose running. 'I'm thirty-seven years of age, an old fecking woman, and I'm having another.'

She smoked and cried. I'd never seen her like this – not in years, anyway. She'd get upset with my father, but never like this.

'Your father's gonna hit the fecking roof.'

'Can't you tell him it's someone else's, Mum?'

'Tony! Fecking Tony! You're a clever little sod. Sure, I tell him he needn't worry because it's a sailor's I met at a bus stop.' She laughed so much she coughed. She grabbed me and squeezed me. 'I'll still have to tell the old man.'

I looked after her that afternoon. I cleaned up for her, looked after Eddy and Richard. I took them out to the park so she could rest and then I brought them back and fed them. My mother said I could be 'a cunt and an angel, at one and the same time'.

That evening, when she told my father, he looked at her strangely, as if he really couldn't believe what he was hearing. Then he rolled himself a cigarette. He sat back, picked up his paper and said no more. She put Richard and Eddy to bed and we all sat on the long couch, watching quiz shows on TV, like it was just another night. But it was the night when we became six boys. There was no fight, as there had been with Richard and Eddy. My father seemed to take it in his stride.

★

Mickey had decided I was joining the gang. Him, Harry, John and now me. He came to my house in the half-term holiday. He knocked at the door; the others were waiting in the square below. Mickey was big – though, like me, only twelve.

'You're joining us, Tone. D'ya wanna join us?'

'Course I do, Mickey.'

'Get your coat, we're going out.'

My mother was angry that I was going out and wouldn't take Eddy with me. It was a Wednesday, the worst day. She was irritable because she had run out of cigarettes. She'd buy cigarettes on a Friday and sometimes, if she left her packet around, I would take a few. I would hide them and give them to her on a Wednesday, when she had none. I had given her two that morning, but that was it: there were no more left.

Harry didn't want me to join. He said I was a weed, I was too easily beaten up. He said I couldn't fight. He was thirteen and tough and whenever I had a fight with him, I lost.

John didn't mind. John was a quiet, good bloke. And now that Mickey had backed me, Harry would have to put up with his decision. Harry, of course, would never stand up against Mickey. Mickey played tough. I never found out if he really was, but he did have a tough family. His elder brothers, Mac and Roy, were 'Fulham Hards'. They knew how to handle themselves. Mac spent much of the time locked up. Roy was a good bloke. He also went round with a gang and he had a black mate called Hubert. They were good and never bullied anyone. My brother Tommy went round with Roy, although Roy had a fight with him once and broke Tommy's nose.

In the park, Mickey asked me what we should do. Harry watched, jealous.

'I dunno. Shoplifting.'

Mickey laughed, told Harry I was brave after all.

Harry wouldn't shoplift but Mickey would steal from anywhere. We walked down the Fulham Road towards Stamford Bridge and Chelsea football ground. On the way, we noticed a house with its front door open. Harry and John waited outside and Mickey and I went in. The place was empty, no one around. In a big room, we looked for something to steal.

Mickey wanted to take a big TV, but it was too heavy – we couldn't lift it. Then we noticed some money on the table, about a hundred threepenny pieces. We gathered them up and left, our pockets full of coins.

Outside, Harry jumped up and down. 'What you get?'

But we rushed up the street, with Harry following behind with John. It was like we'd made a big catch. We stopped at the Bridge Cafe, opposite the Chelsea football ground, and at a table Mickey and I emptied our pockets. Harry tried to take some money, said we were all in it, but Mickey pushed him away.

'No, it's for Tone and me.'

Harry and John had to settle for a cup of tea and a cheese roll, while Mickey and I had a fry-up. I was hungry – it had been bread and margarine at lunchtime. Mickey made a lot of noise eating his, as though he wanted to torment Harry. Harry looked unhappy, but John sat quietly as usual; he didn't seem to care.

IO

She held the brown envelope in her hand and tore it open without care.

'Another fecking bill.'

She read it with a snarl that became concern.

'For the love of God. You're going to court for not going to school.'

Pat and I would stay home to help my mother because she was becoming big with the new child. Eddy was at home and Richard would have to be taken to school; sometimes she couldn't manage it, she was so tired. If I took Richard to school then I would be late for my own school. So she'd tell me to stay at home.

Other times we just didn't have the money for the bus fare. It took an hour to walk to school. We'd help round the house gladly, any chance we got, because we had no liking for school anyway. She liked having us about and we'd make her tea, clean up for her and play.

But it was more trouble, and I'd had enough of it. Miss Ferrier had warned me again about the other teachers. But I could never put my finger on why I was always being seen as 'trouble'. Even Miss Ferrier couldn't put her finger on it; she just said it was my attitude. Miss Ferrier, though, was happy with me. She said she didn't understand why I was so awkward with the other teachers.

I'd been to an exhibition with Pat, at Earl's Court. A bank was giving out cardboard wheels that had the names of all the countries in the world on them; when you turned the wheel it showed you the name of each country's capital city. The wheels were free, and between us Pat and I had taken about fifty of them. When I took one into school everyone wanted it, so I brought the others in and sold them for threepence each. We made good money for something that had cost us nothing.

Miss Ferrier had seen me selling the card wheels in the playground. She praised me, said that I had a bright side to me and I had to work on it.

But the other teachers were not happy. They thought I said wrong things, I wasn't respectful. One day Miss Peck, the current-affairs teacher, got angry with me. We were supposed to bring in old newspapers to cut up for a scrapbook.

'Don't bring in the *Daily Mirror*. That is not a newspaper; it is a comic.'

All our parents read the *Daily Mirror*. So I asked her a very simple question: 'Does that mean that we have to buy the papers ourselves?'

No one else was brave enough to ask that question, but our fathers wouldn't read *The Times* or the *Daily Chronicle*. They were labourers and such like; they worked on building sites or dug roads. She exploded, stuck her face in my face.

'Bird, you ought to keep your beak shut.'

Everyone laughed when she said that, and later I had a few fights as people reminded me what Miss Peck had said. The girls were the worst. They taunted me. And I chased them, but I couldn't hit a girl.

Miss Peck had told Miss Ferrier about my 'downright rudeness'. Then the geography teacher told her that I was always talking out of turn. That was difficult, because I loved the geography class best. But he had said I had to learn to shut up during lessons.

My mother, Pat, Eddy and I got the bus to Harrods in Knightsbridge and walked down the back streets to the court. It was the same magistrate I'd seen before, Lady Wotton. She was grey-haired and had small, half-frame glasses. She looked at us over her glasses as though we were some kind of nuisances. She told my mother off.

'Mrs Bird, you have a legal responsibility to send your children to school.'

'Yes, madam.'

My mother was nervous; her stumbling voice gave it away.

'So you had better see to it that Anthony and Patrick go to school regularly. Otherwise we may have to take the matter further.'

What did she mean, 'take the matter further'? Put us away? Send us back to the orphanage?

Later, we had tea in the Joe Lyons tea shop in Sloane Square. My mother was not very happy and Pat and I couldn't cheer her up.

'Stupid woman. She should try bringing up a handful of children. Feck the bitch.'

I went to school that afternoon. Miss Ferrier knew where I'd been and she shook her head at me when I reported in.

'You're on a downward slope, boy.'

'Yes, miss, a downward slope.'

She smiled.

The following day was the school's annual sports day. I'd nagged my father for weeks and he'd given in: I now had plimsoles, shorts and a singlet. I won three heats in the 100-yard race and everyone seemed surprised, as though they hadn't imagined I'd put myself out. The crowd roared in the small stadium near Putney Bridge, and Miss Ferrier congratulated me afterwards.

I did poorly in the end of year exams, though. But I got good marks in current affairs and geography. Miss Peck was nice to me, said I had really tried. I had – I was interested in current affairs. We had talks about General de Gaulle taking over in France. And the marches of black people in America. There were pictures on the TV of policemen beating black people and setting Alsatian dogs on them. And watercannons. Miss Peck talked about civilised society and said that America couldn't call itself civilised – not if that kind of thing happened there. She talked about Notting Hill; there had been a riot there against black people. She wanted to know if we thought England was civilised. She had to tell us what a civilised society was.

★

School broke up for summer. My mother had the baby. He was called Peter Paul because he was born on the feast day of St Peter and St Paul. He was small and beautiful, like Eddy and Richard had been. We were all excited as he lay in his cot in the front room. Even my father, who didn't really want another mouth to feed.

Tommy would be starting work soon, so he'd be bringing in some money and things wouldn't be so tough. Tommy had long, black, greased-back hair. He looked like Elvis Presley. And he was chasing girls.

Pat, though, was still playing football. He wasn't interested in girls. He always laughed when I told him about girls I liked. He said I was too young and that I should forget about them until I left school. He had got quieter since we'd come to live in Fulham; he was a good boy, always did what he was told. He was no fun and had become really soft: no fights, no nicking, no girls.

One day Wendy Lewis bumped into me as I stood by the fountain in the park. I was waiting for Mickey and Harry. Mickey had wanted to go back to the house where we'd got the threepenny pieces but I'd said we should go down by the river at Putney. There were big houses there, posh, with gardens.

But while I waited for them Wendy Lewis came up to the fountain and nudged me with her hip.

'Hang on, Wendy.'

'Hello, Tony Bird.'

The park was full of kids. Fulham was like a garden – flowers in beds giving off scents and bright colours. Beat said that when she was a kid Fulham was full of countryside. I could imagine what it was like then: fields and rivers, ponds and streams, and country lanes. Old farmhouses, maybe, like Ireland.

Wendy asked me if I wanted to go down to the market with her. I had waited half an hour for Mickey and Harry. They were always late. Now, standing beside Wendy, I was wondering if I should wait any longer. She was the prettiest girl who came to the park. Mickey wasn't interested in girls; he just wanted trouble, wanted to get money and cause fights. Harry liked girls but he just did whatever Mickey wanted to do.

'Well?'

Wendy Lewis had never spoken to me before. She was always with a gang of good-looking girls. Some of them were older, maybe even fourteen, but Wendy, like me, was still twelve. She had very green eyes and light-brown hair. She had a wide face and her hands looked as though she should play the piano, they were so delicate. She had a wonderful smile that lit up the whole of her face. I had followed her home once; I'd walked through the back streets behind her. She'd stopped and looked at me, smiled, and then walked on. When she got to her block of council flats she blew me a kiss and ran in. We hadn't said a word to each other. It was strange, like we were friends but weren't. As though we knew each other but didn't.

We left the park by Parsons Green, up the back way. It reminded me of Geraldine. I still thought Geraldine was the best girl in all the world. She was the girl I had lost. If I knew her again, I wouldn't argue with her so much. But she'd gone on to one secondary school and I'd gone to another, so I never saw Geraldine. But that didn't stop me thinking about her.

Outside Parsons Green Tube, Wendy saw some girls she knew. She told me to wait and she crossed the road to them. They talked and giggled for ages, and they kept looking over at me as I stood on the opposite corner. She talked with her friends for so long, I thought she was going to go off with them. But then she said goodbye and came over to me. She took my hand and waved at the girls on the other side of the street.

'Come on, Tony. Let's go and have some fun.'

Mickey and Harry might be down at the market. And if they saw me with a girl there would be problems: Harry would make a play for her and Mickey would think I was a sissy. So I said to Wendy that maybe we should go to Bishop's Park instead. Mickey and Harry wouldn't go there; they always stuck to the market or the park near my flats. They never went down to Bishop's Park.

We walked down towards the Fulham Road, near the library. Wendy said she went there every Saturday. I could see Wendy chasing boys and talking to girls about hair and make-up. And pop music – Elvis and Buddy Holly and Paul Anka. The latest records in the *Melody Maker* and *New Musical Express*. But I couldn't see her reading books.

She pulled me across the road. I'd never even been inside the library. She let go of my hand as we went through the door. We went straight to the junior library. Wendy told the smiling woman behind the desk that she wanted to show me around. Then Wendy went to look at some books and left me with the woman. She said I ought to join.

'I'd like to, but – '

I couldn't tell her that my father didn't like libraries. That he had borrowed a book from the library before the war and hadn't returned it. He was frightened that if I joined they'd catch up with him.

'I'll have to ask my mum and dad.'

'Yes. They'd have to sign the form.'

The woman was very friendly. She picked up books to show me and asked me what I was interested in, what I most enjoyed learning about at school. When I told her geography, she got excited – it was her favourite thing too.

She left me at the geography section. Wendy was sitting at a table with her nose in a book. She had her legs pulled up and I could see the white of her knickers. I still couldn't believe that a girl like Wendy would want anything to do with libraries. I watched her for a while. She didn't stir. Her knickers looked good. My reading wasn't very good. Miss Ferrier said that as a bright boy I should be reading more; I was slow, but I could get better. I picked up a book on American national parks. It was full of photographs of mountains and forests, rough streams and rivers with salmon leaping. Eagles soared through the air. And there were close-up pictures of the eagles' faces, with their sharp white beaks. I looked over at Wendy.

She was still reading. I sat with the book on American parks, then I looked at an atlas. We'd been in the library for more than an hour before Wendy called me over and said we should go. She asked me if I liked it there.

'I love it. I'm coming here every Saturday as well.'

'I bet you never come.'

'I bet you a thousand pounds I do.'

She whispered. Everyone whispered in the library, except for the small kids. They made all the noise they wanted, even though their mothers tried to quieten them. Before we left, the woman gave me an application form for my parents to fill in for me. Outside, Wendy said she thought I wouldn't give it to them. I said they might not sign the form.

'My dad doesn't like libraries.'

'Then he's silly.'

I didn't disagree. I was sure that after twenty years they couldn't trace my father's book from a library in Notting Hill.

Wendy took my hand again. When we got to Bishop's Park she wanted to play a chasing game, which involved her running and me chasing her. We played on the swings, too, then we had a pinching game.

Then she said, 'You can kiss me if you want.'

She giggled. I kissed her on the lips. She closed her eyes; I kept mine open. Then she pushed me away.

'Love a duck. I have to be home for dinner.'

According to the floral clock in the park, it was twelve-thirty. We rushed off, out of the park and down the Fulham Road. Near to her flats, she stopped walking and looked at me. She was all hot and sweaty from rushing, and she had a serious face.

'Can I see you after dinner, Tony?'

I said I'd wait for her, right where we were standing. I'd stood here when I followed her home that time, months before. I'd turned round and walked straight into a lamppost, cut my face. I had a big bump and bruise on my head for weeks. My mother thought I'd been in a fight; my father said he hoped I'd given as good as I'd got. They didn't believe me about the lamppost.

Wendy turned and ran off into the flats, calling back that she'd bring me some food. I stood for a few minutes then I wandered off up to the main road, past the undertaker's. I stood on a corner, watching the passing buses and thinking about Dominic and his dead mother. I always thought about her when I saw an undertaker's. And about how Dominic was such a good boy.

After a while, I went back and stood outside Wendy's flats. When she came out she had something stuffed up her dress. She quickly ran across the road towards me.

'Let's get round the corner.'

It was as though she was committing a big crime. When we got round the corner she looked up and down the street, then pulled up her dress. Tucked into her knickers was a parcel of newspaper. I must have looked surprised.

'It's all right – you won't catch anything.'

She'd brought me a piece of fruitcake and a hard-boiled egg. I laughed as she gave me the food, thinking it was funny that she'd hidden it in her knickers.

I ate, as we walked down the road, and then I went into a shop and told them I had a dry throat and they gave me a glass of water. It was the best dinner I had ever had. We went back to Bishop's Park. We looked at the floral clock and at the message from the Mayor of Fulham written in flowers. We played again on the swings, and Wendy said she could go higher than me. She could, nearly touching the top bar. Then we went and threw pebbles into the Thames. And in no time she said she had to go home.

As we walked back to her flats I told her about the time I banged my head. She kissed me and ran inside. I wasn't brave enough to ask her if we could meet again. I watched her go in and thought I was stupid not to ask. I stood for a long while, looking at the entrance to the flats, and hoped, really hoped, that she would come out again.

Slowly, I started to make my way home. I knew that my mother would beat me. She would be angry that I hadn't helped her with Richard and Eddy and Peter. As I walked through the park I saw Mickey and Harry climbing a tree. They saw me too, and came over.

Mickey looked angry. 'So where the fuck was you?'

'I waited for ages for you at the fountain.'

He pushed me. He pushed me again. Harry had his fists closed, as though he was ready for a fight. But suddenly Mickey's mood changed.

'All right, Tone – we were late. But don't take the piss. When I say you meet us, you meet us. Else you're not in the gang. Right?'

'Right.'

I got home at about six and my mother went straight for me. She hit me so hard, I tried to get away from her. But she held me. Tommy was in the kitchen and started shouting that I was always thinking of myself. My mother told him to shut up and sent me to bed. I didn't care; Wendy was worth all the trouble, worth all the hits.

But when my father came in he was wild. He came into my bedroom and hit me. He held me by the hair and told me not to fuck my mother around. I told him I wouldn't. I cried and he kept hitting me. Then he sent me downstairs for supper. Tommy was sitting there mumbling. I hated him; Tommy was a creep.

II

A new school year and we had a new teacher. On Mondays the pupils who paid for school dinners handed their money in. Our new teacher had us reading while he counted the money. He'd shout at us, his face red, getting really angry because he had to concentrate. He was old, older than the other teachers. I reckoned he wasn't very good at adding up, because he kept starting again.

One Monday he got very confused. He'd counted the money several times, but it was still a few shillings short. The counting dragged on. We were supposed to have New Testament classes and he was still adding up. And he was in a kind of panic, as though it was a hundred pounds missing.

Then he said: 'When I wasn't looking, someone stole some money.'

He talked to everyone separately. He asked each child if they had taken the money and who they thought might have taken it. When it was my turn to speak to him, I told him the truth: I hadn't taken the money and I didn't know who had. He looked at me smugly, as though he knew something I didn't know.

'Well, we shall see.'

Roxanna was one of the last people to be interviewed. I saw her talking to him and then turn round and look at me. When he'd finished questioning everyone he called me into the hallway. He accused me of stealing the money, said he knew it was me.

I stood looking at this pile of shit, thinking that if only I was bigger I'd hit him. He said that if I owned up he'd be lenient. I didn't own up, because I hadn't done anything. Then he told me to turn out my pockets, and got angry when I refused. He grabbed me. But I wasn't going to empty my pockets for him.

At dinnertime I went home; I wasn't going to be treated like a thief. I was surprised to find my father there, with my mother. He looked angry at first, until I told him what had happened. I swore I hadn't done anything wrong.

Then they were both angry, but not with me. My father told me not to go back to school; my mother would go up there in the morning, tell them to leave me alone.

I decided to go up to Our Lady of Perpetual Succour, down by the gasworks, only a short walk away. I wanted to pray to Jesus, because I had the feeling that if I didn't I'd always be getting into trouble. I'd always be accused of doing wrong.

At the church I prayed for a long time. Then I sat and did some thinking. I wasn't a good Catholic any more; I *was* always doing wrong. But I could be a good Catholic again. I would try. I would try to keep out of trouble.

My mother didn't come to the school the next morning; she was tired, and the kids were playing up. She told me to 'feck off to school' and she'd come up later in the week.

At school I was expecting the worst. My classmates stared at me in the playground. When the bell rang for class, I prepared myself: whatever the teacher said, I wouldn't admit to doing something I hadn't done.

But when he called me into the hallway he smiled. He said he was sorry for accusing me; there'd been a mistake and no money was missing. He put his hand on my shoulder.

'It must have been hard on you.'

And that was the end of it. He didn't actually say I wasn't a thief, and Roxanna didn't apologise to me for lying. In class, I sat down beside Jimmy and cussed. It was going to be hard to be a good Catholic with all these cunts surrounding me.

One Saturday not long afterwards, Jimmy and I went fire-starting. At an old railway station near the football ground there were big poster hoardings. Jimmy and I piled up paper and wood beneath the hoardings and started a fire. Soon it was blazing, climbing up the wooden frame of the hoarding. We stood on the other side of the road and watched as the hoardings burnt down. We carried on watching when the fire brigade came. It was a great event. Jimmy and I had fun talking about it.

At church that Thursday night, I had confession. I told the priest about the fire. I said I wouldn't do it again.

'You must mend your ways, child. What if someone had got hurt?'

The abandoned station was next. We set light to that but the fire didn't spread. I went to church that Sunday and knew that I had to be a better person. But how could I? Trouble just seemed to happen. I knew I had to stop doing wrong, though. My soul was always feeling full up with venial and mortal sin.

When Christmas came, we had nothing. It was like Christmas in Bayswater. My father looked down. His hands were hurting him and he said very little. On Christmas Day he had to work. When he came home we had the chicken, but there was nothing else. And there were no visitors.

Nobody ever came to see us in Fulham. Aunty Kathleen had come once or twice, but that had been because my mother owed her money. No one else came. Tom Dunne never came, and neither did Alma and Ted. We were lost to them. My father never saw his mother and my mother never went to Ireland. We were all alone in Fulham, and it was a miserable place.

I was thirteen now. I had a simple birthday; my father bought me a present of paper and pens. There was no money. Tommy was working and always arguing with my mother about money. He said he wasn't getting value for money: he was paying more house-keeping than he should have been.

'I only fucking sleep here. And have a cup of fucking tea. And a bit of poxy dinner.'

But he never argued in front of my father. He always told Tommy to shut up.

Tommy was trying to get a girlfriend. He and Roy were always after girls, but it was Roy who got them. He was the good-looking one, with his head of curly blond hair. Tommy had his broken nose. Even Roy's mate Hubert got more girls than Tommy did.

I got a job, delivering fruit and vegetables on Saturdays. I started in the New Year, just after my thirteenth birthday. But I didn't keep it for long. They moaned at me, said I was too slow. So they sacked me. When I told my mother, she was angry.

'You'll never make a working man. You'll never earn a living like your father.'

And then there were rent problems, big trouble. My mother was taken to court. She was frightened; so I went with her, for company, even though I should have been at school and I knew I'd be in trouble again.

The London County Council wanted to evict us. We owed a lot of rent. The court magistrate sat higher than us; we were down below. He asked my mother if she disputed the claim that the rent hadn't been paid. She said no, no dispute, and then the magistrate spoke quietly with the man from the London County Council. They whispered. Then the London County Council man stepped aside and the magistrate spoke to my mother.

'Mrs Bird, you have six children and only your husband's income, is that correct?'

My mother said yes, that was true. He played around with some papers, then he looked at my mother.

For a moment, I could see us going back to St Vincent's. But to be honest I didn't care. Fuck it! Life was horrible in Fulham. The fights, the trouble, the lack of food, the arguments; my mother and father appearing to hate us and each other. It didn't seem to me that we'd be worse off in St Vincent's orphanage than we were at home. At least there would be enough to eat. At least there'd be no begging. And at least I couldn't get into so much trouble.

In fact, for a moment I wished that we *would* be thrown out of the flat, that our family would be broken up. And then, at the orphanage, I could be away from all the trouble Fulham gave me. I could see that my mother and father had no time for us; we were too much for them.

So I sort of hoped that this man would tell us that it was all over. And that we would have to leave Fulham forever. But, he didn't. He said we could stay in the flat; the London County Council had allowed us to stay. But we had to start paying the rent, and we had to start paying the rent we already owed: a little bit extra each rent day.

My mother was relieved, you could tell. Tears ran down her face. Her face was very brave, but she was crying.

The Mancinis knew Rocky Marciano. The heavyweight champion of the world had come to Fulham. He had drunk at the Lord Palmerston pub, round the corner from our flats. The Mancinis owned the pub and they knew everyone in the boxing world. They knew Don Cockell, the British heavyweight who had gone fourteen rounds with Marciano. They had met Joe Louis. Don Cockell's fight with Marciano had been aired on the radio; I'd sat up and listened to it. Boxing was the real sport. Not football. And now Tony Mancini was asking me to walk his dog because the bloke who usually did it was away.

For two days I walked the Mancinis' Alsatian. I took the dog over the park, ran up and down with him. He was very well behaved.

Harry was impressed: 'Tony asked you? Tony Mancini?'

Everyone wanted to be the Mancinis' friend. They were the people to be in with. You never had any trouble if you were in with the Mancinis. Morning and afternoon, I walked the dog the length of the park. Tony had told me: 'Whoever has the lead is the guvnor. So remember that and he'll behave.' He did. And people came up to talk to me because I had the dog.

Tony Mancini was pleased. He was pleased that I was a good Catholic boy. He made a fuss of me.

'When you're older, son, you can come and spend your money in our pub.'

Then he laughed and gave me a few shillings. I wished he knew my father; he might quieten him down a bit. But my father had given up drink for years now and he never went to pubs. He never went out. He was home after work and that was it: work and TV.

The summer came and I started seeing a lot of Mickey again. Harry had started seeing a girl called Liz. He would lie in the park kissing her. So Mickey and I would go off and muck about together. One day we all gathered, the four of us: me, Mickey, Harry and John. There was nothing to do. Harry said maybe we should call on Liz.

Mickey couldn't see the point. But Harry said she might lend us a few bob, so we walked round to her house. She wasn't in; no one was in. We hung around and Mickey noticed that a front window was open. He climbed in. Harry tried to stop him, but Mickey turned on him.

'Don't fuck about. Let's just have a look.'

He opened the door and we all went inside. We looked around. Mickey went upstairs. I went to the fridge, found a banana and ate it. Harry then did something strange. There was a bucket on the stairs, with a mop in it. Harry took the mop out, took down his trousers and crouched over the bucket.

'What the fuck are you doing, Harry?'

'Having a shit.'

There was some money on the kitchen table, about five shillings. We took it and left. We shared the money: one shilling and three-pence each.

It wasn't much of a robbery. And I couldn't understand Harry. This was his girlfriend's house and he'd shat in a bucket.

'Why did you do that, Harry?'

'I don't know. Why not?'

In the park, Harry started to get worried. He said if we got caught, we weren't to grass him up – his mother had a bad heart and it'd kill her.

Mickey got angry: 'We're not going to get caught. And nobody grasses no one.'

12

At about six o'clock one evening two policemen knocked at the door. My mother let them in. I was sitting in the front room with the door open. They looked at me as she led them through to the kitchen.

I tried listening, but it was difficult. After a few minutes my mother came in looking worried.

'Tony, these two policemen want to talk to you.'

My throat was dry. I stood up and followed her into the kitchen. The police officers smiled and asked me to sit at the table. It wasn't a table, really; it was more like a long bar. My father had made it from offcuts of Formica he'd got from work. He had this idea that an L-shaped bar was more useful than an ordinary kitchen table. It meant we ate in a row. Now the policemen were asking me to sit at the bar and answer some questions.

They started very gently. The older one did the talking. They told me about a break-in. At Liz's house. I listened, very worried, as he described it all.

'A group of boys climbed in through a window, and then they robbed the house.'

Robbed the house? Five shillings and a banana. It didn't seem like much of a robbery.

'The boys did their business in a bucket on the stairs.'

What he said next almost made me jump in the air: they knew that one of the boys was Mickey. And he'd said I was with him.

My mother was looking at me; trying to read me. Her face was wild. I swore to her it wasn't true and the policeman smiled. He told my mother that I had to go with them to the police station.

He was sure she understood why this was necessary. My mother had to go with me because I was a minor; they couldn't take me without one of my parents being there too. There was fear and anger in her face.

On the way, one of the policemen held back with my mother and the other walked ahead with me. As soon as we were out of my mother's earshot, he started: he knew I'd been at the house. He said that Mickey might have been a sneaky grass, but he wouldn't have said I was there if I wasn't.

We were near Liz's house. I looked down the road.

'Who were the others, Tony? Tell me, who were the other two?'

He went on – telling me that I had to make it easy on myself, that I would have to own up. If I owned up now, there would be less trouble later.

'My mum and dad are going to murder me.'

He patted me on the shoulder, said he'd tell them to go easy on me.

At the police station, my mother was told that I had confessed. She went mad, started hitting me. They had to pull her off. It was a terrible sight.

So Mickey, honourable Mickey was no better than Hayes. No better than all the other sneaks and shits in my life. I was going to get sentenced just for being stupid. Mickey was an arsehole. He had grassed on me, got me in deep trouble. And Harry, well, Harry would get away with it. Definitely Mickey hadn't cared about betraying me; it was Harry he cared about.

I was charged and I still didn't tell them who else had been there. I said I didn't know them; I had never seen them before. The charge wasn't for a banana and five shillings. There'd been money taken from a drawer upstairs; eight pounds. A lot of money. If it wasn't for that, we might have been done for trespassing. I was shocked when they told me about the money, and the policeman realised that my surprise was genuine.

'So you didn't get any of the money? Charming, ain't it – shows what kind of arseholes you've fallen in with.'

Later Mickey denied that he'd grassed on me. It was police guesswork, he said, just that.

Chelsea Juvenile Court. I was seeing the grey-haired lady for the third time. She said that I seemed to be making a habit of it and put me on remand for probation reports.

I was separated from my mother. She started to cry, said what a fool I was. The policeman took me into a room with other boys and locked the door behind me. There were boys of different ages. Some looked hard, others looked frightened. Later, we were taken to a van. We had to sit in it, handcuffed to the seat rails.

When we'd walked up to the court, my mother had carried Eddy. As we walked she'd told me that I was shaming her. She and my father had enough to put up with.

'If you get out of this trouble, I'm sending you to Ireland. They'll beat sense into you there.'

The thought was good. And I knew that when she said it, she meant it. But I also knew I'd never get to Ireland. It would be Fulham, forever.

There were about ten of us in the van. We didn't talk. We sat and looked out of the windows. We were being taken to a remand home in Shepherd's Bush. We drove through the streets, watching everyone go about their daily business, and to me the people looked odd; their normality looked odd. Here, in the green van, I felt anything but normal.

The van drove through some heavy gates that were locked behind it. On the other side, we were let out and our handcuffs were taken off.

'This way, this way.'

Plain-clothes men led us into a room where one of the men read out our names from a list.

The place was like a barricaded school. There was wire mesh on all the windows. And strong doors. We were led into other rooms along corridors that could have been in any school. But then we were lined up and made to strip. A doctor examined each of us. A few of us smiled at each other. Then a man in a loud voice told us the rules: no fighting, no fucking around, and no attempts to escape. If we broke the rules, we'd be put in the cells.

In another room they took our clothes and gave us new ones: underwear, blue-striped shirts, jeans and shoes. In yet another room, we were given books and magazines to read. And told once again to behave ourselves.

'And no talking.'

It was not a prison. That's what they said. They reminded us that we were there to be assessed. If we played around, we'd be assessed badly. And that would affect the way the court treated us.

The new boys kind of stuck together. I sat with some boys from Hammersmith Broadway. None of us had ever been in a place like this. The older boys ruled over everyone. You kept out of their way and you didn't cheek the staff. You went to the classrooms, you listened to instructions and you answered all the questions you were asked. There were a lot of questions, always about the family – 'Is your father working?' 'How many live in your house?' 'Have you got an inside toilet?' 'Do any old people live with you?' They'd ask lots of questions and then they'd ask some more. It was mainly women doing it; older women. There weren't many women to look at in Stamford House Remand Home on the Goldhawk Road.

There were fights all the time. You'd go into the toilets and find someone fighting. At night, though, in the big dormitories, you got punished if you so much as got out of bed.

There was a constant change of people. The remand home was like a street corner – boys were always going back to court, disappearing, sometimes reappearing. Two weeks in, and then out again. Sometimes off to serve a serious sentence. At approved school, or Borstal, or youth prison.

On that first day, I knew that I had to behave for two weeks. I had to do everything that they wanted me to do. I had to impress on them the fact that I was sound, that I didn't have a bad bone in my body.

I knew only Patch. Patch came from the old estate near the gasworks down by the river. It was the roughest estate in all of Fulham. And Patch's family were one of the roughest living there. They had strange faces, as though they lived underground; they had frizzy blond hair. And they were hard. Patch's family knew the scrap-metal merchants, the second-hand car dealers. They knew the villains – were the villains – of Fulham.

Patch was crying. When I asked him why, he said, 'Don't know, Tone. Don't know. But I got myself into trouble here. I hate the fucking place.'

Patch said he wanted to go home; he hated the remand centre and said he might run away. I was surprised. Patch was a year older than me. He knew the game, and he was tough. But now here he was acting like a child. I thought he'd be foolish to run away. He was back in court in a week. I told him that in a week, he'd probably be free – then he'd be at home anyway.

This cheered him up. I realised that he just wanted to have someone around who reminded him of the place near the gasworks. Someone who reminded him of home.

At Stamford House we had a kind of simple schooling. I preferred it to what was done at my own school. Surprisingly, the teachers were nice. They didn't pick on anyone in particular or assume that anyone was worse than anyone else – though perhaps that was because they believed we were *all* bad.

I settled in. Apart from the fights, there were few problems. And the people who fought seemed to want to fight; they went at each other whenever they got the chance. Not like with Fulham and at school, where there would be one boy who wanted to fight and another who didn't. Or when two boys fought but neither wanted to; when it was mutual fear that caused the trouble.

The routine was straightforward. You got up at seven-thirty each morning. You washed, went out to the yard, and then to classes. Eat, classes, recreation and bed.

The yard was the best place. There you could just stand around, even though the screws had their eyes on you all the time. The yard was surrounded by high fences, fences that ran up high. Mesh fencing. Most of us would stand looking at the fence. As though getting over that fence amounted to something really important.

We talked about the fence all the time. It was the challenge. Climbing it and getting out would be like being a bird let out of a cage. We almost wished for people to try the fence.

Occasionally someone did – someone who was set for a two-year sentence might get desperate and try it. But for most of us, it would have been foolish: we would be out in weeks, if not days, so why bother?

I did tests. More interviews. What were they trying to find out? That I was mad, ill, badly brought up? My parents were as good as any. They were loud and violent, but whose mum and dad weren't?

'Do you go to the countryside?' – questions I never thought would help anybody to learn anything about anything.

When I was taken back to court, the magistrate told me my probation would be continued until I was seventeen years old.

Later, my mother moaned at me about all the time she had taken over me. 'Now, you keep out of trouble or I'll send you back to Ireland.'

I still wondered if that would be such a bad thing.

'Do you know the difference between right and wrong, Bird?'

Mr Hindle had a beard. And he combed his hair so that you couldn't see the bald spot he had on the top of his head. He had delicate hands, long and thin.

'I ask you this, Bird, because I have a strong feeling you don't. And I'm going to try and teach you.'

It was the first day of term. It was a new year – the third year at St Thomas More Secondary Modern School. Mr Hindle was our new teacher. He'd heard all the bad things about me – that I was a felon, a juvenile delinquent – and knew I had to be watched.

I still had the same music teacher, Mr Beswick. He tried his usual shit on me but it didn't work. He came up and screamed at me, said I was deliberately singing out of tune. He stood in front of me with an angry red face. I looked at him.

'That's my voice, sir.'

'Loud. Loud and out of tune. You are causing me grief, Bird. And I won't have it.'

He reached out a hand to grab my nose. And right then I decided that I wasn't having this fucker pulling my nose or touching me ever again.

I took my comb from my pocket and smoothed my black, greasy hair. He tried to grab the comb, but I wouldn't let him; I pulled it away and put it back in my pocket. He sent me to Mr McIntyre.

Mr McIntyre told me to bend over. I bent over and he gave me six whacks of the cane.

'There, Bird – that'll teach you.'

I stood up. 'Thank you, sir. That's very kind of you.'

His eyes bulged. He told me to bend over again and this time he really hit me. A few strokes missed, hit my back instead of my arse.

I couldn't walk properly on my way back to Beswick's class. And sitting down brought tears to my eyes.

'There, Bird, that'll get some of the fight out of you.'

'Thank you, yes, sir.'

My mother sent me on an errand after school. She stopped me on my way out the door.

'What's the matter with you? Why are you walking like that?'

She laughed when I told her I'd got the cane. She said I'd probably deserved it.

Later that night, though, when I was on my way to bed, she noticed the welt marks on my back and my arse.

'For the love of God, what happened to you? They've cut you to pieces.'

She looked closely at my sore skin and told me to go downstairs; I had to show my father.

He was shocked, angry. They both were angry. But I had been caned before: obviously this time it looked bad.

My mother wrote a note for the headmaster. She told me she would go to the school the next day to sort this out. But I went to bed knowing that I wouldn't deliver the letter. And that my mother would find some reason for not going. And that I didn't want the headmaster looking at my arse.

I didn't deliver the letter. And when I got into school I said nothing to anyone about my parents' anger.

Mr Hindle was a religious man. He told us all about how Henry VIII had wanted to divorce his wife but the Pope wouldn't let him so he became a Protestant. Mr Hindle said that the Catholic Church was the true church. Henry VIII, to serve his own interests, had dumped the church that was founded by Christ and the Apostles.

He told us about St Thomas More, whose name our school had taken. St Thomas had lived down by Chelsea Bridge, near where the houseboats were later moored. If you went down there you could still see the tree under which he'd said goodbye to his family before he was taken to the Tower of London to be executed because he wouldn't support Henry VIII against the Pope.

Mr Hindle was so religious that he wanted us all to be good Catholics. We weren't. Most pupils didn't care about Christ; they didn't even go to Communion and confession unless they were forced to. I didn't need to be forced. I loved the Lord and I loved going to Our Lady of Perpetual Succour. However much I did wrong, however many times I caused trouble in my life, I still believed in the love of the Lord and I believed in the goodness of Jesus. And no one could stop me believing, even if it made me strange, different in their eyes. I understood that those who considered me strange had no love of Jesus in their hearts.

They took our TV away because we hadn't paid the instalments. It was like the end of the world. We would have nothing to look forward to in the evenings. My father said we would get the TV back as soon as we got the credit back; we had only to wait a week or two.

Beat came in one day and said to my mother that we could watch TV in her place – 'No one watches it in the evening except Shirley and Colin.'

They talked among themselves and decided that I should go in to Beat's.

'Keep him out of trouble, Beat.'

'Any time, Eileen. He can come in any time.'

I went to Beat's most evenings. The nights were dark early and there was nothing else to do.

Beat's old husband had just died. Her brother Len still lived with her and so did her daughter, Shirley. Shirley was eighteen. She worked at the gas board showroom. She was beautiful and kind. Beat and her were great friends; they shared everything together. You could see them sitting in the living room, chatting and smoking. And Len would come in and join them. They were a kind family.

Colin was a carpet-fitter and Shirley's boyfriend. He had a good manner. He and Shirley never seemed to mind me sitting there in the armchair. They'd sit on the sofa and every now and then they would look over at me. We would talk sometimes. I thought that Shirley was a beauty, and that Colin was a lucky man. Shirley was a redhead with a great body.

When I was at home on those dark evenings, we played cards and other games. We played Monopoly, and snakes and ladders. My father played well – he was good at most games. He seemed happier. He said, 'I think we'll get rid of the TV forever. This is more fun that the telly.' And it was.

And then I would be in Beat's, hoping to get a look at Shirley's knickers. And hoping that I wouldn't be discovered, walking round and thinking about girls all the time.

I would lie in bed at night thinking about Betty in my class. Betty wasn't good-looking. She was tough – if she hit you she hurt you. But Betty had something the other girls didn't have: a grown girl's body. When when the classroom was rearranged and we had to decide who we wanted to sit next to, I chose Betty. Betty wanted to sit next to Jimmy, though. And good-looking Jimmy appreciated Betty too.

I ended up with Patricia, who had asked to sit next to me. She was nice, red-haired with great legs. But she wasn't as advanced as Betty.

Dave was as interested in girls as I was. We were in Earl's Court one afternoon and Dave pointed out a shop near the station.

'See those magazines, Tony? Now I'd love to get my hands on them.'

We went in and pretended to be looking at the regular magazines. It was the girly magazines we were after, though. The shopkeeper was busy, customers coming and going. We flicked through some other magazines until he wasn't looking; then I took a girly magazine down and pushed it into my jacket.

Down by the side of the station we looked at our prize. It was a black-and-white magazine. Society girls in suspenders and bras. And a few nudes – but without any hair. Nothing: they had painted out all the naked women's lower parts.

Dave was beside himself.

'Tony, I think I'm going to be a dirty sod when I grow up.'

'I'd like to be a dirty sod before I grow up.'

We walked up to Gloucester Road and managed to get another magazine. Then we walked up to Kensington Gardens, sat by the Albert Memorial and looked at them.

Dave had an elder sister and he'd seen her naked. She'd screamed when he walked into her room and he had just laughed about it.

But I had never seen a naked girl before. Whenever I went round his house and saw Dave's sister, I'd try to imagine her with no clothes on.

We exchanged magazines and talked about what it must be like to be married and have sex whenever you wanted it. Dave knew more about sex than I did.

'Men like sex a lot. Girls not so much.'

I thought that must make life difficult. I told Dave he should ask his sister how often she liked to have sex. I said he could tell her he was doing something for school and he'd have to ask her questions.

He laughed out loud at the thought of it. 'We could say that. You could ask your mum.'

Now I laughed. Imagine it! I'd never ask my mum; I didn't even want to think about my mum and sex.

At school we never talked about sex. You didn't get told about it at Catholic schools. Only when you got married. Then the priest would talk to you about sex. He would tell you what you could do and what you couldn't do.

We went down to Barkers department store in Kensington High Street, to the ladies' underwear department. The floor managers looked at us. We didn't look like the kind of people who'd usually be there. But we walked round and looked at the underwear. There were photographs of women in bras and knickers. We hung around the changing rooms, hoping to catch a glimpse through the curtains.

Eventually we were asked to leave and out in the street I begged money from people. I told them I was lost. I pretended to be foreign; I spoke like a German. We knew how Germans talked because of all the war films. I got a few shillings and Dave was very impressed.

We had a fry-up in the Black Cat cafe on the Fulham Road. Dave was happy. We'd had a good day: dirty mags and money.

The old lady at the cafe admired our appetites. 'You been working, boys?'

We told her we'd been doing some magazine work, and the joke made us laugh out loud.

*

Once again, we had a poor Christmas. All Christmases seemed poor now. There was never any money. Pat said we would have a good Christmas next year. Next year he would be working and his money would make all the difference.

On Christmas Eve, Pat and I made decorations out of newspaper. Pat was good at it. My mother laughed at us. We said the rosary and then she said that we should pray for a good Christmas next year.

I was not too sad. At least we had Peter. At least we had everyone in good health. And the Lord Jesus Christ had his ways. He knew about our suffering. He knew we would one day enter the Kingdom of Heaven, however poor we were.

I also knew that when the New Year came I would turn over a new leaf. I was sick of being a rogue, a person from whom everyone expected the worst. I probably did talk out of turn sometimes, and I'd done some stealing, but I wasn't a bad person. Anyway, in the New Year I would turn over a new leaf.

Next year, 1960, would be the year when I grew up and stopped behaving like a child. I would be fourteen. Fourteen was almost like being a man. I thought that fourteen was the age when I might get myself a serious girlfriend. Someone I could love. Someone like Geraldine, perhaps. Or even Wendy Lewis. Surely there were plenty of girls around looking for a boy like me? I might not have been the best-looking boy, but I had charm; I was good with words. There was bound to be a girl out there that I hadn't met. A girl who could love a good Catholic. A good Catholic who had turned over a new leaf.

13

My toe was hurting. I came home from school with blood in my sock. My mother thought I was foolish.

'Go up to the fecking doctor and get it sorted.'

Dr Scriven told me I had an ingrowing toenail. I had to stay home from school for a few days to let it clean up, and he'd book me an appointment at the hospital.

I had a legal reason to stay off school. Now neither the school nor the court could say anything; they couldn't touch me. With a bit of luck this ingrowing toenail would be around for a long time.

Back at home, my mother was dying for a cigarette. She sent me round the corner to try and get some on credit. Round the corner was the fat tobacconist called Mr Bird – no relation to us. He often gave me sweets on credit – because, unlike my mother, I always paid off my debts. Still, though, I wasn't sure he'd give me cigarettes.

I was right. He smiled at me when I went in, hobbling on my sore foot. But when I told him what I wanted his expression changed from friendly to angry. He went completely mad, told me to get out the shop. I tried to protest but he kept shouting at me.

'Get *out*! You'll have time enough to learn how to smoke – and I'm not going to encourage you!'

I limped from the shop as quickly as I could. I was angry. Damn my mother. Damn adults – damn them all.

I stood in the street for half an hour and begged money. It wasn't the best place. The best place was further down the King's Road, by the Town Hall. But I managed to get enough for a pack of Woodbines: the cheapest of all cigarettes.

When I got back to the flats she was looking down from the balcony.

'Did you get any?'

I felt like swearing at her. Me with a bad foot, begging outside the Lord Palmerston and the Wheatsheaf. Telling some lie about having to get back home to Croydon to get my foot sorted out. One man asked me if I had any idea where Croydon was. I said yes, it was by the seaside somewhere. He gave me tuppence for the cheek.

But later, when my father came home, she said how good I'd been to her. She told him about my suffering and about my sacrifice. He smiled and ran his hand through my hair and smiled. His best smile.

I stayed off school for a week before I went up to the hospital for an operation. I was only in for a morning, but I was off school for another week. And then my toe was better. I had hoped for another week, but I had to go back to the school. And the problems.

I was keeping away from Mickey and Harry because I didn't trust them. They would stick the knife in. Whenever I saw them, I walked the other way. I had a new friend now. Gill was younger than me. He had a beautiful sister, Pauline. She would lie in the park with her short skirt on. And I would lie there too, trying to look up it. She would sit up and move around. Gill and I would be talking, but I was thinking of Pauline all the time.

Gill and I would walk round, like Mickey and Harry and I used to. But we didn't try breaking into cars or houses. I wasn't going to get into trouble any more. That was the past.

One afternoon, Gill and I found two bikes by the gents' toilet in the park. We took them and rode round on them that evening. Then we put them back where we found them. The next day, after school, they were still there. And that evening we rode them again.

A few days later, two policemen came to our house about the bikes. It was the same routine as before. By this time, though, I had wised up and admitted little. Or so I thought. My mother sat in the kitchen with the two policemen, looking angrily at me.

The policemen thought we'd stolen the bikes. I told them no, we'd just ridden them – they'd been lying around by the gents' in the park. But they didn't believe me. One of the policemen asked if I knew about stealing by finding.

Again: 'No, sir. I rode them and I'm sorry for it but I thought they'd been thrown away.'

He looked at me. My mother sat watching my face, looking for a tell-tale sign. He told me it looked suspicious. He said they'd been nicked from a school two miles away – my school.

He leant forward. 'And *mysteriously* they end up almost on your doorstep. Now *that's* a coincidence.'

They questioned Gill, too. Gill told them what I'd told them. Nothing happened for a while. A few weeks. And then they called us into the station. They charged us with stealing the bikes. They didn't believe that anyone would steal bikes and then abandon them.

In a month I would be before the grey-haired old lady with the half-rim glasses. Telling me I was making a habit of it.

In court we were told we were guilty. No discussion. No pleading. No argument.

The magistrate asked me why I'd taken the bikes. Gill stood beside me looking worried. I could have told the magistrate that I hadn't stolen anything – told her what really happened. I could have told her that I'd taken the bikes because I wanted to ride them. But I felt that she'd think I was laughing at her – and I didn't think what I said would make any difference anyway.

So I simply said, 'Because I was bored, missus.'

She looked at me oddly, then got up from her table and went into a back room with some other people.

My mother called over: 'You said the wrong thing, Tony.'

A few minutes later I was told that I needed a short, sharp shock. Perhaps three months in a detention centre would teach me something. That in future I should avoid stealing because I was bored.

My mother was crying as we were led by a policeman down Walton Street to Chelsea Police Station. No vans, no lock-ups. Just me and a policeman. And my mother. She cried the length of the street. I was upset for her.

I could have run off. The policeman was an older man and I doubted he'd be able to catch me. But I wanted to get this sorted. I didn't want it hanging over me.

When she was told to leave me, my mother waved goodbye sadly, tears streaming down her face. But I wasn't frightened. In a way I was looking forward to the next three months. At least I wouldn't be going to that shit school.

I was put in a cell. I sat there thinking that I had to straighten my life out. I was always in trouble. I had to get out of it; I had to stop making a fool of myself. I did such stupid things, always the most stupid things.

I sat in the cell and thought about how far I had come since the orphanage. How far I had come since the time we went to the farm in Ireland. How my life was just rubbish. I thought about my poor mother going home on the bus on her own. Poor thing that she was, with me breaking her heart. Always breaking her heart.

There was no sense to my life. I had to get this sentence out of the way. And then I could be good again – I could be a good Catholic again. Now I was a bad Catholic, always in trouble. Jesus wouldn't be happy with me. He would look at me and think I had to learn to be good again. Like when I was a child. I'd been good back then; I would be good again.

A young policeman was going to take me on the train to Campsfield House Detention Centre in Oxford. He was new to the job and I was told not to arsehole about.

We were taken in a police car from Chelsea up through Hyde Park to Paddington. I was excited, being driven to Paddington. I hadn't been there since the days before the orphanage. It made me think about Ireland, about those days that were good. They were good even though we were poor.

The new policeman was shy. His ears were red and he stuttered when he spoke. When we lined up for the rail tickets he looked lost. He took me for a tea and a bun while we waited for the train. I could have run off when he went up to the counter. But he was a good sort; I couldn't have done that to him.

He wanted to know something about me. I told him that I'd ridden an abandoned bike, that I'd been in trouble before. He was a Catholic. We talked about God.

'Seems you're not a bad lad.'

'No. I don't feel bad.'

He laughed, said I'd just have to find a way to stay out of trouble.

'I will. I'm turning over a new leaf when I get home. In three months.'

We talked some more and he bought me a magazine. He told me about his fiancée. I asked him why he'd wanted to become a policeman and he smiled. He said he'd asked himself that question. He'd wanted to do something useful.

We sat at the back of the train. He explained why the lines came together in the distance – how perspective worked. He was easy to talk to and he told me again that I wasn't a bad boy; I was just stupid.

'I feel stupid.'

When we got to Oxford we took a bus to the detention centre. It was bleak. Big fences, with barbed wire. It looked bad. At the gates the policeman left me with a warder.

'Look after yourself, lad. And keep away from the trouble.'

When he was gone, the warder got me to empty my pockets. He put my things into a brown bag. I was taken through a series of doors. It was grim. This was prison. I knew it was going to be a hard three months.

I was fourteen years of age and being treated like a real criminal.

★

I was naked. The warder checked me over. He shone a torch up my arse. I was given clothes: grey trousers, blue-striped shirt and a dark-blue jerkin.

The warder explained things to me. I'd be seeing the governor tomorrow. Here, all officers were to be addressed as 'sir'.

You didn't slouch; you stood up straight. You didn't saunter; you walked briskly or you ran.

'And you salute officers when they talk to you.'

He went on like this for a few more minutes. Lights out in the cells by nine-thirty. Up at five-fifteen. Exercise, wash, breakfast . . .

The warder looked old. He said sharp things, but he didn't say them sharply. He was using tough words, but he wasn't tough.

As I walked behind him down a corridor I could see the other boys. They looked big and hard. And they looked at me as though I was a piece of shit. The warders shouted, screamed.

'Get your fucking arse into gear.'

A boy rushed past and a warder kicked him.

'Faster, you arsehole. Get your fucking head up.'

I was taken to the dining room. I was told to stand in the corner while they got me a place to sit. I was surprised at how old the other boys looked. Many were not boys at all – they were men.

'Right, boy. What's your name?'

'Bird, sir.'

I saluted. Everyone had their eyes on me.

'Bird, well, no twittering here.'

All the boys laughed at this. He pointed me towards an empty seat.

I got some food and sat down. A boy who looked like a small man spoke to me.

'Where you from, Twitty?'

'Bird's the name.'

He smiled. He had tattoos on his arms. He looked rough, in a small way.

'All right, Bird. Where you from?'

I told him Fulham and he screwed up his face.

'Where the fuck's that place?'

The biggest boy on the table leant forward.

'Religion?'

'Roman Catholic.'

The boy smiled. 'Good. You get any trouble, you tell me. I'm the top Catholic. We don't get fucked around. I won't have it.'

He too was covered in tattoos. He had greased-back hair. He looked like a tough version of my brother Tommy.

After dinner we had to sit for an hour in total silence. This was called the 'quiet hour'. You could read one of the books they had, or write letters to your family at home. I got a book by Baroness Orczy, *The Scarlet Pimpernel*. I hadn't really read a book before, even after I'd been to the library with Wendy Lewis. Comics, yes, but not books. But I thought I'd start now with this one, about the French Revolution.

I sat at the table and read. Everyone was quietly busy. No one seemed interested in what I was doing. That suited me. I didn't want to get into any trouble with the other boys. It wasn't like in the remand house, where there was plenty of opportunity to get into more trouble. This was a place where you didn't play around.

After quiet hour we filed off to our cells. A warder led me upstairs and told me that there was a cell inspection each morning. Our cells had to be tidy, everything exactly right. He'd get a boy to show me how to do everything.

The door was locked. It was about eight-thirty. I lay on the bed in the cell and thought about my poor mother, about how she must be suffering. I thought about Fulham. Now it didn't seem such a bad place after all. At nine-thirty the lights went out. I thought that perhaps cells weren't so bad. At least you were on your own. At least there were no problems.

The bell rang. It was the first thing I heard. Then the knocking started. I could hear the warders knocking on the doors.

'Up, up, up!'

The lights went on. A warder opened the cell door.

First we had to 'slop out': empty our piss pots. I hadn't used mine in the night, but I still had to go with the others while they emptied theirs into the toilets.

Next we had to go down to the yard. I followed the others and lined up. Boys pushed me. Everyone seemed to be pushing or being pushed. It was cold and mist covered most of the yard. We were there to do exercises: jumping, running on the spot, press-ups. I was soon exhausted.

The warder walked among us, making sure that we kept going. It was hard. The warder kept on at us. Most of the boys seemed to be doing OK. A few of us were no good.

'Get that arse up. No dropping.'

But I was so tired. I stopped moving and the warder came up and hit me. He snarled: 'I told you, lad, get on with it.'

'It's my first day, sir.'

'I don't care if it's your last day.'

In line for breakfast in the dining hall, I was pushed. As if from nowhere, someone punched me. I turned round to see who had hit me, but I couldn't tell. I understood the order of things: new boys were beaten and pushed around. That was the way this place was run.

I was pleased with the breakfast, though. It was bacon and eggs, better than the breakfast I had at home. I ate it quickly and went up for more. It seemed strange that we were being fed so well.

As a boy of school age, I had to attend classes. There were about ten of us in the classroom. A big boy was telling everyone else what to do. He seemed angry.

'Sit down at your fucking desks. Get your fucking books out.'

The way he walked around the class snarling at everyone made me think he was the head boy. When the teacher came, though, he quickly jumped into his seat.

The teacher was a woman. She seemed polite, very unlike the

warders. We spent the morning studying maths and English. I listened but I couldn't understand much. Everyone was so well behaved. Not like at St Thomas More. And we worked. We listened to the teacher as she went from one subject to another.

At lunchtime we left the classroom. Royce, the big boy, pushed everyone around. I knew he would bully only those boys he could frighten. I knew I would have to stand up against him, or he'd treat me like he treated the others.

After lunch we had more lessons. And then we'd have to work for two hours. Out in the boilerhouse or whatever. The warders arranged it so that we were under their watch most of the time. You could see there were things that they did to make our days difficult. Like the early-morning exercise. That was supposed to make us feel that we were under pressure all day. And then there was the ordering us about, pushing us, swearing at us. It was their job to do this. We were there to be punished. We were there to suffer.

Flash Callow was about as bad as screws came. He'd hit you whenever he got the chance. He pulled your hair, got you to repeat 'sir' so many times. He was like a pig: short and fat and pink. With a permanent snarl on his face. This was the kind of person that we were supposed to learn from. Learn what? How to be mad nasty bullies, like them?

A boy from the remand home was at Campsfield House. Croker. He was a soft boy. He'd been at the detention centre two weeks longer than me, and he'd already become part of the system. He'd been pushed around and now he was one of the ones doing the pushing. He could spot the new boys. And he made it hard for them, even though he was soft.

On my second day he got me beaten up in the showers. He told two boys I was a grass.

'He grasses up his mates.'

That was enough. I was attacked and kicked to the floor. Croker stood watching. The two boys were his protectors. As they hit me he encouraged them. Before they could really hurt me a warder came along. They broke off and went into the shower cubicles. I watched Croker and I knew that I'd get back at him.

Smith was in the school group and came from Bristol. He was very posh. He walked and lined up like a posh boy. Royce tormented him more than anyone. But Smith did no harm. He was just out of place and Royce took advantage of that.

One day in the classroom before the teacher had arrived, Royce was hurting Smith. I was sat at my desk across the room. I suddenly felt I had to say something.

'Leave him alone.'

Up till then, Royce had ignored me. Now he came over to me. He was mad with anger. He threw his arms around, stuck his face in my face.

He screamed: 'Who the fuck are you?'

'Bird. And you should leave him alone.'

I was hoping the teacher would come in. She didn't. I was frightened, but I wasn't going to allow Royce to see that. Royce shouted. He looked at me as though I was some kind of fool he was going to crush.

Everyone was looking at us. They were silent. I was still sat at my desk. Royce was standing in front of me. His fists were clenched and his forehead was sweaty. He looked as though he was holding back from killing me.

'Who the fuck are you? If you're so fucking brave.'

'Leave him alone.'

Royce snarled, went and sat at his desk. He was calling me all the cunts under the sun, but I knew I'd called his bluff. He was big and strong-looking, but he was just a bully. Bullies only go for people they know they can beat. And he didn't know if he could beat me.

The warders in the exercise yard were bullies too. I learnt to get the exercises right; I got better, stronger. And I watched the warders. They always seemed to hurt the people they could confuse. If you took their kicks and punches without looking confused, they left you alone. I realised that they were not strong in themselves. They were no different from Royce. Royce would probably have made a good warder.

Croker continued his own bullying. We hadn't been friends in the remand home, but nor had I ever done anything against him. So when he got me hit for a second time I planned for the day when I could hurt him. I thought about getting the tough Roman Catholic boy on to him. But I didn't want anyone fighting my battles for me; I would have to put up with this.

One night, as I walked up the stairs to my cell, I saw Croker alone, without his protectors. I went up close.

'Croker, I'm going to make you pay. You're going to pay for your lies.'

He laughed at me, called me a cunt. Then one of his cronies arrived. He chased me to the cells and hit me on the back of the head. I wasn't so much hurt as angry. I had to sort this out.

It wasn't just Croker. Campsfield House was full of arseholes.

Atkinson was a Scotsman. He made the lumpiest porridge. He was the centre's cook and he was also a screw. One night during quiet hour he decided to give us a lecture. He stood at the front of the room and told us all to pay attention.

'Listen. What you must remember is that the lowest form of life on earth – the ugliest, most evil form of life – is not the black. It's not the Indian. It's the Jew. The Jew is always there. The Jew is the scum of the earth.'

Occasionally the screws would talk to us. They would tell us how we should behave. They'd say we needed to get work. And we needed to keep out of trouble. But Atkinson, it seemed, had a different kind of thing to talk about.

He said the Jew was the worst thing we'd ever meet on this earth. And then he turned and pointed to me.

'This boy is a Jew. This boy is one of them.'

I was shocked. No one had ever called me a Jew before. Whatever a Jew was. But he pointed at me and told me to stand up.

'The Jew is an animal. The Jew is the most evil person you're ever going to meet.'

I didn't understand. I was lost.

'I'm not a Jew, sir. I'm a Catholic.'

'Shut up! You'll always be a Jew to me.'

And that was it. We returned to our reading and writing. Atkinson walked around the room but he said no more. I was still lost. What did he mean, I was a Jew? I didn't know anything about Jews. I didn't know what kind of people they were, or where they came from. But now I knew that they were hated.

Atkinson never picked on me again for looking like a Jew. And after six weeks at the centre I was an old hand. I knew the drill. I knew how to get on with things. I wasn't going to cause any trouble. Only the new boys were picked on. And some of the screws didn't trouble you.

My mother came to see me once. She cried when she saw my shaved head and my uniform.

'God love you, what have they done to you?'

Pat and Richard were with her, and, surprisingly, Tommy. He didn't have much to say; he just asked me how I was doing.

'Horrible.'

He smiled. 'Serves you right. You shouldn't get into trouble.'

My mother and Pat told him to shut up.

'How's Dad, Mum?'

'He's all right. But Tony – you look like a convict.'

Even I had to laugh. 'I *am* a convict, Mum. That's what I'm doing here.'

The visit was only half an hour. When they left I waved and once again felt sorry for my poor mother, having to put up with all this trouble from me.

When I'd been there two months I felt like an old boy. The place was full up with the new intake. Boys who had been frightened and cornered like me. Nobody hit me any more.

Croker generally avoided me. As we walked out of the showers one morning, though, he walked past me with a stupid smile on his face. I turned round and punched him in the mouth. His lip split and he dropped to his knees. He looked surprised.

I stood above him. I told him that whenever I got the chance I'd do the same thing again.

Later that day, he was going down the stairs as I was going up. He cringed as he went past me. I pushed him hard and he fell all the way to the bottom of the stairs.

Croker's latest protector came to see me, but not to threaten me or beat me. He wanted to know why I was picking on Croker. What had he done to me?

I laughed and told him the full story.

'That's fucking awful,' he said. 'I didn't realise.' That was it.

In the gym I hit Croker across the face with the rope that hung from the wall bar. He begged me to leave him alone.

Croker was a piece of shit and I told him so. When he left the centre, I hoped I'd taught him a lesson. I hated him. A weak boy who picked on the weakest.

The time came for me to leave. In bed on my last night, I knew that I never wanted to find myself in a madhouse like that again. In the morning I was up earlier than usual. I got all my kit together and was taken to the room where Atkinson would sign me out.

He made me strip naked and stand to attention. He came up to me. Looked me all over. And then went back to his desk. I stood naked for about fifteen minutes. He was doing other stuff. When I was finally taken away by another screw, I looked back at Atkinson and knew that I'd like to kill him if I ever saw him again.

The old screw that I'd met on my first day was taking me to the station. He was still kindly. He came for me after breakfast and led me through many doors, out to the screws' car park. It was a cold and grey autumn and there was mist on the ground. I could smell the trees. I could smell the grass. Everything seemed so different. So fresh. Soon I would be back in Fulham. Never to get in trouble again. I had learnt my lesson.

'In the back, son.'

We got into the screw's car and were soon out the gates. The screw didn't talk to me. He hummed to himself. We drove for about a mile and then stopped in front of a house.

'Now don't you go nicking my car.'

'No, sir.'

He went inside the house and when he came back out he had a young woman with him. She sat in the front seat. She turned and said good morning to me. I could see the steam of her hot breath. And I could smell the toothpaste in her mouth. They talked. She kept calling him 'Dad'. He smiled and laughed. I felt good about him and his lovely daughter.

He dropped his daughter at work and then we drove to Abingdon Station. He took me up on to the platform and said he was supposed to wait with me for the train.

'You don't have to, sir.'

'Good.'

He gave me a ticket. And he gave me a pound.

'All right, lad, it's up to you now.'

He shook my hand. We were the only people on the platform. He started to walk off, but he stopped and turned to me.

'Now you keep out of trouble, boy.'

'Yes, sir.'

Then he was gone.

On the train, I looked through the window as the mist and dark lifted. I was happy that I was on my own.

My mother was beside herself with happiness when I arrived home. I had been away for only a few months, but it seemed like a lifetime.

147

She was even more happy when I went down to the shop and bought bread and milk and cigarettes with my pound. It was a Wednesday.

14

Helen was making eyes at me in the playground. She was a good-looking girl with reddish hair. She was posh. She looked good in her school uniform, a green blazer and grey skirt. No other girl looked so good.

Helen was pure-looking. She was soft. When I kissed her she closed her eyes. I wanted to find out what was going on under her clothes. I had a feeling that I would never find out. What could she want with someone like me?

We would meet after school and walk through the streets, up to Knightsbridge. Then down Park Lane to Marble Arch. She lived in Wigmore Street. She never took me into her house.

'I don't think my mother would like you.'

It was all walking, talking and kissing. I was always trying to lift her dress. We sat on benches in Hyde Park. I'd try to touch her breasts but she'd keep moving my hand away.

'At least show me your knickers.'

'Tony, I can't. What's the point?'

I would laugh. 'But we like each other.'

'We do.'

Then she'd kiss me lightly on the lips. It was always the same.

It was December. It was bitterly cold, but we had nowhere to go. We couldn't go into pubs – we were too young. And there were no cafes; Knightsbridge was too posh for cafes. It was no man's land. So we stopped meeting straight after school. Instead we would meet at seven at Sloane Square and then walk up to Knightsbridge.

I couldn't quite understand why we were together. But it was something to do. At least I wasn't hanging around and getting into trouble. And she looked happy most of the time. I liked the idea that she was happy. She just wanted to be with me now from seven until nine o'clock.

One night we sat on a bench by Hyde Park Corner. For the first time, she allowed me to run my hands over her.

Then I kissed her.

'This is dirty, Tony. It's not right.'

'Then why are you letting me?'

She hesitated. Then: 'Because it's what you want. I don't want to lose you.'

I was annoyed. I told her not to do me any favours.

'But Tony, I like it. Even if it's dirty.'

I pulled up her dress. But I couldn't go too far. She kept putting my hand elsewhere.

'Do you love me, Tony?'

'Course I do. I wouldn't be going out with you if I didn't.'

Those endless nights, just walking in the cold December air. Me telling her stories, jokes. Playing around, pinching her, chasing her, catching her, squeezing her.

I got a job as a butcher boy. Cobb and Co. of Knightsbridge were the Queen's butchers. I worked there on Saturdays throughout December. The money was good; the work was good. It meant getting up early but it suited me, working in the cold. There were always jobs to do. Lots of deliveries. There was always a cup of tea and a roll or two when I got back. The tea was strong. The rolls were crusty, with thick butter. I worked hard and was left alone. Apart from the odd bit of trouble with the foreman, I enjoyed the month. It was a good industry. Cutting, packing, and delivering to wealthy households. Getting tips for my labours.

Helen would wait for me after work. She would turn up perhaps half an hour before we finished. The other boys and men laughed at me, in a friendly way.

I got two pounds in tips one Saturday. When I finished that day I really felt like I'd worked. I was aching with tiredness. But I didn't mind; I could lie in on Sunday morning.

I took Helen up to Piccadilly Circus on the bus. It was cold and dark, but there were lights everywhere. Tonight, I didn't care. I could spend two quid without anyone saying anything. We kissed on the bus as it moved along down Piccadilly. The lights and the people made me feel happy. And Helen was good. Even though she still thought touching and exploring was bad.

'I love this, Helen. I love all this. This is what I'm going to do every Saturday. Get on a bus and come up here, to Piccadilly.'

'With me?'

I told her of course with her; who else?

It was about six o'clock. I was supposed to go straight home after work. But I didn't know what for. To sit in front of the dead TV with my dead family? I'd rather get told off and beaten and be with Helen.

We got off at the Circus. I even paid the fare. We walked round looking at the lights. We went into a Lyons Corner House. We were like a proper young couple. A few people looked at us. We ordered tea and cakes. Helen got excited. The big cafe was full of men and women at tables, gazing into each other's eyes. I was happy just to sit and look around, not even talking. I just wanted to look at this adult world. It was not my world, nor was it Helen's.

Helen was talking about the future. In a concerned way, as if she cared. In one year's time, she would still be at school but I wouldn't – what were we to do? I hadn't thought about what would happen in a year's time. I might join the army, or the navy, or become a farm boy. I wasn't going to work on a fucking building site. Really all I knew was that soon after Christmas, at fifteen years of age, I would be saying goodbye to school.

'Don't know, Helen. Who knows? We may not be together in a year.'

She looked sad when I said this. I took her hand. A nearby man and woman looked at us and smiled. The man raised his teacup to me.

'More power to your elbow, son.'

I raised my cup to him.

I told Helen she mustn't be sad. I took her hand. I had a feeling that she might cry. It was good that a girl wanted to cry over me. Probably no one had ever cried over me. I blew her a kiss. She laughed. We laughed together. Across the room the man held up his cup again. Helen and I held up ours.

I said out loud to the man: 'More power to your elbow, mate.'

'And yours also.'

We must have been in that place for two hours. We sat and talked. And fussed and ate cakes. In a few days it would be Christmas and Helen would be going to France to see her father. And then I wouldn't see her for a few weeks. Not until we started back at school.

Next year was going to be the best year. No school, just work. My own life. No one could tell me what to do once I started work. Fourteen was better than any other age except for fifteen. You just needed patience, because soon you would be away from idiots and fools. Soon I would be what I'd always wanted to be: in charge of myself.

I went to a party at Ray's house and got drunk on cider. Ray went to the youth club in the World's End and knew loads of girls. My mother and father would never have allowed me to bring friends back. But Ray's parents let us have a party without them. I got drunk on one glass of cider. But it was great. Josephine from school was there. She was tall and had dark frizzy hair. She was dark-skinned. She was Gibraltarean. We kissed in the kitchen. She was drunk as well. It took me ages to walk home. I stuffed my mouth full of peppermints as I climbed the stairs to the flats.

In just a few days it would be 1961. The year when they could no longer treat me as a child.

She hit me, as she always did. I was an hour late. But I didn't care. And I didn't want any stupid presents for Christmas. I didn't care about Christmas any more. It was for kids. It was for them. Fuck

Christmas. But I went to Mass on Christmas Day, and had Holy Communion.

A few days later I went for a long walk by myself. I walked along the river through Chelsea all the way to Blackfriars. I had this feeling in my head that I had to be by myself. That I would go crazy if I had to stay with my family any longer. I couldn't help but think that they were a strange bunch. Mad, in a way.

Late one night I saw Colin near the flats. He had a man with him. Colin owned the bike that I'd ridden the year before and ended up in detention centre because of. But I didn't hate Colin. He was just a big soft boy.

Colin said the man was his brother. His name was Phil. He didn't look like Colin. Colin was big and fat; this man was tall and thin. He had long black hair, like a girl. He was unshaven and wore an old coat and had a scarf round his neck. He looked like a tramp.

Phil shook my hand. 'Ugh, another proletarian friend of my prole brother.'

Colin laughed. 'That's what he's like. Knows a lot of words.'

Phil seemed interesting. Not like the rest who lived in grey Fulham. I asked him what 'proletarian' meant.

He made silly noises. 'Proletarian: of the working classes. I am ashamed to say I come from the Irish labouring masses. Despicable group of people.'

Colin laughed even more. Phil lived in Paris. He was a poet.

He and Colin were like chalk and cheese; I couldn't see them as the same family. We hung round on the corner a few more minutes and Phil insulted me some more. He made me laugh, the way he described Colin and me as 'peasants' and 'the scum of the earth'.

That night I went to bed and thought about Phil, and about how interesting he seemed. More interesting than the sort of people that I came from.

I had my fifteenth birthday a few days later. I was on the road. A few years of work and then I could leave this dreadful place. I could say goodbye to my dreadful family. I could be my own person. I wouldn't have to listen to moaning older brothers and parents. All of them like donkeys; working and thinking of work. Getting excited when they got a shilling payrise or found a bit of wood that they could nick and bring home. What scum I came from. What a dreadful life. All they wanted to do was work.

I had broken up with Helen. Charlie, the best footballer in the class, took up with her. But he kept checking that I wasn't angry with him about it. I told him I didn't give a toss, but he said that Helen loved me; until I told her I wasn't interested she'd be stuck.

I wrote a note and gave it to Charlie: 'The bearer of this note has my permission to tell Helen to fuck off. Signed, this day, while of sound mind, Tony.' I told him to show it to Helen.

Charlie wasn't happy, but he did what I said. A few minutes later Helen rushed over to me and threw the note in my face.

'You are mean. Nasty. Evil.'

In a way I found this all funny. I didn't need these people. I'd spent years trying to make friends at school. Now all of them, Helen included, could disappear. I didn't need any of them, ever again.

Mr Murphy, the headmaster, had seen me in Sloane Square. He later said to me that if I wanted to leave school he would cover for me. He would make sure that the register was filled in. So I wouldn't get into trouble for truancy. He said not to worry; he realised that the school and I didn't see eye to eye.

His suggestion may have suited him, but I wasn't in the mood to help. I would go to school up until the very last day. So that when I left I would remember everything. I wasn't going to assist them by getting out of the way. They had treated me badly; now I could get my revenge.

I took great pleasure in taunting Mr Beswick. Mr Beswick who had made me suffer. I sat in his class with my feet up on the desk. But now he was kind and tried friendliness. It didn't work. Where was the friendliness when I needed it. Where were the compliments then?

Bert lived round the corner from the school and was always playing truant. I'd go to see him at dinnertimes and we'd have cheese sandwiches and play Elvis on his sister's record player. We would meet after school and shoplift down the King's Road or go to the youth club at the World's End. He wasn't as interested in girls as I was, but he could fight; he was brave. And he didn't care about school.

I told him my plan: on the day I left school I wanted to go back there in the evening and wreck Murphy's office.

Bert laughed. 'You're an evil little fucker.' But he said he'd help me. He was a good friend.

We sat our exams in March, then had little else to do. The teachers let us read books and make scrapbooks of newspaper cuttings. The school term was ending without anything much happening. I was glad that I'd soon be out, but I knew that I wouldn't be leaving with good exam marks. I couldn't see the school ever giving me a reference if I needed one.

When the exam results came out during the last few days of term I didn't even bother looking at them. I didn't gather round the notice board in our form room like the rest of them did. I had no interest. I felt a bit flat. As though there was no longer anything to fight against, now that the school had no power over me. I had nothing to stand up against. Mr Bridges, the PE and technical-drawing teacher, took me aside one afternoon. He said he was dumbfounded: I'd come fifth in my year in the technical-drawing exam. I had nothing to say. The result didn't mean much to me, but I was nonetheless surprised by it. Mr Bridges and I stood for a few minutes without a word passing between us. We'd never liked each other, and nothing was going to change that now. He seemed to be thinking about something, though; perhaps trying to work me out.

He gave me a wry smile and shook my hand. 'Good luck, Bird – you may need it.'

I shook my head. I said: 'No, sir. I have Jesus; I don't need no luck.'

He laughed, said good – at least they'd given me something. But that wasn't true and I told him so: 'No sir, you didn't give me Jesus. I had him all the time.'

On the evening of the last day of term, as planned, Bert and I went down to the school. We climbed up on to the bike shed and dropped down into the playground. Carefully, keeping to the shadows, we made our way to the back of the school. A board covered a broken window. We pulled away the board and climbed in. I led Bert to the headmaster's room. The door was locked, so I kicked it open. With the lights out, we threw paper from the desk all over the floor. We threw ink against the wall. We rubbished the office as much as we could. Then we left. And that was the last time I set foot in St Thomas More Secondary Modern School.

PART TWO

Dreaming Bonaparte

15

The offices of Thomas Crapper and Sons were on the King's Road. I was to be paid three pounds a week. My parents moaned: if I worked on a building site I could probably earn five pounds a week. But I didn't want a building-site job; coming home covered in cement dust, with my hands all raw and torn. I didn't want to be like my father. My father said I should get a job in a factory. But I wanted to work in an office.

I was in charge of the post and the paperwork that went down to the warehouse. As soon as I started I knew it was going to be boring. The office had no good-looking girls, for a start. There were just office boys, like me, and a few old men and women. The best part of the job was going to the post office. I would gather up the letters and take money from the petty-cash tin to buy the stamps. That suited me: I'd post only a few of the letters, keep most of the stamp money and spend it in the Chelsea Dining Room. Sometimes I'd have three breakfasts; other times I'd spend the money in the evening. I'd tear up the unposted letters and throw them into rubbish bins.

On my third day, the office manager called me into his room and told me I was very slow doing the post.

'Sorry, mister. It takes a bit of getting used to.'

He smiled at me. 'Well, let's hope you can quicken up.'

That dinnertime – now called lunchtime – I was put on the switch-board. I loved answering the phone. Most people were out of the office for lunch, so I had to take messages. I wrote them down very carefully, though my handwriting wasn't good. I tried to be helpful.

Chris, who was two years older than me, said I was turning into a creep.

'You want to be nice to everyone.'

'Why fucking not? There's nothing wrong in being helpful.'

Chris was a laugh, always joking about everything. He wore a suit with a shiny arse and a shabby jacket. But he always wore a clean white shirt and his hair was neatly greased back. At the end of my first week, he wanted to know if I liked it at the office.

He said he couldn't see me lasting more than another week. I told him I thought he might be right.

Saturday night, I went to a party. I borrowed Tommy's suit jacket without telling him. Terry from the youth club had invited me; it was his sister's twenty-first birthday. When I got there I realised that everyone was a lot older than me. There was lots of drink and soon I was drunk, talking to all the older girls. I was sitting in an armchair and a girl I'd been talking to came and sat on my lap. We were both drunk and we played around. I kissed her and put my hands on her breasts. She moved my hands and told me to behave myself. Then Terry's sister called me out into the hall.

'Someone wants to talk to you.'

About five blokes grabbed hold of me. They beat me up and threw me out the door on to the pavement. My face got cut and Tommy's jacket got torn at the shoulder so the arm hung off. I went mad, started kicking the door, and the blokes came back outside and beat me up again. Now they threw me into the road.

I walked home feeling annoyed about the way I'd been treated. Where was Terry? Why hadn't he stopped them? The house was dark when I got in. In the kitchen I started washing the blood off my face. My mother came down, took one look at me and started shouting at me.

'What the fecking hell happened to you?'

I laughed – I couldn't help it. She started pulling me around and smelt my breath.

'You're fecking pissed!'

I cleaned myself up as she moaned about what a load of trouble I was. She said Tommy would go mad when he saw his jacket. Then she laughed. She took the jacket from me and went upstairs to hang it up. When she came back down she was beside herself with laughter.

'God in Heaven's name – wait till he takes that jacket out to put on. With the fecking arm hung off.'

We both really laughed now. She had forgotten about my trouble and the cuts to my face. I went to bed laughing. But when I lay down my head started to spin and I had to get up to be sick.

Chris had been right: I wasn't going to last at the office. On the Monday after the party he took me to the pub at lunchtime. I had a glass of cider and felt drunk. Back at work I went in to see the manager and sat on his desk. He shouted at me. And when I asked him for a payrise he got really mad and slung me out. I handed in my notice the next day and he accepted it without complaint. He then asked me to leave immediately; I would be paid until the end of the week. Chris said he wanted to keep in touch. He thanked me for bringing some fun to the place.

I went to the youth club that night. Allen was there. He was a noisy bloke who always seemed to be trying to impress people. No one was impressed, though, and most people ignored him altogether. He shouted and boasted, but he was always left out of things. I kind of liked him – he was just a lonely boy. So I started being nice to him; I included him. I didn't care what anyone else thought. I didn't need anyone's permission to like someone.

And there was Lilly. Lilly was sixteen, still at school and beautiful. She and a girlfriend always danced together at the youth club. Allen and I stood and watched her. That night her friend came up to me and whispered in my ear: 'Lilly fancies you.'

I looked into her face to see if she was joking. She didn't seem to be. Then I looked across the dance floor. Lilly was smiling at me. She waved. I turned to Allen and told him I wanted to leave.

I couldn't face the idea that Lilly fancied me. She was good-looking, but she was two levels up – too good. I got cold feet. Allen and I went to the Man in the Moon pub. As we sat there I talked to

Allen about his big mouth, about why he was always boasting. I told him that from now on I'd call him 'Mick the Mouth'.

He screwed up his face. 'Mick the Mouth? Why?'

'Because you're a mouthy git. So why not use your greatest asset? You're saying to people: "Fuck you, I've got a mouth. So what? That's why I'm called Mick the Mouth."'

He liked it.

Late one Saturday afternoon, I went into a bookshop. The woman who ran the shop eyed me suspiciously. I'd been in the shop many times and she knew I was a shoplifter – I'd robbed from all the bookshops along the King's Road.

'Anything on Adolf Hitler, missus?'

She looked down her nose at me and directed me to the history section. I looked at a few Hitler books. No one liked Hitler – you talked about him and people were put right off. And that made me like him.

The woman watched me until other customers started talking to her. I made my way down into the basement and looked at dozens of books on the shelves there. One book got my attention, though – a collection of Beat poetry. Inside was a poem by Leroi Jones that I liked. It was so simple:

> Let's do something.
> Let's go into Central Park.
> And piss on the first person we encounter.

I was struck. I could write this stuff; it was simple, and rude. It was the kind of stuff I could feel good about.

I slipped the book into my inside pocket. The poet Leroi Jones was right up my street. His stuff was about not giving a shit about the grown-up world. It was about fun. Leroi was my kind of poet.

As I left the shop the woman looked painfully at me. She would have loved to have searched me, but I would have told her to go and screw herself. I read more of Leroi Jones as I stood at the bus stop:

> Let's do something.
> Let's go into Central Park and
> give a prize to the first person
> Who can copulate with their
> Clothes on.

It was beautiful. I didn't understand the word 'copulate', though, so I decided I'd ask somebody at the youth club what it meant.

I became a poet. I didn't want to look like a little worker; I wanted to look like a poet. Like a beatnik. A bohemian. I grew my hair longer. I wore torn jeans and black shirts and an old overcoat. I wanted to look like Colin's brother Phil. As I walked through Fulham at night people would look at me. With my longer hair, all curly, they didn't like what they saw. Sometimes people would spit at me. I didn't care. Who wanted to be a worker? Living for brown ale and cigarettes. And watching TV. Not doing anything, not living for anything.

I was falling out with my mother and father all the time. They didn't like the new me. They didn't want to see their son turning into what they called a tramp. My father would get angry with me just looking at my hair.

'You look like a fucking girl. Go and get a fucking haircut.'

But I wasn't frightened of him any more; he could say what he liked.

So here I was, fifteen and going in another direction. Slums. Orphanage. Detention and probation. I wasn't going to be doing anything that the British working class would want of me. They were the aliens, not me.

I carried a notebook and in it I wrote poems. I wrote a poem to Lilly:

Lilly seize my arm,
Down the King's Road,
Myself and charm,
A fad of hair upon her face,
Puts shine and grace in
Every place.

Usually boys from council houses didn't write poems. But I did.

It was an art shop on Kensington High Street. The man interviewed me and gave me the job.

'You've got to keep all the shelves filled and well ordered in the basement. And then you have to fill up the shelves in the shop.'

It was dusty in the basement warehouse. I unpacked boxes; I unloaded and loaded; I kept the shelves filled. After the first week, the manager seemed pleased with me.

There were some good-looking girls working in the shop. They came down to the warehouse for special items. I talked to them and they were friendly. But more friendly than them was an older woman called Marie. She was like a gipsy. She had long, jet-black hair and wore black dresses and coloured blouses. I could tell she liked me. She would come down and talk to me.

'So, Tony, what do you want to do with your life?'

Whenever she sat down I'd try to look up her dress. She sat with her legs crossed and occasionally I'd get a flash of leg or knickers.

I told her I wanted to be a great poet. I showed her my book of Beat poetry and read her Leroi Jones. Once she'd explained to me the meaning of the word 'copulate' I liked the poem even more.

Marie said she found it strange to hear someone with an accent like mine talking about poetry. She meant that I was a working-class boy and I talked like one; she said that usually it was middle-class people who talked about culture.

Marie would talk to me at teabreaks and at lunchtimes. We went for walks together, up to Holland Park. She told me about her love for art. Paintings. I couldn't see the point of them; I preferred words. I told her that I had been interested in art when I was younger but that words were the thing for me now.

She was beautiful, very beautiful. Maybe forty years of age. But Gregory, who worked with Marie, didn't like me. He was very posh and was always trying to annoy me. He called me a fraud. He had just left the airforce. He wore a suit and thought I looked like a tramp. Marie would tell him to leave me alone, but one day at teabreak it all blew up. We sat at the table downstairs drinking tea. Gregory was, as usual, against me that day.

'You know, you're not really up to much. You talk rubbish – you're just a little oik.'

Marie told him to shut up, but already I was mad; I couldn't stand what he said. I screamed at him: 'You think I'm nothing? Well, I could just go out there now and kill a copper – just kill someone – just like that.'

Gregory laughed at me, but Marie quickly got up and left the room.

I told Gregory that, one day or night, I was going to whack an iron bar over his head. Then he lost his temper, pulled off his jacket and offered to fight me. He was a muscular man of twenty-nine; I was fifteen and half his size.

But still I just laughed at him. I told him to hit me, but that if he hit me he'd better kill me – because I'd have him, one way or another.

Gregory didn't hit me. But Marie never spoke to me again. Except once, when I apologised for having shouted.

She looked at me with bitterness and said, 'I almost thought you were civilised. God, you're just an animal like the rest of them.'

So I lost her friendship. And Gregory knew that if he hit me it wouldn't be the end of it; I would find some way of hurting him. For all his airforce muscle and his public-school accent.

Neville had me stealing painting materials for him from the art shop. Each night I would load up a bag and he'd pay me for the stuff. Neville was a funny eighteen-year-old who went to the youth club. He talked like a girl. I asked him once why that was and he looked embarrassed, said maybe it was because he worked for a ladies' hairdresser. He said that he'd become a hairdresser to be near all the women and girls.

'I just love it – washing their hair, being near them, pressing myself against them. I think they think it's safe, 'cause most hairdressers are queer.'

I laughed at that. We were sat in the San Tropez cafe on the King's Road. Neville always had lots of money because he got great tips at work, even though he was still an apprentice. He always bought the hot chocolates when we went out.

Neville wasn't queer; he loved girls and they seemed to like him. Lilly used to look at him in a strange way. He was a good bloke and I liked him, even if he did talk like a girl.

I lasted three weeks at the art shop. I left one Friday afternoon and went walking down near Gloucester Road looking for job notices in windows. I saw mainly delivery jobs, nothing special, and then I passed a hairdresser's and saw a sign saying they needed an apprentice. Gigi's of Gloucester Road. I went home, put on my best clothes and went back.

Mr George looked at me as I stood in front of him. He looked puzzled. 'You want to be a ladies' hairdresser?'

I could see that he didn't quite believe me but I told him yes, I'd always wanted to be one.

He seemed to think about it for a moment and then smiled. I got a month's trial, starting the following Monday morning, two guineas a week.

How could I tell my parents that I was on my third job in just over a month? And that the new one was for a ladies' hairdresser? My father would fall over; my mother would call me a little queer. And I was on even less money than before. My brothers would laugh at me.

Mr George was very kind. He was probably queer but he never

came anywhere near me. He was just kindly – though he did sometimes get pissed off. He put me on shifts with a Polish lady who treated me like a son. She showed me how to wash hair.

'See, Tony. Make sure the customer doesn't get wet.'

I worked with her for a few days. I cleaned the floors; I took the towels to the launderette and sat and watched over the machine. In my second week, I washed hair myself. Mr George praised me, said I was very thorough.

One afternoon I took a woman into the cubicle where we washed hair and she got undressed. She took off her jacket, and underneath she had on a small black bra that her breasts bulged out of. Then she took off her skirt. She was wearing stockings and garters with small black knickers. I nearly fainted. I had never been this close to a full-grown woman – one who was almost naked. She must have been about thirty. And as I started washing her hair I understood what Neville meant: this was the place to be.

She said nothing to me and I couldn't have said anything to her. But when I'd finished she thanked me and gave me a shilling.

I got a few other tips, most of which I gave to my mother. I had to try and make up for the fact that I wasn't giving her much regular money. They'd accepted that I was doing the ladies' hairdressing, though they'd all laughed and thought it hysterical. My mother had guessed why I wanted to do it.

'You're fecking cunt-struck. That's your problem.'

My father had laughed. 'He's cock-happy, that's for sure.'

I had avoided Lilly and that made her want me more. She sent her friend one night to see me again. The friend was annoyed, said that no one fucked Lilly around. Lilly could have anyone.

I arranged to meet Lilly and her friend at the San Tropez cafe with Mick the Mouth. He was excited, thinking it could be me with Lilly and him with her mate.

Mick the Mouth was brave, would try anything. He was good company. We sat upstairs at the cafe. I recognised some of the waitresses. One kissed me on the cheek and Mick the Mouth was impressed. Lilly came in with her friend. Lilly had this big smile; she was beautiful.

She asked me why I'd been avoiding her and I told her I'd been busy writing a book of poems. She laughed and sat next to me. Mick the Mouth offered the friend a seat beside him, but she ignored him. She looked as though she was there to referee the evening.

I read Lilly my poem about her. I had to read it a few times. She was so pleased.

'I don't think I've ever had a poem written about me.'

She kissed me, on the lips. She then took my hand and we walked off out. She told her friend to keep Mick the Mouth entertained. Outside we walked down towards the river.

'I still want to know why you fucked me about. I don't like that.'

We stood near St Thomas More's tree, by Battersea Bridge. I told her that I didn't want to be just another one of the boys she had after her all the time. She looked serious. She kissed me.

'You're different, Tony.'

We played around down by the river. Lilly said that I was out of place in the World's End and Fulham; I should go off to Paris and be a real poet. I read her a few more poems. When we arrived back at the cafe, both the friend and Mick the Mouth looked annoyed. Lilly wiped some lipstick off my mouth. I thought she did it to let them know we'd been kissing.

I made a big mistake. One day during my third week at the job I went into work in jeans. Mr George hit the roof. I told him that my other trousers were dirty; they were covered in mud.

'You can't come into the studio in jeans, Tony. You'll have to go home.'

He wouldn't listen to my pleas, so I turned on him. I told him to stick his job up his arse.

He was dumbfounded. He went to the till, took out two guineas and told me to leave. I was angry with myself. I had been getting on all right. There was the opportunity of being near to girls, and I kind of liked the place.

I walked off down the road so annoyed with myself I felt like crying. How stupid. I could have gone home and cleaned the trousers. They'd got muddy when I was lying in the grass by the river with Lilly. Now I was out of work again. Heading for my fourth job in less than two months.

I walked along the Brompton Road towards South Kensington, once again looking in shop windows for job notices. I found one: the Peppermill was a small supermarket advertising for a boy to help out. I went in and saw the manager. He had a sour face and he looked at me warily, looked at my hair. He was probably short of staff; he wouldn't have given me a start if he'd had a choice.

I could start the next day, four pounds. He wanted me to work in the fruit and vegetable section. All I had to do was weigh out people's stuff and put it in a bag with the price written on. I filled in a form and left. I was kind of happy again – at least I had a job – but I was still annoyed that I'd blown the best job yet.

I spent the rest of the day walking round the museums at South Kensington. I wrote a few poems and looked at the paintings and drawings. I liked Constable, liked his drawings of trees. I sat in a canteen and did some more writing. And then I went home at the usual time, so that it looked like I was still working at the hairdresser's.

16

Tony, the African man on the meat counter, smiled at me. He and the Polish lady at the till were the only ones that smiled. Misery was all over the place. Tony told me to listen to Peggy Lee's 'Till There Was You'. He sang it for me. It made me feel good. He sang it up and down the shop all day.

The manager often walked through the shop. He looked at everything with suspicion. He rearranged things. He picked up pieces of paper. He told me that when I had nothing to do I should clean up. He didn't like me. But I reckoned he didn't like anyone.

I went to see Mick the Mouth one evening and met his big brother, Brian, for the first time. He shook my hand. They lived behind the Watneys brewery on the King's Road. Brian played around like a boy, though he was almost twenty. He annoyed Mick. He pulled his hair and punched him. Brian was like a man and he had just come out of prison.

Brian was bright. He talked about communism and fascism. And about poetry and other things. He was full of words.

He asked us what we were doing that night. I told him Mick and I were going to Battersea Park to pick up girls, and Brian said he'd come along. When he went inside to get his coat Mick looked at me like I'd betrayed him; he was annoyed. He didn't want Brian hanging around with us all night.

Walking over Albert Bridge down to Battersea Park, Brian told us about all the girls he'd pulled. I knew he was bullshitting and I had a feeling that really he would be shy. I was right. In the park, I started talking to girls and Mick and Brian just watched me; they stood back while I performed. I talked to all sorts of girls that night, just stopped them and chatted for a while. Like a game. I wanted to show Brian and Mick that you had to be brave with girls. You couldn't just wait for them – you had to go after them.

Later, at the San Tropez cafe, Brian bought me a hot chocolate. Mick looked miserable, sitting looking at me talking to Brian. Brian told me I was good at chatting up girls.

'And you're not, even though you're five years older!'

The reason for that, he said, was that he'd been in homes and nick; he'd never had my chances. I laughed, though: my life didn't seem like a set of good chances.

Being at work was like being at school. Except that they paid you to tell you off. The money was good even though there were no chances to steal from the cash till. But the manager was a miserable man who made people miserable.

It was hot in the shop. One afternoon I noticed that the dates were going off. I took one and ate it – and that moment the manager came round the corner.

'You're fired. Get out.'

I shook Tony's hand and left. The manager said I could pick up my three days' pay at the end of the week.

The heat made me lazy. I sauntered down the Fulham Road towards Sloane Square. I knew I had to get another job. If I didn't my parents would explode. I was looking in windows on the King's Road when I saw a bloke I'd known at school. He was standing around outside a pub. His name was Phil. I hadn't seen him since I'd left St Thomas More.

I shouted so loud that people in the street looked around. When Phil saw me he threw down the cigarette he'd been smoking and ran towards me.

'Tony! You've saved my life.'

He grabbed me as if he was in some kind of panic. He shook me. His hands were shaking and he was sweating.

He took me round the corner to Markham Square. From his pocket he pulled a small booklet: a shop-savings book that belonged to his grandmother. He had to explain what it was, because I'd never seen one before.

'She puts money in the shop each week. She's saved up £5 already.'

His grandmother had gone home to Ireland and he'd nicked it from her flat. Trouble was, he couldn't cash it because the people in the shop knew him. I laughed when he told me that. All that fuss over this book.

We agreed to split the money fifty-fifty if I went in and cashed it for him. I didn't hesitate. The shop was on the King's Road; I told Phil to wait in the square and went in. The woman inside took the book from me when I said it was my granny's. She was young-looking. She walked to the other end of the counter and spoke with a small man who'd been serving someone else.

The man came over and spoke to me. I told him my story: my granny was in Ireland and wanted the money sent. The man looked at me. I could tell that he didn't believe what I was telling him. But still, he told me to come back at five o'clock; he'd give me the money then.

I left the shop without showing fear. I knew I had to keep a brave face, because otherwise they'd be suspicious.

In the square Phil was unhappy when I told him the news. He was ill-looking, his eyes rolling in his head. I had never seen him like this. He was just so nervous.

'They'll nick you. They'll fucking nick you. If you get nicked *I'll* get nicked.'

I stopped him, told him to calm down. I told him there was one thing I'd never do: grass him up.

We had three hours to kill before I could go back to the shop. He didn't calm down at all. He was like a cat that had been scalded. We walked up towards Hyde Park and climbed the fence by the Serpentine and lay on the grass. It was impossible to calm him, so I ignored him.

I wrote a poem in my notebook. I turned my back on Phil and watched girls as they lay on the grass near us. Phil sat still, staring at the water. He looked tortured, thinking about the savings book.

Five o'clock came and we went back to the shop. The manager gave me the money, after some more questioning. And he gave me back the book. But I could tell he still didn't believe me.

Outside I crossed to Markham Square where Phil was hovering. His eyes lit up when I told him everything was OK. But then I gave him half the money and he started.

He said he'd let me keep £1. You couldn't argue with Phil, so we started to fight. He hit me hard in the face and I hit him back, as hard as I could. The money dropped on the ground as we hit each other and rolled around. He scratched my face and tried to bite my ear. But I was so annoyed at him I wouldn't let him get the advantage.

In the end he shared the money as agreed, fifty-fifty. But we spat at each other when we parted. And I knew that if we'd been somewhere other than the street near the shop Phil would have fought to the very end.

My next job was in a wine merchant's in Knightsbridge. I delivered wine to the posh houses of Kensington and Chelsea. Mr Lindsay who ran the shop was very kind. He sat in his office in the basement drinking port and sherry for most of the day. He took snuff and the front of his jacket was covered in it. He always wore a suit and had a coloured hankie sticking out of his breast pocket – yellow, blue, green or red; never white.

He said he'd teach me about the wine trade, about ports and sherries and wines. I told him I only drank cider and he rolled his eyes at me. 'Such common taste.'

But he never did more than show me various bottles, really. And tell me about his adventures in the wine trade. His time in India, and in Portugal. And the girls he'd known in his youth. He'd offer me a glass of wine, now and then. But I would just sniff it; it smelt and looked too bad to drink.

Mick the Mouth came to work for the summer, before he went

back to school in September. Mr Lindsay welcomed him. Mick was better dressed than me and more polite and Mr Lindsay took a liking to him. But I didn't care. I was more interested in robbing bottles of whiskey. I would leave each evening with at least one tucked in my coat. Sometimes I'd drink it, but other times I'd sell it – to Brian or his mate Mad Roy. There was always someone in the World's End who could do with a bottle of whiskey.

Mick also took bottles home, but he was more frightened than me; he always had a guilty look as he left the shop. One night we got drunk on a bottle of Olde Granddad and went to the Hammersmith Palais. We were thrown out. Out in the street I was so drunk I tried to push Mick in the path of a bus. I was that mad. Mick laughed it off and then tried to do the same with me. When I got home in the early hours my mother beat me for being drunk and late.

One evening in August the police came to the door as I was about to go out. I heard them talking as I stood in the bathroom with the door open.

They were from Gerald Row Police Station and they wanted to talk to me about reports of a Roman-looking boy cashing a stolen savings book at a shop on the King's Road.

I looked at the floor. I knew they thought they had me, but I wasn't going to make it easy for them this time. I was going to deny everything: I was going to plead innocence.

My mother and I were taken by police car to Gerald Row, near Victoria Station. My mother looked worried. The shopkeeper was already there.

'That's the one.'

And then he left. My mother turned on me, hit me.

I was charged with receiving money under false pretences. It was back to Chelsea Juvenile Court. Back before the grey-haired Lady Wotton.

I pleaded not guilty and said I wanted a jury trial. Against police recommendation, I was remanded on bail for the sum of twenty pounds.

As I left the court the arresting officer didn't look happy. He came up to me and said, 'You better turn up, lad.'

On the way home my mother cursed me for all the trouble I'd caused her.

Mr Lindsay asked me to leave. He said he didn't need two boys; he'd promised Mick the Mouth work for the summer so he would have to stay. I was pissed off: I had got Mick his job and now I didn't have one and I had the court thing hanging over me too. But in a way it was good. They would soon do a stock-take and discover a lot of stuff missing.

I was fed up. I got a job delivering fruit and vegetables from a shop in the King's Road, but they fired me within a few hours; they said I was lazy and didn't put my mind to it. I didn't care. I had made up my mind what I was going to do next: I was going to run away from home. I'd had enough of all the work stuff. And I'd had enough of living at home. It was killing me. They had no life.

I went round to Brian's house. We stood outside and I told him. I was running away: I asked if I could stay with him for a few nights.

'Sometimes. But don't make a habit of it.'

Brian was a good bloke; he would help me out. But I could stay only occasionally because his and Mick's dad was around. Other times I slept in doorways off the King's Road. I wandered round through the night. I always avoided well-lit places. Whenever I saw policemen, I'd run off.

Then I found a cement shed behind the World's End pub. Brian had given me his father's airforce overcoat and I looked like a tramp now. Or a proper beatnik. I would get into the cement shed and put cement bags over the door. I was safe in there. I always came out covered in cement dust, but that didn't matter. I got in after midnight and left before six, so I wasn't discovered. Sometimes I had bad dreams, though; once, I woke up screaming. I'd always had night-mares, but now they were worse. Especially in the shed.

There were queers who'd ask me to go places with them. They'd smile at me, ask if I wanted to earn money. Tramps, too, who wanted me to wank them off. They frightened me because I was always on my own in the middle of the night. I was always having to tell them to fuck off. Sometimes they did but sometimes they'd follow me around.

Some nights, I walked down by the river towards Victoria Station. I would sleep in the waiting room there, under the big bench.

One night, it was late – gone midnight – and I met a bloke called Nick in the San Tropez cafe.

'You look like the young Bonaparte on a retreat from Moscow in that coat.'

I didn't understand what he meant.

'Napoleon Bonaparte.' He said I was the dead spit of him. I was pleased, even though I didn't know who this Bonaparte fellow was.

Nick was working for the Campaign for Nuclear Disarmament. He laughed when I told him I hadn't heard of that either.

Nick said I was a little simpleton. And he gave me a nickname: Boney. When I told him I had nowhere to stay he said I could sleep in his car if I liked. Nick was a good bloke; I liked him.

'It's parked in Oakley Street. You can sleep there so long as you don't get seen. If you do I shall have to say I don't know you.'

I got into the small black car. I got in the back seat and squeezed down on the floor. I covered myself with the overcoat. I had been sleeping rough for about three weeks by this time and this was the best of places. If I kept myself covered I would never be seen.

In the morning Nick went off to do some work. But first we had a bacon sandwich in the Black Cat cafe on the Fulham Road.

'You are a strange boy, Boney.'

'Why?'

'Well, you write poetry and yet you talk like a delivery boy.' He said that my class weren't interested in those kind of things – just football and darts and stuff like that.

We became friends. Nick had only just come to London. He was a student as well as working for the CND. We would drive around in the little Ford car and then he'd let me sleep in it at night. But sometimes he had to go away in the car and then I'd be wandering around again. I started to wander away from Chelsea, up to the West End. It was easier to sleep there. I wouldn't go anywhere with people who asked me to. You never knew who they were, or what the dangers were. It was always better to sleep in stations, or behind the Empire Cinema in Leicester Square. Or there were clubs, like the Nucleus, that stayed open late and were full of beatniks. They were all right, they left you alone. The 2Gs by Charing Cross Station closed at about four in the morning; you could stay there with a cup of coffee and be left alone. Sometimes I'd go down and pick up fruit at Covent Garden.

I lived by begging. That's how I got food money. I could always get something. Most people said no but a few helped me with coppers or a couple of shillings.

One night I met Brian in a generous mood. He wanted to go to the pictures so we went to a cinema on the King's Road. He bought me a Coke and some chocolate. When we left, we were playing around outside the cinema when I saw my father standing watching me. He was on the other side of the road and had a bike with him. I walked over – I wasn't frightened of him any more. I didn't care if he hit me.

'Get on the bus. You're coming home.'

He told Brian to piss off. I got on the bus and my father cycled after it. He couldn't keep up; I could have stayed on the bus and he would never have caught me. But I was in an angry mood. Let him do what he wanted to me – I wasn't going to put up with it. Never again.

I waited outside the flats for him. When he came we walked up the stairs, with him carrying the bike. I said nothing. I wasn't going to say sorry for anything. Those days were over. In the flat he sent Tommy and Pat into the kitchen. My mother was in Beat's flat. He closed the front-room door and took off his belt. He had a wild look on his face. As he came towards me I jumped on him, hit him with my head. I knocked him over the couch and he landed by the fire. Then he called out for Tommy and Pat.

'Hold the little cunt down.'

They grabbed me and pushed me to the floor. And as he beat me with the belt they held on to me. I shouted at him. He kept beating me and I kept calling him a working-class bastard. Then he stopped. I got up, pushed past them and went out the door.

I got down to the square. He stood with my brothers, looking down at me. My mother came out of Beat's and started screaming.

I shouted back. 'Fuck the lot of you, you fucking working-class cunts. I'll never see you again.'

And then I walked out of the square. I walked up to Brian's but couldn't raise him. So I went to the cement shed and shut myself in.

I didn't care. He had beaten me for the last time. I hated them all – Tommy, Pat and my parents. They would always be arseholes. My life with them was over and they could do nothing about it.

I said my prayers before I went to sleep. At least I had Jesus on my side; he would understand what I had to put up with. He would know that I wasn't a bad person and that I had to have a life of my own.

Sunday morning and I went to the service at Westminster Cathedral. That was the good part of being on the run: I could go to any church in London I chose. And, to me, Westminster Cathedral was the best of churches. Big and full of people. It was like being in the middle of something important. Not some shit church down by the gasworks in Fulham. I could see people coming to this church with doubts and coming out firm believers.

Later, I walked back towards Chelsea. I kept getting drawn there. I went to the Cafe Des Artistes and fell in with a French woman. That evening we went to the all-night hamburger bar in Earl's Court. I had a fight with one of the French woman's friends. He told me to piss off because the woman was his friend and not mine. He was a grown man but I stood up to him; he didn't worry me.

We sat until early morning. I walked the French woman home and then went and lay on a bench in a square near a church. I slept there until the evening and then went round to Brian's.

He slammed the door in my face, said he had no money. I was angry with him now; I thought I'd never call on him again. I walked down the King's Road furious with Brian.

And when I reached the Man in the Moon pub I saw the policemen who'd arrested me for the savings-book fraud.

I'd broken bail and that was it: with smiles on their faces the policemen called for a car to collect me.

Later, at the police station, my mother beat me in the cell. But I didn't care. I just told her to fuck off. I was transferred to the remand home the next morning and I still didn't care. Nothing much mattered now; they had me. I knew I was being sent down, so I didn't care: let them do what they wanted.

I went to the London Quarter Sessions and knew I would get sent down. It didn't help that I went for trial with a jury. It was all sorted. I got three years. It was that straightforward.

I was not yet sixteen years old. I could be away until I was nearly nineteen. But I put that out of my mind as I was led out of court that day. I just thought it was a good thing that my crying mother wasn't there to see me go. At least I didn't have to put up with her grieving about my foolishness and how I was killing her. And what had she and my father done to deserve such an arsehole for a son.

17

The car drove slowly up the gravel driveway, away from the main road. Stones bounced up and hit the underside of the car. I remembered the joy with which I'd greeted the countryside when we were sent to the orphanage. I knew I was not about to make the same mistake again.

Cows came to a long, low fence. Trees swayed in the wind. We came to a bend and I could see an old bridge and, beyond that, something unexpected: a big house, like a mansion. Like the one in Bishop's Park by the river.

The house sat by itself in front of large green lawns, flanked only by more trees. It took my breath away. I had expected it to be like Campsfield House Detention Centre. I had not expected a country house – a posh-looking house surrounded by greenery.

Miss Foster noticed my surprise. I told her, 'It don't look like a reformatory.'

She said it wasn't supposed to be a place of punishment; it was a place of change. 'Park House has a very good record. People leave here and never get in trouble again.'

The car stopped in front of the main door and we got out. Now I could see what looked like the dipping banks of a river. No barbed wire fences. No gates. No plodding warders. Just this great big house that looked as though it had been built for some well-placed family not for delinquents.

Miss Foster led me inside and introduced me to a man who was dressed like a schoolteacher – no bunch of keys, no uniform. Miss Foster said goodbye. She smiled. She had beautiful grey hair. I was left with the man who looked like a teacher.

I was taken to meet the headmaster in his office. He told me that my new life would begin today. He wore a heavy tweed suit. He had thick hair and his face was tough-looking, almost brutal. But I thought he was kindly. He also had very bad breath. And his teeth stuck out of his mouth – badly organised teeth, I thought.

The headmaster said that I'd get a lot out of being at Park House if I behaved myself.

I was shown around by a boy with wild blond hair. They didn't shave your head here, like they had at the detention centre. The boy didn't talk to me and I had nothing to say to him. He was dressed like a schoolboy, in a blue shirt, pullover and tie and black trousers. He took me to what was called the sewing room, where I was given clothes just like his. The uniforms weren't like prison clothes, but they made us look like grown-up schoolboys.

Next I saw the house room, where you went before and after meals. Where you hung out when you weren't working or in classes. Then the boy showed me the boot room, where you kept your shoes and plimsoles, and the bedrooms. The bedrooms were small and neat. I left all my stuff on the bed.

He took me back to the house room. It was big, with big windows overlooking the lawn and the trees. He left me there without saying anything else, without explaining anything else. I'd wanted him to tell me what was required of me. I wanted to get through this place as soon as I could, to get back to being a good Catholic. But I stood in the house room with its big windows and was happy that at least I wasn't in a place of madness. At least I wasn't back in the detention centre.

There was a ping-pong table. I was messing around with the ball and a bat when suddenly the door opened and boys rushed in. One boy with greased-back hair snatched the bat from me.

'Fuck off somewhere else before I give you a whack.'

Another boy took up the other bat and they launched into a game.

The room was now full of boys, all of them ignoring me. I

watched the two boys playing ping-pong and had a feeling that I might have trouble with them.

Later, at lunch, I was given a place at a table of eight. There was a big mantelpiece in the dining room, and pictures on the walls.

The blond boy who'd shown me around sat at the head of our table. Opposite me was another boy with greased-back hair. He introduced himself to me. His name was Clive. He had a smiling face, and tattoos on his arm and hands. When the food arrived, in metal trays, I helped the blond boy and Clive give it out. The boy who'd taken the ping-pong bat from me was at the end of the table. He had a kind of wicked smile on his face as I served him food.

Clive was the only boy who wanted to talk to me. He explained the system at Park House. There were five 'grades': novice, lower, middle, upper and senior. Everyone had to work their way up through the grades to senior; only then could they leave. Clive had been at Park House six months and was at lower grade. I asked him how long it would take to reach senior grade.

'Maybe eighteen months – that's if you're doing good. Mostly twenty months. Maybe two years, maybe even longer. Depends on how much of an arsehole you are.'

He said they could keep you even longer – till you were twenty-one if they wanted to. Twenty-one seemed a long way off. It was a lot of time to think about.

After lunch, I had to see the headmaster again. He said I was a bright boy who kept getting into trouble. He said that at Park House stupidity wasn't allowed. I would learn a trade. I would learn to work, to be responsible.

'Have you any idea what you want to work at?'

I had no idea. I couldn't imagine telling him that I wanted to be the greatest poet in the world. That I wanted to be the Adolf Hitler or the Napoleon Bonaparte of poetry, to crush all the other poets. I didn't want to be a plumber. I didn't want to be useful, or responsible. Could I tell the headmaster that?

'No, sir. I just want to earn a living, sir. And never get into trouble ever again.'

He looked sharp at me and said never to tell him what I thought he'd want to hear.

A boy called Jim was in the bed next to me.

'D'you wank, lad?'

'No.'

'Fucking liar. Everyone wanks.'

Norman also talked to me. He looked like a weight-trainer. He was big, seventeen years old. He told me to be prepared: after a few days, I'd get pushed around. He said that if I fought my corner, hit back a bit, no one would touch me.

It was always the same story. It was all about bullying. No one touched anyone they thought could beat them in a fight. But I was braver than this fucking lot. I'd fight anyone, no matter what the outcome might be.

Norman was right, though. The trouble soon started – the tripping up, the kicking, the threatening. The blond boy tried to be tough with me but I could tell he was weak, just throwing his weight around. Trevor, the greasy-haired boy, was different.

At dinner one day I was told to serve the vegetables. Trevor wanted more than I gave him. I said that if I gave him more, everyone else would be short. He said nothing. Smiled. I shared out the vegetables evenly. The blond boy laughed. Clive looked at me as though I was stupid, but he said nothing.

Later on, in the house room, Trevor walked up to me and punched me hard in the face. He punched me so hard that my nose split and I fell down. Then he kicked me in the head. I lay on the floor covered in blood.

'When I want extras, I get extras.'

Trevor was eighteen years old; I was fifteen. And no one said or did anything.

As I cleaned myself up all I could think about was revenge. I thought I would get a knife. I could stick the knife in his throat as he slept. Or in his heart. No one could stop me. They couldn't hang me.

I stood sobbing. I was powerless. There was nothing I could do.

You had to learn a trade, as the headmaster had said. To begin with, to determine which trade would be yours, you spent a week on each one. Plumbing, carpentry, building, gardening, painting and decorating, catering and tailoring. During my first seven weeks I learnt a bit about all these different trades. It was boring. I'd tried hard to get out of the working classes and now I was back among them. Now I was going to have to put up with building sites and other places of rough work. I thought it was a waste of time. I would probably never use the trade that they taught me; I had no plans to get a job as a labourer. I was going to get out of the working-class stuff as quickly as possible.

After seven weeks I decided that the best trade for me was catering. It was indoors and you were left alone. And Mr Drury, who ran the department, didn't complain. I was no more interested in catering than I was in building, but at least I wouldn't be outside getting covered in shit in all weathers.

My mother came to see me. She brought Peter, Richard and Eddy. We walked round the grounds, down to the river. Richard and Eddy had a great time throwing pebbles at ducks. Peter looked beautiful.

My mother said I looked different – in a good way, not so skinny. I asked if my father was ever going to come and see me, but she said he was always working. We didn't talk about the fight between him and me.

'Now, Tony, you're not to feck around here. This could be your big chance.'

The visit ended well. I was pleased to have seen them, but I didn't feel bad about them going.

Mr Hepworth was one of the housemasters and also a teacher.

He told me I should join the GCE English class. He thought it would be good for me, that I'd learn something. He said I was a bright boy.

I may have been bright but I wasn't educated. After I'd left school I'd read some books, loads of books. I had brought a few with me to Park House: *The Romans in Britain, Angelo in Italy* and *The Catcher in the Rye*. Also some poetry by Leroi Jones and Lawrence Ferlinghetti. The staff had been impressed that I had books, but I didn't want them to think that I was educated.

Chester Flaws was the boilerman. He was Canadian. Canadians had lived in the house and grounds during the Second World War and Chester had stayed on. He was small and shrivelled-looking. He called everyone 'cock-sucker' and was great fun with his insulting tongue. He saw me reading Leroi Jones and Lawrence Ferlinghetti one day.

'Hey, cock-sucker. Lend me the book.'

A week later he'd read it and brought it back. He said he'd loved it. It was covered in ash marks from the boiler house. I didn't mind. I liked the fact that he liked what I liked.

I joined the GCE class and soon realised that I didn't understand a lot. Mr Hepworth taught us about books and poems. He talked about grammar and style and about books and writers I had never heard of or didn't know much about: Thomas Hardy, D. H. Lawrence, Arnold Bennett. We read and discussed. On my first day we read 'The Snake', a poem by D. H. Lawrence. All I knew about Lawrence was that there'd been all the interest in *Lady Chatterley's Lover*. That he'd used the word 'cunt' a few times in the book.

'The Snake' was interesting but it was a very deep poem. Mr Hepworth had to explain it all. The boys in the class didn't seem brighter than anyone else. Clive was there. He spoke a lot, had opinions. Hepworth listened, but he still had to tell us how to truly understand the poem. That the snake was a piece of nature that visited the water hole. And the poet had thrown something at it, regretting it later.

The class was better than the trade work – not that there was any real work in the catering department. But it was also interesting and Hepworth tried hard to keep our attention. I had nothing to say when he asked me my opinion, though. After the class he asked me if I'd enjoyed it. I told him yes, but that I didn't know anything; all I could do was read and write a bit.

'Don't you worry. That's a good start.'

As winter came I began to feel that I could stomach Park House after all. I'd had no more problems with Trevor, but I still thought he deserved to be punished. And he was, one bitterly cold day in the house room. Brooks came in. Brooks was big and strong. He walked up to Trevor and hit him, kept hitting him. Trevor gave up; there was no contest. Brooks said nothing, just silently hit him again and again.

The house room was hushed. When he'd finished the beating, Brooks left. Trevor lay on the floor, a changed man. He had two black eyes; he had cuts to his cheeks and his chin. He was in a bad state. Probably the humiliation was the worst thing. He must have known that there were people, like me, who had silently cheered. Because the bully had been bullied, was down and defeated.

Christmas. The coach left the school full of London boys for the break. The coach seemed slow getting into London. But as we moved through Wandsworth, and I began to recognise places, I became happy. Dreary, damp London looked great to me. The coach dropped us at Waterloo. As I walked away from the others I thanked God that I would be a good person again.

I took my time getting home. I had not seen my father since the fight. Would he still hate me? Would he feel that I had treated him badly? I was worried as I crossed Westminster Bridge. At Parliament Square I thought about all the times I had walked through there, begging or looking for a place to sleep. I was glad that I'd got out of trouble, that my slate had been wiped clean. Now I was doing my penance. No one could go to my mother and tell her that I'd done a new wrong. It was a good feeling, not having anything hanging over me.

By Parliament I felt happy that, despite all the wrongs of my life, I seemed to be getting things straight. I was reading and learning more than anyone else in my family knew.

The day was still dreary and cold. The lights were on, though it was only early afternoon. I got on a bus and was soon passing down through Victoria and Chelsea. I kept my eyes open for St Thomas More boys and girls I might know. That life didn't seem so bad, now that I was out of it.

At home they were all happy to see me. The kids screamed. My mother almost cried.

'You're beginning to look normal, Tony. Not like a tramp or a tinker.' She always had an opinion. Always wanted to give it. I didn't like her saying that I might look normal again. 'Normal' meant joining them; it meant talking and thinking like them. And watching TV, like them. I may have wronged my family but I wasn't going back to be one of them.

I needed to go out. I needed to see Brian, and Mick the Mouth. I wanted to go to the San Tropez to see if any of the old waitresses were there, or any of my other friends. But I had to wait for my father to come home.

When he came, he looked at me warily. I could tell that he hadn't forgotten everything. The calling him a stinking working-class bastard was a difficult thing to face.

We said hello and he just looked at me. He knew I wasn't frightened of him any more. He could do what he liked but I would never let him hit me again.

Brian was working in a theatre. Mick the Mouth was even bigger-mouthed. They didn't really want to know me; I was yesterday's news. But I had this feeling that whatever was happening to me was important. That it wasn't time wasted. That whatever Brian and Mick the Mouth were, they weren't as important as me. They wouldn't have important lives.

Brian almost told me to fuck off, said he was doing things and I wasn't. That's how it was with him – like some kind of rotten competition. I didn't care about all that. I was going to turn the world upside down. And fuck Brian and Mick, they were nothing.

One night we walked through Earl's Court.

'So, Tony Bird, get us into a party.'

Brian was pushing me. It wasn't going to be easy to be sensible. To be thoughtful, careful. But I knew that I had to keep out of trouble. I knew that 1962 was going to be the year in which I'd learn how to be sensible. I would be sixteen. Jesus was expecting me to be good, and telling me not to waste my life.

But Brian was driving home how stupid my life was now. He said, 'You just use people. You're all about Tony Bird. I think I fucking hate you more than I hate anyone else.'

I didn't have to listen; I didn't need this shit from Brian. I walked home, feeling glad that I didn't need him as a friend any more. I was on the road. I was going to be a great poet. I was going to get out of Park House in record time and be sensible about my life. Brian was the past. I wouldn't see him again. If he couldn't be a friend, then I could do without him.

I spent the rest of the holiday taking the kids out. I took them on buses all over London, up to Fleet Street and into the City. I felt better about my family, even my father.

My father was working by Waterloo Station, converting some offices. When I went to meet the bus to go back to Park House, he was standing around waiting for me.

'Here you are, son.'

He handed me half a crown. He looked sad. Maybe as his son I made him sad. Maybe he'd been sad all his life. Sad that he had nothing, nothing except a family to support.

He waved to me as the bus drew away. At that moment I loved my father more than I loved anyone. It was his life that made him bad.

★

Park House was not going to be easy. But I could see that I just had to stay out of trouble. The bullies would rule; that would never change. Very occasionally, a bully would get beaten. But there would always be another to take their place. There would always be cowards and weaklings. There would always be people whose lives made them bad.

18

'How would you get away, then? If you're so smart.'

'I wouldn't go up the main London road.'

Green gave me a worried look.

We'd been back for a few weeks. It was January 1962. Already I'd been taken out of the catering department. I'd got bored with the simple, stupid things we had to do. Now I was in the gardens – no more interesting, but you were still left alone. But it was freezing outside. I walked around and slapped my thighs, trying to keep warm.

Before Christmas, I had told Green that I was thinking of running away. Green wouldn't go unless he had a partner. Now we were discussing how best to go about it I was in two minds.

I had been there nearly three months. It wasn't as bad as the detention centre. Here you got a bit of normal life. I hated the system. The bullies, the cowards, running the place. But now I wasn't sure that I wanted to run away.

For Green it was different. He was big, tall. But he was not one of the hard nuts. He was pushed around. Because he was tall and big, he was picked on. He had a worse life than me. I knew that.

So I told him that, if we did it, we should go the way that no one would expect us to go.

You could get away from there any time. There were fields and open roads. A river and a bridge. You could go anywhere; there was nothing stopping you. No big fences, no walls, just the open country. And then the main London road half a mile away. It was just a question of planning.

I got sick. I had heavy flu and was soon stuck in the sickbay. I couldn't shake off the illness; it just got worse. I was hallucinating. One night I woke up screaming, thinking I was being murdered. It didn't help that I was in a dark little building set away from the main house. Surrounded by trees that rustled and knocked at the window all night.

I was in sickbay for five days. When I came out, I felt all right but was still weak. I sat in the house room like a real old invalid. Green came in, impatient to run away.

'Tomorrow night, Birdy?'

I didn't want to go now; I'd changed my mind. But I'd promised him, and he was desperate to go. I had made a promise and I couldn't go back on it.

It was another two days before I was strong. It was a Wednesday. Before supper Green took our own clothes out to the big cedar by the small fence. At six we met in the boot room and left through the basement door. There was no turning back. We ran across the dark lawns to the tree and dressed in silence. Green had left my shoes behind in the boot room. I had on a pair of house slippers. We laughed at the thought of running away to London wearing a pair of slippers. And then we fell quiet again.

The school was lit up but we were in shadow. It was a good dark night; there was no moon. I led Green across the field towards the hill behind the house. From the top, you could see the London road.

We walked down to the main road, and when we were sure no cars were coming we crossed it. On the other side we took a smaller road to Godalming, where we could get a train. We whispered as we walked along. Green wanted a cigarette but I told him he couldn't light up. Whenever we saw headlights approaching we left the road and hid in the ditch or in a field beside the road.

We had to move quickly. We needed to get on a train for London by seven-thirty, when our classes would start and we'd be reported missing.

It took us more than an hour to get to the station. We held back near the end of the platform, by the guards' office, and waited for the train to come in. Green was shivering with cold and fear. He stood smoking, looking nervous. I felt nothing.

When the train pulled in, at quarter to eight, we waited until it had stopped, then waited a few minutes more. We walked through the gate and got on the train just before it pulled away. We didn't look around, just made our way straight to an open carriage. I thought it was best to stay in the open, not try and hide. To act as if we had nothing to hide.

We sat opposite some girls. They smiled at us. I talked to them, but Green just sat and looked on. He still looked nervous. He looked like someone who had done something wrong.

When the ticket inspector came into the carriage I rushed up to him, interrupted him as he clipped tickets.

'Inspector! I'm in a terrible pickle. I've left my wallet with my tickets on the bench at Godalming. Can you stop the train?'

'What?'

He must have thought I was crazy. And he looked irritated as I contrived to badger him with my story. But it worked. He said there was nothing he could do; he said I'd just have to explain my situation to the inspectors at Waterloo.

When he'd gone, I sat down and Green winked at me. And the girls sitting opposite smiled.

The train finally drew in at Waterloo Station. I noticed that there was an empty train on the next track along.

'Come on, Green. Let's get out this side.'

We walked over the track and got on to the empty train. Then we stepped down on to the deserted platform on the other side. I told Green to pretend we were train enthusiasts. We walked back and forth looking at the carriage. Then we made our way towards the exit, talking to each other loudly about the train as we passed by the guards near the barrier.

We got through, and left the station. As soon as we got outside, Green jumped for joy.

'Birdy, that was fucking marvellous.'

He shook my hand. He couldn't believe how easy it was.

We took a bus towards Chelsea. Green knew about stealing cars. He knew how to hot-wire cars. We would find a quiet road and get ourselves one. It didn't take long, once we'd got off the bus at the King's Road and headed down a side street. I didn't care what kind of car we got; I just wanted to get going, out of London. But Green was looking for something nice, with a bit of push. In a cul de sac by the Fulham Road, he found just what he wanted: a sports car; an Austin Healey Sprite. He opened it easily enough, hot-wired the engine and then we were off.

The little sports car could really move. But I made Green go slowly, said we didn't want to draw attention to ourselves. We drove aimlessly through the streets. Down the Fulham Road towards Knightsbridge, and then on through Piccadilly. Green loved it. He said he wanted to go to see a friend in Walthamstow. As we drove we sang. This was fun, we both agreed.

Then we got lost. We were in east London and a police car suddenly started following us. I could tell that Green wanted to race off. I told him to take it easy, not to go mad.

'They're behind us.'

'Keep it easy.'

He turned down the first side road. The police car turned as well. Green put his foot down and the car leapt forward. I looked over at him. He looked possessed; the car was out of control now. He turned a corner and we hit a road sign. At the end of the road there was a dead end. Just before it, on the right, was a turning. Without slowing down, Green took the corner. The car skidded and crashed into a fence.

I was shocked, but not hurt. Green jumped out of the car.

'Come on, Birdy.'

He was off. I managed to get out but I felt funny. My legs didn't seem to be working. I tried to run but one of the policemen soon caught up with me. He tapped me on the shoulder.

'You're not going anywhere, lad.'

★

The policeman who'd caught me was smiling.

'Well, you brightened up our night. Nothing ever happens in Barking Creek.'

I sat in a cell at Barking Creek Police Station and realised that I'd been stupid. I'd been getting on well at Park House, and I'd thrown it all away. I had probably put my release back a good six months.

Ashford Boys' Prison. I was sent there until my court appearance. I was in a cell by myself. It was a luxury. I realised that if I had my way I would spend the rest of my sentence in a cell on my own. The warders were kind. They gave me paper and pencils. They treated me like a serious person. They didn't treat me like a boy, even though I was not yet sixteen. I wrote stories and poems. I had neglected my writing at Park House, and now that I was on my own I felt like writing again. I wrote a letter to my mother. I told her that I'd been stupid again. And that it wasn't anyone's fault but my own. She wrote back that she knew it was my own fault; she could never see me being misled. She said that I was a wilful boy who cared for no one. And that in the name of Jesus I should get myself sorted out.

The only times you met the other inmates were in the exercise yard and the dining room. On one occasion a boy started getting flash with me. I turned on him and a warder separated us, took me aside.

'That bloke's an arsehole. Ignore him.'

Back in my cell, I realised that I wanted to be treated like a grown-up. That was one of my problems: everyone treated me like a boy.

Green was caught a hundred yards from his home. We both ended up back at Chelsea Juvenile Court. The headmaster of Park House was asked to speak. He said that Green and I were very different: Green was a troublemaker and had led me astray. He was prepared to take me back, but not Green.

He talked about my innocence and Green's bad influence. I felt I had to say something, and asked if I could speak. When the magistrate said that I could I told her that Green hadn't misled me. We had both decided to run away; I was younger than Green but I'd had a lot of experience and made my own decisions.

Green then told the court that he and I were good friends and he hadn't meant to cause any trouble.

The magistrate said, 'Well, there was trouble. The car that was taken and wrecked – that was trouble.'

She sent Green to Borstal and me back to Park House.

When I got there the headmaster and his deputy caned me. I refused to bend over so they beat me more. I shouted at them that Jesus was on my side. But they just scoffed at me; Jesus couldn't help me right then.

It took me three months to become a full person again. Up until then I was treated like a leper by boys and staff alike. The boys didn't like runaways, because life was made harder when people tried to escape. But by spring I was being left alone once more and was no longer considered to be such a risk.

I worked in the gardens again. Mr Jones was the one-handed garden leader and he kept on about how unreliable I was. He said that I was a troublemaker, and he had me working by myself.

We had been shown how to properly dig the earth. Deep, careful digging, breaking up the soil and taking out the weeds and couch grass. I preferred working by myself. I worked in a big walled garden, with a serpentine wall in the middle. There was a small orchard. I would look around and think about the fact that every building, every piece of wall was more than 200 years old. It was strange to think that I could have been doing what I was doing all those years before; digging a garden with a spade.

Jones had his own way of training. He picked on you, challenged you, saying, 'I bet you can't do that'. And then you would do it, just to prove that you could. It was his way of encouraging you to change. Jones believed that work changed you, that we were put on earth to be workers. Jones had a method of making you want to do your best.

Whenever I worked hard in the gardens, getting the ground even, pulling out all the weeds, I'd know that Jones was happy. But still he'd talk in his funny way: 'Well, I suppose we'll just have to put up with that.' Playing his strange game.

McGee, Jones's deputy, was different. He was Scottish and also a Catholic. On Sundays he'd drive us to the Catholic church in Godalming. He knew all the Latin names of plants. He loved flowers and plants; wherever you went with him, he'd point out plants and trees. And he would ask you to repeat the plant names he had taught you.

McGee was always full of stories. He would tell you stories about nature, and he would talk about God as though God was everywhere. He would break into song in the van. He was a happy man, just working, bringing bad boys back to life.

'Bird, you should remember that you are a Catholic in an un-Catholic land. We have a responsibility to create the best impression.'

I went to jazz-appreciation classes. We listened to music most nights. But I wanted to learn how to draw and paint. I'd been drawing in exercise books for a few months. It was good, doing something that didn't involve anyone else. I wanted to learn more than anything now. I told Mr Ran, a tall, thin master with a wet, drippy nose. When he spoke he closed his eyes and rattled the coins in his pockets.

'Well, that is capital. And I know just the person to teach you.'

He was smug. But I liked him because he was so funny with his smugness. And he was fair; he didn't want anyone punished on the word of another.

'Who, sir?'

'My wife, Mrs Ran.'

So Mrs Ran arranged to teach me at her house. The first night, I walked past the churchyard in pitch darkness. I was frightened, and ran the rest of the way. I had never met Mrs Ran before, but she welcomed me as if I was a friend.

She was short and fat. The small house had low beams and

everywhere were floral decorations – even the wallpaper was floral. We sat in the living room and I showed her some of the drawing I had done.

She said she was impressed, that I was good. We talked about art and whose work I liked.

I told her I liked Constable; they had some of his pictures in the Victoria and Albert Museum. She seemed very excited. I got the feeling that she liked doing this kind of thing. She'd once been an art teacher and felt starved of it now.

We talked for an hour. We looked again at my drawings. Then she asked me to do a few sketching exercises. My drawings were of pot plants, geraniums. She wanted me to go out on Saturday afternoon and draw a tree.

'You should spend all your spare time drawing, Bird. If you're serious about learning.'

Later she led me into another room. Laid out on a table was a feast: ham, chicken, boiled eggs and corned beef, bread and cakes and a large pot of tea. I was surprised. Mr Ran came in and we sat down. Mr and Mrs Ran tucked in but I was more careful; I didn't want them to turn me away in future because I'd eaten too quickly.

After that, I went every week. Another boy joined me. Davis said he wanted to do art, but I never saw him do any. He never brought any with him when we went to meet Mrs Ran. And he wanted to talk about the Renaissance. I knew nothing about all that history.

Mrs Sherman, who worked in the surgery, came up to me one day. Her husband was also one of the staff. He was the kindest man I had ever met working in an institution. He would wake everyone up in the morning by calling out their first name. I thought he was testing his memory; he could remember everyone's Christian name and never got any wrong.

Mrs Sherman was shy and, like her husband, kindly. She asked me if I'd ever heard of the Impressionists. She smiled when I said no.

'Then I shall have to lend you a book I have. But you must look after it.'

She brought me the book a few days later. I was astonished by it. The bright colours, the flowers and the countryside. I couldn't believe how there could be such bright paintings.

Mrs Sherman said that I should visit the National Gallery and look at the Impressionist paintings there. I knew the National Gallery. It had been a good place to have a wash and brush up when I was sleeping rough in the West End.

I did as she said. When we next went on home leave, I took Mrs Sherman's book with me. I went to the National Gallery and looked at the Impressionist pictures. More than ever, I knew I wanted to be a painter. Afterwards I walked down Charing Cross Road and bought *Lust for Life* by Irving Stone. It was a novel about Van Gogh. It stunned me. I was determined to be like Van Gogh.

It was strange being back at home for leave. Everyone was so pleasant. Even my mother stopped shouting. But I felt that in order to be the next Vincent Van Gogh I had to learn to be by myself more. I had to be sullen, quiet. And maybe mysterious. I had to stop talking to people and think only of my art.

I read in the book that at one time Vincent had lived in Clapham. He used to walk down to the river through Wandsworth, then on to work in the West End. I decided that I would do that also. So I went to Clapham and walked to the river, trying to follow Vincent's footsteps.

But I had a problem: I was too talkative. I went looking for Brian. We went chasing girls down the King's Road and in the Cafe Des Artistes and the San Tropez. I knew that I could never be like Vincent because I couldn't be that shy and withdrawn. Maybe, because I was so talkative, I would never be a great painter. Or maybe I would be the first great talkative painter of all time.

One night Clive was shivering in his bed. The small dormitory was cold. It was spring, but it was colder than it had been in winter. We lay in our beds and Clive was moaning about the cold, telling me to give him my counterpane.

'Come on, Birdy, I'm fucking ill.'

'If I give you my counterpane *I*'ll be ill.'

He shouted at me: 'You cunt.'

'I'm not the only cunt here.'

Clive crossed the floor from his bed. I looked up and in the gloom I saw a raised fist. And then I felt a smack in my face. That's all I felt. Clive and I rolled around hitting each other in the dark.

Suddenly we heard footsteps down the corridor. We jumped into our beds, pretended to be asleep. The duty master came running in. He turned on the light and then pulled back covers. When he pulled back mine, he seemed shocked.

'What the hell has happened to you?'

There was blood on the wall and the bedclothes. Yet I felt nothing.

I was sent to clean myself up. I looked in the mirror and had to laugh. My nose had been smashed flat; it looked like a pancake.

Clive was badly beaten by some other boys. He was terrified. He kept telling me that he didn't mean it. And he didn't, I knew he didn't. And anyway, the damage to my nose meant time off, for many hospital appointments, away from Park House.

They reconstructed my nose. I was happy, though it still looked slightly bent. Clive and I laughed about it all a few months later. He had overreacted, that was all.

In the summer I put my name down to go off to the hills and moors of the north. Mr Hepworth was leading the expedition. I was now so trusted that I was put in charge of others who were not trusted. I had finally got back all that I'd lost by running away at the beginning of the year. I was born anew. Even Mr Jones started to see some change in me.

'Bird, from under that pile of stupidity you may be getting somewhere.'

Mr McGee thought it was because I was becoming a better Catholic. Certainly I felt better. I was not doing harm to anyone. I was thinking about my family. I was going to church and Holy Communion. I wasn't chasing girls, because there were none to chase. And I was reading good books.

And when I did my drawing and painting I knew that I was being blessed by the Lord Jesus Christ. If I became a great painter it was because the Lord had prepared me. He had blessed my efforts.

19

My ingrowing toenail had been causing problems again. More hospital appointments, and eventually I'd been told it would have to be removed. It meant an operation. Another few weeks off, doing nothing in hospital. I was happy with that.

When I woke after the operation, nurses Marie and Inez stood looking at me, smiling.

'Get up, you lazy bugger.' This was from nurse Inez.

Nurse Marie commiserated: 'Poor boy, will it affect his art?'

My lies were catching up with me. I had told them I was a famous artist. That I'd injured my foot building the sculpture of Christ that overlooked Rio de Janeiro. They had soon found out that I was just one of the bad boys from Park House. And they'd laughed at me.

Later, nurse Inez spoke to me alone. She asked me if I really was going to be a great artist.

'Inez, I'm going to be famous. I'm going to wipe the floor with everyone.'

She sat on the bed. She looked around the ward. It was getting dark. She leant forward.

'Can you do me a picture?'

She said she loved art, and had wanted to paint. But there was no future in it as a job.

I scoffed. 'Artists don't need jobs. They just need canvases and paints.'

As she walked off to speak to another patient, I watched her in her tight-fitting uniform.

I loved the gullibility of girls. As soon as you told them you were an artist they were interested in you. I knew there would be countless girls. Girls who wouldn't notice my big broken nose or the fact that

I was skinny with spots, not the most beautiful of boys. My art would open doors for me, that I knew. As soon as I'd left Park House.

It was August. Nearly two years since I'd begun my sentence. They would have to let me out soon, even though I would never meet their standards. If only I could stay straight for a few months I would be free.

A few days later I was up, hobbling around the hospital wards. I did a drawing of some flowers for Inez, but she wasn't that impressed.

'It's all right, but it doesn't look like the work of a genius.'

I was getting better, but I still needed more practice.

'For fuck's sake, Inez, give me a chance. I'm only seventeen.'

'Then how do you know you're a genius?'

'I know. I just know.'

She didn't even take the drawing; she left it on the bed. I was angry, and tore it up.

Back at the school I tried hard to be a good person. Stupidly, though, I was still saying I was going to be an artist. My housemaster told me I should give up on art. That I should make it a hobby, not a job. He said I needed a real job to keep me out of trouble.

In late August the committee met to decide which senior-grade boys could leave. I was told I was to meet the committee. But although I had reached the senior grade, they could keep me there for another five years if they wished.

I was nervous on the evening of the committee meeting. I waited to be called into the big hall. I paced back and forth. They would all be there – the headmaster, the deputy, my housemaster, someone from the gardening department and other board members. When the time finally came, I walked into the room and stood silently.

They were sat at a big table. The chairman spoke.

'Well, Bird, you're a rare fish.'

They all laughed. I thought it would be polite for me to join in, so I laughed along with them.

The chairman said that I was always getting along well and then mucking it up. 'You're not consistent, Bird. What do you have to say to that?'

'I'm sorry, sir. I know what you mean.'

'I'm sure you do.' He said it was me keeping myself in the place; I could have been out six months before had I behaved. Then McGee spoke up, said I did good work. I was one of their best workers.

They talked among themselves as though I wasn't there. It seemed that I would be kept back. Nobody was saying good things about me. The headmaster spoke about my obsession with art, and I knew I had to play it down. They talked about keeping me back for another few months. I remembered what Clive had said when I first arrived – that those last few months were the most difficult.

The chairman shuffled his papers. He said, 'Well, Bird, there's no enthusiasm here for an imminent release.'

He pondered some more, then he asked me, 'Do *you* think you should leave, boy?'

I was surprised by the question; it seemed like a stupid thing to ask me. But I thought I'd better answer seriously.

'No, sir. But I would like to.'

It was the best thing I could have said. They all laughed, said at least I was honest.

I was asked to leave the room and wait outside. Again I paced the floor. After a few minutes McGee called me in. He had a smile on his face and I knew I must have said the right thing.

The chairman, however, was not smiling. He said that they would release me, but only when I'd got a job. Mr McGee thought he could get me placed. Everyone except the chairman seemed happy with the decision.

He said, 'You are leaving this school very much under a cloud; you must bear that in mind. Any trouble and you'll be right back here.'

I thanked him and left. I was elated. Outside, I ran out the front door and down towards the gardens. Soon I would be rid of this place. That night I wrote to my mother. It was a short letter: *Dear Mum & Dad and the kids, I'll be out soon. They've released me. Love Tony.*

McGee kept his word. A few days later, he took me up to London in his car, an old Bentley. We visited the gardening department of the Royal Borough of Kensington and Chelsea. He went off and talked to some people for a few minutes, then came back to me smiling.

I would start in less than two weeks.

The last days were wonderful. I got my stuff together. I got all my drawings and paintings in my portfolio. I didn't realise how many I had; my portfolio bulged. Suddenly everything seemed good. I even began to feel that I might regret leaving. But the feeling soon disappeared. Now I could begin to become the great artist I knew I could be. Of course I would have to work. But in my spare time I would devote every minute to my art.

The Saturday morning came slowly. When it did I picked up my things and walked out the front porch for the last time. My portfolio was very heavy and I had a bag as well, but I didn't mind. I said goodbye to the boys working out the front and set off. I would have to walk the three miles to Godalming, and I didn't mind a bit.

I walked down the drive, looking back occasionally. As I turned the bend I knew I was out of sight and that no one was coming after me. I screamed with happiness. Cows looked at me.

I'd almost got to the gate by the main road when McGee's Bentley appeared. The top was down and he called to me. He said he'd drive me to the station.

My heart sank. I was happy walking; I didn't want a fucking lift.

'It's all right, sir. I don't mind – honestly.'

He chuckled. Mr McGee had an obvious chuckle. He pulled the door open for me.

'Nonsense. You'll give yourself a hernia with that stuff.'

I tried to protest but he wouldn't listen. I almost told him to mind his own fucking business, but McGee was a generous man.

We drove to his house first, so we could have tea and biscuits with his wife and daughters. They were very kind to me. Mrs McGee smiled at me. Their two young daughters kept giving me ginger snaps. But today I didn't want to see anyone. I just wanted to be left alone.

Eventually we all got into the car and headed towards Godalming and the station. I couldn't relax until the school was in the distance; I had a feeling that something might still go wrong.

McGee drove slowly and talked all the time. Telling me I had to keep going to church. That I had to behave at the Royal Borough of Kensington and Chelsea. That other boys would come along later and I shouldn't screw it up for them.

Finally we reached the station. After they'd all shaken my hand, McGee gave me a last piece of advice before he drove off: 'Behave yourself now, laddie. Remember you're an ambassador for us.'

I stood alone on the platform with my ticket. I kept looking at it. I couldn't believe it. I had left; it was all over and nobody could stop me.

It was only when I got on the train that I fully relaxed. I took my seat and breathed a sigh of relief. I looked at other passengers. None of them were having a day like I was. In the month of September 1963.

My mother was very pleased to see me. I offered to take Peter out. He was five and great fun to be with. I took his little hand as we walked out on to the street.

'Where we going, Tony?'

'It's a surprise.'

I wanted to go to Westminster Cathedral and say a few prayers. And I wanted to take Peter up the tower. We got on a bus and I savoured every minute of the ride, along the King's Road, past Sloane Square and Victoria. We passed places where I'd slept when I was on the run. We stopped at a cafe and I bought cakes and tea. Peter loved it; he talked all the time. He was the best company.

'Tony, are you going to be good now? Mum thinks you are.'

I laughed. 'Course I am. I don't ever want to get nicked again.'

I said prayers in Westminster Cathedral. Peter was restless, looking forward to going up the tower. I thanked the Lord for allowing me to be free again. I would pay back his trust in me. And I prayed that I would be the great artist I wanted to be. My talent would be a form of praise for the goodness of the Lord.

We took the lift to the top of the tower. Peter held my hand tightly. He had a little raincoat on and he looked like a very small man. I kissed him. He was the best. At the top we ran around. We looked out at London and I pointed out places I knew. We spent half an hour looking and then we went back to the lift.

Waiting for the lift was a bloke called Ammon. I couldn't believe it. He had been at Park House and had left earlier that year. I looked at him; he looked at me and then he turned away – he didn't want to talk. The coincidence surprised me. My first day out in this big city and I meet an old boy, at the top of a tower that I'd never before been up.

I hung round the house all weekend. My father was pleased to see me. He looked at me every now and then and smiled. His rotten black teeth didn't stop him having a good smile.

I got to the garden headquarters in North Kensington at seven-thirty on the Monday morning. All the men and a few boys stood round in their municipal overalls. No one spoke to me until the deputy came out of his office. He said I should go with two others to the glasshouses at Kensington High Street.

He had a face that reminded me of my brother Tommy. It was a complaining kind of face, as though he didn't really like anything. But I noticed that he tried smiling at everyone else. And he called them by their first names.

'Mr Slattery's the name, Bird. You'll be seeing a lot of me.'

I didn't like him. I knew he didn't like me. I was a crook, a wrongdoer. His boss had probably imposed me on him.

I'd be working with Matt and Simon. Simon was about my age;

he was black and he had a very pleasant smile. Matt was an old Irishman. I thought he looked like a boss's man.

'Well, boy, let's be off.'

Matt walked ahead and Simon and I followed on. Simon was friendly. He shook my hand. I was surprised – I hadn't expected anyone to be good to me, because I'd been in trouble.

I told him my name was Sean: 'It's Irish for John.'

It was a long walk across the borough to the glasshouses. We would do this every Monday. Simon told me there was supposed to be a kind of meeting between all the gardeners and tree staff, but nothing ever happened. We'd just meet and then go on our way.

Matt walked in a strange, plodding sort of way. Every footstep was heavy. As he walked he hummed. I asked Simon what Matt was like.

'He's all right. But he can be awkward. We do all the shit jobs. He gets to do the glasshouse stuff. The easy stuff.'

When we got to the glasshouses Matt talked to me, said I'd have to work hard and do as I was told. They'd had a Park House boy before who hadn't done too well.

When I told him to call me Sean, though, he smiled and his eyes lit up.

'Ah, a little Irish boy.'

'London-Irish.'

'Still, that'll do, Sean.'

Sean was a good Irish name. And I was a good Irish patriot. One day I would help Ireland to free itself from the English. So Sean was my new name; I didn't want to be Tony ever again.

The glasshouses were set beside the new library. Matt, Simon and I were the regular workers there; other people would sometimes come from the depot, but mostly I would be working with them. I preferred it that way, because I could see myself getting into trouble with lots of people. I knew that I wouldn't be popular. These were ordinary people, workers who would not like someone artistic.

People like my family. I knew that they would get annoyed with me. I could put up with two but more wouldn't be good.

Simon and I were given our first job: we had to tidy up gardens round the back of the Town Hall. I was happy that it was just Simon and me. An old lady was waiting for us when we got to the gates. She was small, with a fur hat and a fox stole. She smiled when we arrived.

'Good morning, boys. I'm so glad to see you.'

Simon smiled at me, and when she wasn't looking he indicated with his finger that she was mad in the head. As soon as she got into the gardens she started throwing pieces of bread on to the ground for the birds.

I set to work, and soon Simon came over to me, told me not so fast – we had to take it steady. So I began again, slower this time.

As we swept I looked around and I knew I would enjoy working here. There were always girls passing by. Simon saw me watching them and laughed. There were children playing in a school playground next to the gardens, and the noise they made was pleasant to hear. I looked up at the children playing and thought everything seemed to be as good as it could be.

We had a break mid-morning. We put the tools away in a corner and left the gardens. The old lady was trying to feed the sparrows at the same time as frightening the pigeons away. Simon found this very funny. He said she hated pigeons and loved sparrows.

'But when she frightens the pigeons she frightens the sparrows.'

'That's why it takes her all fucking morning.'

I found a few art classes to go to in the evenings, three nights a week. I joined Fulham Library and spent the other nights there reading art books. I ordered other books, too; among them was Brendan Behan's *Hold Your Own and Have Another*. I started reading *Borstal Boy* by Behan and I bought a copy of James Joyce's *Portrait of the Artist as a Young Man*. I had a lot of books I wanted to read.

At the library a girl with red hair smiled at me. She worked there and our eyes kept meeting. I had only been out of Park House a few weeks but I was desperate to get a girlfriend; I kept dreaming about girls. The red-haired girl looked like a possibility.

One Friday night I was in the library when it closed. I hung around and waited for the red-haired girl to leave. I stood on the other side of the road until she came out. She didn't notice me; she just walked down towards Parsons Green. I was nervous but I still followed her. I caught up with her as she crossed the road near the station.

'Excuse me.'

She stopped and turned to look at me. She must have been about my age. She stood looking at me, just at the spot where I used to play with Geraldine Osbourne. And where Wendy Lewis had talked to her friends all those years ago.

I told her I'd seen her in the library. She didn't look too friendly until I said I was an artist and I thought she'd make a great painting. She looked surprised at this and let me walk with her.

'I knew I was being followed.'

'I'm sorry, but I couldn't tell you in the library so I thought I'd tell you after.'

As we walked together down the road we chatted and she seemed more relaxed. She even said she'd come for a drink with me. But when we went into the White Lion I was petrified. I'd been acting all confident and I wasn't sure I could keep it up. All the skills I'd had for chasing girls had been destroyed by the school. Now I was like a novice, having to start again. I bought her a glass of cider and I had a beer. We sat at a table and she looked hard at me.

'So you're an artist?'

I told her I was a student at Chelsea School of Art on the King's Road. She was impressed, and relaxed even more. I tried to reassure her that I wasn't someone who followed girls home all the time. We talked about art. I told her about Gauguin and Van Gogh; I told her I loved Paul Klee and Matisse. She looked closely at me.

'A lot of art is a mystery to me.'

She said she was lost with Picasso, asked me to explain.

I tried; I said that abstract art was different, all about space. But I couldn't keep it up. I couldn't even explain Matisse. Only that I had gone to the Tate Gallery and loved it. But I couldn't say why.

'Well, I'm not convinced you're not some con man.'

'Perhaps we can go to the Tate Gallery and I'll try and explain.'

For a moment she didn't answer. Then she said something that floored me.

'I don't suppose my boyfriend would like that.'

I managed to pretend to take it in my stride, said he could come along too.

She laughed at that. We finished our drinks. I had hoped to spend the next hour in the pub, but our time came to a quick end.

When she left the pub I got another drink and opened my *Portrait of the Artist as a Young Man*, thinking that perhaps James Joyce would cheer me up. He didn't. Later, as I walked across the green towards home, I felt drunk and foolish. I went to bed with a spinning head.

Saturday night I went over to my Uncle Tom's. He was pleased to see me; as the father of two girls he'd always wanted a son. He took me out with him selling the *United Irishman*. We went to a number of pubs around King's Cross and sold a few copies. I was proud of my uncle. Proud that he was an Irish patriot. The IRA had not been defeated – my uncle was the proof of that.

'I'm Sean now, Uncle Tom.'

'Then that's fecking fine by me. But stop fecking calling me Uncle fecking Tom. Just call me Tom.'

'OK, Tom.'

He slapped me hard on the back.

Later we met up with his wife, Patsy, in a pub by his house. There were other friends there. They poured drinks into me. Soon I was drunk, and after a while I said I'd have to go home because I was pissed stupid. Tom laughed, told me just to go to his house and sleep.

In the morning everyone was up before me. I felt bad and was given aspirin and water. I lay on the sofa and my cousins came in, jumped on me. They were wonderful girls of ten and twelve. Soon I got up and went off with Tom to a pub while Patsy made Sunday dinner. I didn't drink and Tom made a joke out of it.

'How can you be an Irish patriot without a drink in you?'

'Eamon de Valera doesn't drink.'

When I said that, he grabbed hold of me by the shirtfront. He said, 'Don't ever mention that fecking blackguard in front of me. Ever again.'

I was confused. I didn't understand Irish politics and I was showing it. Tom said that de Valera murdered the finest man in all of Ireland. I felt stupid asking who he meant, but I had to.

'Why, Michael Collins. As great a fecking Irishman as there ever was. And a great Cork man as well.'

Tom wasn't sullen, though. He forgave me my ignorance.

'It's a pity everything you draw ends up so small. Can you not try and draw bigger?'

I wasn't enjoying this. The class was made up of housewives who liked drawing flowers. They talked nonsense about curtains and lawn mowers and the teacher encouraged them, laughing and giggling together. The class was in a school in Parsons Green; it was an evening class for Sunday painters. I hated them. They hated me.

'But that's the way it is – I can't do it any other way. Does a drawing have to be a particular size, missus?'

She didn't like me calling her 'missus'. She wanted to be called Dot, or Dotty. I was never going to call her either. She said that a drawing could be any size; the problem was that I'd start with a big sheet of paper and draw something the size of a walnut.

She was insulting me. I hated her for not saying anything positive about my drawing. She got annoyed with me. She never got annoyed with anyone else. She encouraged the others, said nice things about their shitty, prettified work. I realised that this woman made her living out of these people so she couldn't say to them that their work was crap. Which it was. But fuck that, I thought, let them do their little pieces. I was going to be the greatest painter. And the greatest Irish patriot.

Simon was very interested in my art. He'd ask me about it as we worked in the gardens at St Mary Abbot's. I told him I was obsessed, painting, drawing whenever I could. Simon didn't have something like that. He just went home after work and watched TV. At weekends he lay in bed, or went down the market at Shepherd's Bush.

We were talking about all this one day and I was watching the old lady trying to feed the sparrows. I thought she was a bit like me: she had her obsession. That day there were more pigeons than ever. She tried to kick them, and then she suddenly fell over. She lay on her back on the grass.

I rushed over to her and picked her up. She was a strong little woman. I got her to her feet and picked up her bag of fallen bread. I wiped some grass off her coat.

'That's very kind of you young man. But those pigeons – '

I got her to sit on a bench. She was a bit confused.

'Maybe you should go home, lady.'

'Perhaps I should. I do so hate pigeons.'

'If you need help, I'll always help you; I'll help you frighten the pigeons. But you have to be careful.'

I was tired, real tired. I had come in from work and was lying on my bed before I went off to the evening class. I heard a noise on the stairs. It was my mother running up, screaming, shouting. She came into the bedroom and her face was white.

'Tony, Tony, they've shot him.'

I lay on the bed wondering who had they shot. My father?

She knelt down by the bed. 'They shot the president.'

There was only one president. The President of the United States of America. An American Irishman and a Catholic. I sat up, shocked. I put my arms around her. She was shaking.

'I just heard it on the television. They shot him in Texas.'

We sat for a few moments and I couldn't think of what to say. Eventually I asked her if he was dead.

She looked at me. 'They only said he was shot.'

I stood, got my bag of drawing materials together. I put on my coat.

'Tony, for feck's sake can't you stay in?'

She never asked me to stay in. She was glad that I'd been good since I'd left Park House. No going out all night, no trouble with the police. I was changed. I was more serious; I went to work, and I did my drawing and painting.

I knew she needed company now. Tommy and Pat wouldn't be much use to her. Neither would my father. She needed me because she needed a good Catholic with her. But I left the house and went to my class.

It was a cold night, November. There was a mist around and the streets looked empty. I went to the sweetshop opposite the flats. The bearded lady who ran it tried to talk to me.

'Terrible, terrible, shooting that nice man.'

I said nothing. She looked like a Protestant to me and I didn't want her Protestant sympathy. I bought a choc-ice – I liked ice cream in cold weather – and left the shop. I felt angry at the woman's interference in the life of a Catholic. In the street I knew I had to make a sacrifice so that the life of John F. Kennedy would be spared. I took the choc-ice and placed it in a rubbish bin.

'May this offering, Lord, be for the life of John F. Kennedy. May he be spared and may his good work be rewarded.'

I passed the launderette where mothers washed clothes. The newsagent's was full of people buying cigarettes, crisps. The greatest Catholic on earth was perhaps dying, was hanging on grimly to life, and these people washed clothes and bought cigarettes.

I walked through the dark streets towards my art class hating what someone had done. At the class people hung round in groups, talking, whispering about John F. Kennedy.

I drew bigger because I didn't want Dotty talking to me. Not knowing whether he was dead or alive. Dotty came and looked over my shoulder. She made an 'umph' noise and I felt like knocking her down. She tapped my arm and spoke softly, as if she was in church.

'Good, good.'

We were silent in the canteen at break. An Indian woman came over to where I sat.

'Have you heard? Kennedy's dead.'

They had killed the greatest Catholic in all the world – even greater than the Pope. I felt like crying. May the Lord Jesus Christ strike down dead whoever did this thing.

At home, later, my mother was beside herself. Even Tommy managed a sad comment. Pat said that he thought Frank Sinatra would be very upset. He had seen a photograph of Kennedy with Sinatra.

'They were friends.'

Tommy laughed at him. I went to bed sadder than I had been for a long while.

One wet Friday lunchtime I left Simon in the cafe near the glass-houses. I wanted to be by myself. Matt was pissing me off. He ordered us around as though we were stupid children. And Simon didn't object. I used to push Simon to tell Matt to stop treating us like stupid kids.

'Stand up for yourself.'

'He doesn't mean it.'

'It doesn't matter what he means. The bloke is a prize cunt.'

So I left Simon in the cafe because I was annoyed at how stupid he was about Matt; he wouldn't be a man with Matt.

I stopped outside a bookshop. They had a row of old books out front. I picked through them, paying no attention. I just wanted to take my mind off the soft Simon. Then a blue Penguin book caught my eye. It looked like a pre-war book, small, dirty, dog-eared. *The Pre-Raphaelite Dream*. I started to read it. It told a simple story, about a group of students defying the Royal Academy and producing a new art. Dante Gabriel Rossetti, Sir John Everett Millais and William Holman Hunt with some hangers-on. In 1848, 115 years before – 98 years before I was born. A different world, a lost world.

I bought the book and another one by the same author. I was late back to work and Matt was standing looking at his watch with Simon obedient and slave-like beside him.

'Sean, this isn't good enough. You're allowed an hour, not an hour and ten minutes.'

I looked at Matt savagely and pushed past him. The boss's man was not going to tell me what to do. He tried talking to me but I ignored him. He stood over me as I brushed the paths between the potting sheds at the depot. He became increasingly angry. Still I said nothing, even when he shouted at me.

Later, Simon said I'd handled it very well.

'Well, you didn't. If you don't watch out, Simon, you're going to turn out like Matt.'

'Sean, it's all right for you. I'm not angry like you.'

I got obsessed with the Pre-Raphaelite Brotherhood. Winter 1963. No one seemed interested in the PRB. I tried talking to Dotty at the art class, but she turned up her nose when I mentioned it.

At the Tate Gallery they didn't display many of the Brotherhood's paintings. It seemed that no one was interested in their weird art.

I finished *The Pre-Raphaelite Dream* and started reading Gaunt's *Aesthetic Dream*. It was another wet week. Simon pushed the barrow along the pavement as I walked beside him, reading. We got to the big house with the big garden to give it a winter clean. The Royal Borough had charge of the gardens of the house and it was one of the best of jobs. Spending the whole day away from Matt and the public.

We worked all morning in drizzle. The rain stopped and we took a break. Simon read the *Daily Mirror* and I read the book.

Suddenly I couldn't believe what I was reading. Lord Leighton, President of the Royal Academy, had a visitor. The painter James Abbot Macneill Whistler had been accused by the critic John Ruskin of 'throwing a pot of paint into the public's face'. Ruskin said Whistler's paintings were little more than splashes and stains on the canvas. Whistler visited Leighton at Leighton House to ask him to be an artistic witness. Leighton agreed to be a witness as they walked in Leighton's garden.

At the precise moment that I was reading this, I was sitting in Leighton's garden.

'Simon, can you fucking believe it – I'm reading about something that happened in this garden eighty years ago.'

I was so excited. Sitting in the gardens of Leighton House, now a museum owned by the Royal Borough of Kensington and Chelsea.

My reading got Matt so mad he nearly hit me. But Matt was annoying; I couldn't stand the man – I had to show him he couldn't push me around.

He stood over me in the potting shed one day, told me to put down my book and get to work. I ignored him, said nothing. He tried to take the book from me but I carried on reading, pulling it away from him.

'You carry on, Matt. I'll be along in half an hour.'

He left the yard with Simon, angry. As soon as he left I picked up a broom and a rake and left the yard. I watched them walking down the street. I turned the other way, ran up to the corner and took the back route to the gardens. I climbed the fence and started sweeping the path. A few minutes later, Matt and Simon arrived. Simon let out a hoot of laughter. Matt was beside himself with rage. I turned as he came up to me.

'Matt, where've you been? You know we're supposed to be on the job by seven-forty-five.'

I looked at my watch. Matt stuck his fist in my face.

'You blackguard. You little bloody blackguard.'

But Matt stopped treating me like a stupid boy. Things improved. I had proved to Matt that I was not like Simon.

I was drunk with my uncle.

'Have another drink, Tony.'

'It's Sean.'

'What the fuck.'

We sat, ten of us in Tom's living room. I could hardly make sense of anything or anyone. Suddenly my head spun. And then I was sick on the floor. Tom went mad.

'You dirty little git.'

I tried to stand to get to the bathroom but couldn't make it. Patsy told him to leave me alone, said I was only a boy.

We had been out selling the *United Irishman*. It was just before Christmas. We'd walked from King's Cross to the Angel, drinking as we went along. Now, back at Tom's house, I was out of it.

'Bloody fecking git.'

I woke later on the sofa with my head still spinning. It was dark. I fell back to sleep, but at first light I got up, got dressed and snuck out of the house. I couldn't face Tom and Patsy. I took the bus to Fulham, feeling ashamed – ashamed that I could not hold my drink, ashamed that I was not really a man. I was just a boy, even though I would soon be eighteen.

At home my mother sat smoking in the kitchen. She looked at me with her nose turned up. She said I smelt like a brewery.

I stayed in bed for most of the day. I couldn't eat. In the evening I went to Mass at the Servites. The service was good. We sang in Latin and I felt good. But I knew that I couldn't visit Tom again until I was over the embarrassment of not being able to hold my drink. And being sick on his front-room floor.

20

I could see the tops of her stockings. She sat drawing on the floor in one of the Japanese rooms. I walked past with my board and pad. She looked at me and smiled. I smiled back at her, turned and walked over.

Her name was Liz. I introduced myself as John. That's what I had settled on: John. Sean was gone; Tony was gone.

We walked through the galleries and spoke about art.

She was studying at the Chelsea School of Art. I felt like lying but for once I didn't. I told her about my job as a gardening labourer and my evening classes in Fulham.

'Are they good?'

'Crap.'

'Well, let's have a cup of tea.'

Liz was a woman. Dark-haired, tall, beautiful. I felt childish. But for some reason I didn't feel like exaggerating my age or my skills. As we sat over tea she told me she was in her last year at art school.

She looked at some of my drawings and showed me hers. Hers were superior. I talked about the fact that art was everything to me; I had no other life.

It was January. Nothing was going right. I wasn't enjoying my job and I still didn't have a girlfriend. Home life was bad – how could I be an artist living in a block of council flats in Fulham? And here was a real artist. An art student, well on the way.

We took the bus together. Liz lived off the King's Road, close to the art school. She invited me back to her room. It was small, crammed with a bed, books and paintings. The only place to sit down was on the bed.

'This is great, Liz. It's like a real artist's place.'

'It's all I can afford.'

We shared a lone bottle of warm beer. And we talked. She had an idea; her eyes sparkled. She suggested that I should go along to the drawing classes at Chelsea. People came and went, no one needed identification. She said she'd take me.

She sat on her bed with her legs drawn up. I saw her stocking tops again – a good sight.

We finished the beer. Before I left, we arranged to meet the following night so I could attend my first real drawing class.

So at six-thirty the next day I waited outside the school for Liz. She arrived with a smile, said she'd thought I wouldn't turn up; she thought I might be nervous.

We walked into the school and down a long corridor. I had to pretend to be a first-year student if anyone asked. The place smelt of paint. Students milled about. There were many badly dressed but good-looking girls. At the end of the corridor was a big room, full of easels, with students drawing and a naked model standing on a plinth. Liz and I each took an empty easel and set to work.

It was weird and very serious. No one spoke, they just drew or painted the model. I furtively looked round the room. There wasn't a Dotty walking round talking about curtains and holidays and dinner parties. Everyone just worked away. Liz occasionally looked over at me.

The instructor talked to other students but he said nothing to me. I was pleased, not feeling confident that I could bluff.

I drew the model as big as I could, using charcoal. I didn't want anyone to see how bad I was so I kept changing the paper. It took me an hour to settle down.

'So, how was that?'

'The best feeling in the world.'

Although I didn't feel good about my achievement, I had survived the first trial. We left the school and Liz told me there were classes every night, Monday to Friday. I decided I'd go to them all.

★

I was leaving the depot one night in a rush to get to my drawing class. The last thing I had to do was lock the glasshouses. I was about to lock one when Matt called out from the other end of the glasshouse: 'Don't lock it, Sean, I'm still working here.'

Boss's man. I locked it anyway and he started shouting. As I walked off down the path I could hear him banging on the glass.

At the art school the instructor started talking to me. I was getting used to the place. The instructor was a grey-haired man called Mr Villaincour. He wore a shabby overall and his hands were dirty with paint and charcoal. He showed me how to create perspective in my drawings.

Liz went to some of the classes but I went to them all. This meant that I did nothing but work and draw. I hardly spoke to anyone in the classes. But the night I locked Matt in the shed one of the students spoke to me. Like me, he came every night. His name was Anselm. He looked like a serious person. He had frizzy, almost-ginger hair, and thick lips. His features sort of looked African. He spoke slowly. I looked at his work. He wasn't drawing the model; he was drawing some thick black lines on big sheets of paper. He told me it was a kind of abstraction – he was drawing what he knew was there.

Later, when the class was finished, a group of students hung around Anselm as he walked along the corridor. He saw me and called out, asked if I wanted to go for a drink.

I stood and looked at Anselm, surrounded by girls. I envied him.

We went to the Six Bells on the King's Road. I sat with Anselm and his friends. They didn't talk to me, but every now and then Anselm remembered me and that was enough. Slowly I was getting somewhere.

I arrived late for work the next morning. I was more than an hour late and the deputy was there. Matt, too, in the background. The deputy questioned me, asked me if I knew that I'd locked Matt in the glasshouse the night before. I was in trouble: Matt knew I'd heard him shout; he was still furious.

I gave the deputy my most innocent face, looked confused, said I hadn't heard anything. But this was a trial. If I got the sack I'd be sent back to Park House. Playing the arsehole had got me into danger.

Matt and the deputy talked among themselves, then the deputy spoke to me. He said that he'd forget the incident. But I was being transferred to the tree department.

I watched Matt walk off to work with Simon and I felt stupid. I was out of the gardens and now the simple pleasures would be gone. I'd be working in a gang with men who wouldn't like me, men whose passions were football, horseracing and TV. What a fool I had been. I cursed myself as I walked across the borough to my new department.

I kept quiet on the tree gang, did as I was told. Neither the foreman nor the head man liked me. They took all the risks, had all the fun. Climbing trees, hanging from support ropes, swinging out to cut off branches. We cleared up the dropped branches. We went out in the back of a lorry to do this boring job, day in, day out. There were no quiet moments. I couldn't sneak off to libraries or visit the bookshops on Kensington High Street.

The only fun bloke was a queer called Allan. He took the piss out of everyone. Allan talked to me about art and theatre. He talked about poetry at break time while the others ate their sandwiches and talked about last night's TV.

'They're all wankers, Sean. Don't pay attention to them.'

And they paid no attention to me. For a while, at least. I managed a few weeks without trouble, then one of the blokes started picking on me. It boiled over one day when he pushed me aside as he walked past me. I punched him hard in the face and the foreman saw me.

I was sent back to the yard and I knew that their patience with me had worn thin. Nonetheless, I was transferred again, to grass-cutting and flower-beds.

The job was good. Now I was on my own most of the time and no one troubled me. Some days I worked with Old Bill. He would walk with me as I pushed my barrow, telling me about his life in the war.

But usually I was alone, and I loved the work. Sometimes I'd be the last one back to the yard at the end of the day. I just kept working. Working late impressed the superintendent and at last I was in his good books. Even the deputy smiled at me occasionally. Everything was good again.

At art school Mr Villaincour spoke to me. He had a strong French accent and a kind manner – a careful manner.

'I like the way you work. You use very little colour.'

I wasn't interested in colour – only greys, blacks and white. Mr Villaincour looked for a long time at the painting. He said that my work was coming along, but I knew I wasn't getting far in becoming a great painter. I was eighteen and at a standstill.

Later I talked to Mr Villaincour again. He took me into a corner and I asked him if he thought I should go to art school. He looked at me with surprise. He thought that I was already a student; I had to explain. He didn't mind that I wasn't really a student already. He told me to enrol, if I could, for the next term. 'You must go to art school, John. It would be wrong for you not to.'

I was pleased, excited. I met Liz and I told her what Villaincour had said. I showed her my latest watercolour and she praised it.

The following morning, I went to the college office and got an application form. The man in the office added me to the list.

A week later, I went before the interview committee. They stuck every one of my drawings and paintings on the wall. I was overwhelmed when I walked in. The interview reminded me of Park House, and I was nervous. But the leading man smiled, said I had a phenomenal range. I was asked about my job with Kensington and Chelsea.

'So, you're a horticulturalist?'

'I think I am. But I'm an artist first.'

They nodded me through. They said I would get a letter in the post. Before I left the room, I looked around at the many images I'd made. It was something special.

My mother was angry.

'Working-class people don't go to college.'

I held the letter in my hand. 'But they say I can go.'

'Don't be stupid.'

My father looked at the letter. 'It says he can go.'

'But he'll only feck it up.'

A grant-application form had come with the acceptance letter. My mother said she wouldn't fill it in. I was so angry. Fuck this working-class thing. I went upstairs and lay on my bed. I was tired and annoyed. If they didn't fill in the form I couldn't go.

My father came into the bedroom. 'I'll fill it in; don't worry about your mum. I'm proud of you – really, son.'

He shook my hand and took the form. I went out, walked down to the World's End where Brian was staying in a basement flat. I'd decided to call on him and tell him my good news. He opened his door, looked at me and closed it again.

I banged on the door and shouted until he came out.

'What, yer mates let you down? You got spare time on your hands?'

'Don't be stupid. I thought we could go out.'

'Why would I want to go out with an arsehole like you?'

'Because you admire me.'

As we walked down the King's Road I told him I'd got in to art school. He wasn't very encouraging; he said he wasn't surprised, the way I crept up people's arses. But he gave me his blessing.

'Think of all the nice middle-class girls you'll meet while I'm digging holes in the street for the London Electricity Board.'

'You'll get out from the proletariat one day, Brian. They'll discover your talents.'

'No, Bird, never. You see, I can't stand the taste of shit on my tongue. Not like you.'

We ended up at the Cafe des Artistes and looked around for girls. But we weren't doing well, so we left. Outside the Servite church I blessed myself.

'Still believe all that Catholic stuff?'

'It's my faith.'

'Your faith, my arse. You've just been indoctrinated; you'll grow out of it some day.'

'Jesus is still my saviour.'

We spent the night arguing. When we started hitting each other I drifted off home. But I knew that it had been a special day.

21

I was frightened. I walked into the art school as a first-year student. Liz had graduated, and so had Anselm. The teachers weren't the ones I'd met in the previous year.

I was in a class of smart, clean, public- or grammar-school boys and girls. Before, I'd posed as a knowing student; now, I was an apprentice.

We were taught in a new building. The old dirty, paint-stained classrooms had gone. We were in a place that looked like a furniture store. Careful greys, clean whites. I preferred the dirt and mess and the paint stains. I preferred the confusion and clutter of the old building.

I had a big argument with my mother. She said I treated our home like it was a hotel.

'I'm at college, Mum.'

'Feck the college. You're getting above yourself. You're just a working-class boy.'

I had to get out of the house. The owner of Brian's flat was away. Brian said I could sleep in the front room – 'But no fucking about.'

We shook on it. It seemed better, being an artist, to live an independent life. To sleep on a strange sofa that was called a *chaise longue*.

When I told my mother I was leaving she went mad.

'After all your father and I did for you! Get out – feck you, get out.'

When I got down to the square she called to me from the balcony: 'D'you have to do this, Tony?'

I left, saying nothing.

The painting was good. We had whole days of it. The teachers walked around talking to us, but largely left us to ourselves. And then there was the drawing; this was all I ever wanted to do. The teachers were friendly. They were artists, really, just doing a bit of teaching. My course was getting better the more time went on.

Tony, or 'Greaseball', moved into Brian's as well. He was short, wore a black leather jacket and black gloves. He was always up for stealing. He would go out early in the morning and come back with pints of milk and sometimes yoghurt, or newspapers, bread or rolls.

I had no money. I'd got an £83 grant for my first term and had given my mother £60. Greaseball was generous. If he got money he shared it. His speciality was robbing from the gas meters in big houses full of bedsits. He'd come back to Brian's flat laden down with hundreds of pennies and sixpences. He shared the money with me because he knew that I had nothing.

The art school was full of girls, but the best weren't in my year. There was one girl who particularly caught my attention. She was beautiful, tall and blonde. She had a good face with a good nose. Her name was Jane. I stood watching her reading in the library one day. I walked up, looked at the book.

'Brancusi. He's one of my favourites.'

She made a rude face, handed me the book and walked out.

It was the same whenever I saw her. I'd try to talk to her and she'd ignore me. One night in the Six Bells pub she was standing at the bar. I stood beside her, asked her if I could buy her a drink.

She just said, 'Piss off,' and went back to sit with her friends.

There were good-looking girls all over the place. They all looked as though they knew what they were doing; they had confidence. But I was just a new boy, a first year. I was a student. They were artists.

One afternoon I was building an armature in a sculpture class when the studio door opened and I saw Jane standing there with a group of friends.

She pointed to me and spoke to a tall man beside her. He crossed the room towards me. I thought I was about to get a punch in the face. I thought of the embarrassment of being beaten up in front of my fellow students. But he stopped in front of me and invited me to a party.

It was at his place the following night. I couldn't quite believe it. He just gave me the details and left. As Jane closed the door she had a smirk on her face.

I thought I had arrived. I wasn't just another student. My drawing and painting were good; I was the best. And now other students, from senior years, were taking an interest in me. I didn't have to bother with my classmates – they were just kids. I was a real artist now.

When I arrived at the party everyone ignored me. They ignored me the entire time. They sat and drank vodka and talked among themselves. Jane didn't even look at me. The big man who had asked me to the party didn't speak to me. I sat like an idiot all night and I knew that I'd been fooling myself: I was a kid to them; Jane had wanted me at the party so she could humiliate me. And I was humiliated. They talked about art, about sex, about their friends. And I was nothing. I didn't exist.

The tall man was Jane's boyfriend. He gave me a lift home in his small van and as we drove along he talked about Jane.

'Jane's great. Lovely girl.'

'I know.'

I felt low, depressed by the night. I didn't feel like talking but he carried on.

'You fancy her, don't you? Course you do – everyone does. But she's got something about you. You may be a kid, but she likes your cheek.'

That cheered me up. Then he told me about his dad. His dad made things; he was a natural sculptor. He made wheelbarrows that were too heavy to use. The boyfriend didn't seem to mind that Jane might have had a thing about me.

He dropped me at the flat. He shook my hand and I felt better.

She had set it up to see how I would manage. I hadn't managed –
I'd looked like an idiot – but that didn't matter now.

The door to Brian's flat was open. The man who owned it was
there, and as soon as he saw me he started screaming at me.

'You fucking bastard!'

Brian and Greaseball looked sheepish. I was surprised at the
bloke's anger. I'd met him before and he'd always been friendly.

He stuck his finger into my chest. 'You little thief. You've been
selling my fucking bric-à-brac. Get out of my house.'

I didn't know what he was talking about. I looked at Brian and
Greaseball. They had silly little smiles on their faces.

He kept on. He told me to get my stuff together and get out. It
was two o'clock in the morning. I tried to reason with him but he
wouldn't have it. Brian's girlfriend came in from the kitchen. She
gave me the key to her room in Kilburn, said I could stay there.
Greaseball was told to go as well.

Out in the street Greaseball explained all. It was, of course,
Greaseball who'd been selling the bloke's stuff.

'But I got the blame.'

'Well, he wouldn't listen to reason.'

'And you didn't tell him the truth.'

'It was difficult. He was so angry.'

I had to laugh.

At college the next day I saw Jane. She tried to walk past me
without saying anything.

'God, you're an arsehole.'

She stopped. 'Why?'

'You know why. You only invited me so I would end up looking
like a cunt.'

'Well, you certainly managed it.'

'And you looked like a spiteful child.'

Greaseball and I were homeless. We slept in different places each
night. Sometimes we just wandered round all night. We'd sit in the
all-night hamburger bar in Earl's Court where I'd sat when I was a

runaway at fifteen. Or we'd stay at students' places, just for one night at a time. I could have gone back to my parents but I wasn't prepared to put up with that life any more. Greaseball and I decided that we would stick together. He got money during the daytime so at least we ate. One night we picked up two girls in South Kensington. They were staying in a hotel and we went back there with them. I convinced Greaseball that he should sleep with the girls while I slept in the other bed. I woke up every now and then and heard Greaseball screwing each girl in turn. The noise was terrible, with a lot of giggling.

One afternoon I was talking to the owner of an art shop on the King's Road. I'd known the woman for a while. When I told her I was homeless she rang a friend of hers and before I knew it we had a room in Putney – a big room with two single beds. The landlady allowed us to pay the rent at the end of the week instead of up front, so Greaseball spent a few days going round doing gas meters. We were excited about having somewhere to sleep.

It was nearly Christmas. The college office had told me that I should try to get my A level art; it might help some day. The exam would be on the last day of the autumn term. I wasn't looking forward to it – if I failed, I might look stupid.

We always had problems finding the rent. By this time he'd already got into most of the bedsit houses in Earl's Court and Gloucester Road. One Sunday night in December we walked around Knightsbridge looking for cars to steal from. We got nowhere. At the back of the Victoria and Albert Museum we went into a church. Evensong was playing. Behind a door was a woman's bag. Inside it were ten shillings, a toothbrush and some clothing. We took the money and the toothbrush.

It was a depressing night. We got the Underground at South Kensington. Greaseball had suggested that there was a petrol station near Gloucester Road that we could rob. We were going to check it out, but I didn't really like the idea.

We got the lift up to the street at Gloucester Road and Greaseball pointed out a good-looking girl. I went up to her, asked her for the time.

She looked at her watch. 'It's six-twenty-five.'

I looked at my watch. 'Sorry, love – you're five minutes slow.'

She laughed. We chatted and introduced ourselves. I was pretending to be posh; I told her my name was Jonathan.

She was called Linda. She had a soft Scottish accent and was a beautiful blonde. She looked at Greaseball and me in a friendly way. We asked her to come for a drink, and in the pub when she went to the toilet Greaseball wanted to know what the Jonathan thing was about.

'I felt like telling her a few lies.'

'She's beautiful.'

'Gorgeous.'

We sat in the pub for an hour and then we walked her home to her room near the station. She invited us to meet her sister, Kim. She was as beautiful as Linda.

On the last day of term I went up to the West End to do my art exam. The first part was a still life. We had two and a half hours. After twenty-five minutes I was finished. The invigilator took me out into the hall. She thought I needed the toilet and when I told her I didn't, I was just finished drawing, she looked shocked.

'But you have another two hours.'

'Is there a rule that says you can't go when you're finished?'

'Well, no.'

I left. I knew I was kind of showing off – I was a real artist; I didn't need to hang around. I went back to the art school and went to the Six Bells with some other students.

Graham from my class was the funniest, the best. We started drinking and soon I was drunk.

'How's the exam?'

'Crap. They're all a bunch of schoolkids.'

'And you, of course, are this wonderful, mature artiste.'

Graham had this way of showing up the stupid things I said.

The pub was full, everyone celebrating the last day of term. Suddenly I realised I was supposed to be back in the West End for the second part of the exam.

Graham had a powerful motorbike, a 1000cc Vincent that he'd ride at more than a hundred miles an hour. He never wore a crash helmet. He was just mad about speed. In minutes we were roaring through the streets. I clung on to Graham feeling drunker than I had been in a long time.

I was lost in the second exam. I spilt my paint and at one stage I nearly fell asleep. I was the last to leave. I staggered out of the exam room and went to Russell Square, where I slept on a bench. I woke a few hours later and went back to the Six Bells to find Graham. He was still drinking, looking no worse for wear.

'I can't drink any more.'

'Then don't fucking drink.'

'I'm going home to Edinburgh for Christmas.'

'Really? Funny you should say that. I have family up there. Maybe I'll go and see them.'

'Really?'

Linda believed anything I said. I had become a full-time liar. I had become Jonathan De La Rue, part of the wealthy printing-business family. I was the black sheep; I came from money and class. Linda seemed to believe it all. She was sixteen. I was eighteen. She was very impressed that my family owned the Luncheon Voucher company and printed bank notes for African countries.

Linda wanted to hitch up to Edinburgh on Christmas Eve. First we would go to see her family. Then I might meet up with my Edinburgh family. But I had no family in Edinburgh. I had working-class Irish-Scottish cousins in the Gorbals in Glasgow. But they wouldn't fit my rich De La Rue image, so I didn't mention them.

We left town after she finished work on Christmas Eve and

headed north. We got lifts from trucks and cars – it was easy with Linda on my arm. We arrived in Newcastle in the back of an Indian's van, lying on carpets listening to Oriental music. We ate in a cafe by the station. I told Linda to wait outside while I paid the bill. But I did a runner and we had to run down dark side streets to avoid capture. Near the Scottish border we ran into a spectacular snowstorm. In a small town we walked across a little ancient bridge and down by a river. I was so excited I jumped around in the snow.

Later I was worried that she might discover that I had no Edinburgh family. As we hitched closer to Edinburgh I struggled with the thought that I should tell her the truth. That I was a boy from council flats and slums. But how could I break the spell?

At six in the morning we arrived at Linda's house in the suburbs of Edinburgh. She didn't have a key. She rang the bell and her mother eventually answered.

'Hello, Mum. D'you mind if I bring Jonathan in?'

Her mother looked down to the ground as if she expected to see a dog. Then she saw me and laughed.

'Well, come in, kids. Don't catch your death of cold.'

I slept in a small room in the loft. Linda's parents didn't seem to object to me much. Late on Christmas Day I pretended to go to a phone box to call my posh Edinburgh family. I'd even written down an imaginary phone number. When I returned to the house Linda looked at me expectantly. I told her my family had gone to their lodge in Northumberland; there was only a servant at the house.

We had a good time over Christmas. I was happy being with Linda. She was the kindest person I had met in a long while, if not ever. I was in love. A thought crossed my mind occasionally. An image of my family crammed in their front room, eating their dinner. Watching the Queen on the TV. Watching bad programmes in silence, half-sleeping, half-waking. I was glad I was out of all of that.

Back in London, I wanted to celebrate my love. I wanted to tell everyone about Linda. I couldn't. No one was really interested. Their dull lives continued and I had found love.

Within my first week back at college I knew I couldn't work as hard as I'd done before Christmas. Instead of going to the evening classes I would go to see Linda. We'd eat and talk and do nothing. We went to expensive restaurants and quickly spent my grant money. I always wanted Linda to myself; I didn't want to share her with anyone. Linda and I were one. The art school seemed like rubbish; the people seemed small. I didn't want anything except Linda. She was everything to me. She was worth more than anyone I had ever met. I'd be happy just looking at her. I made her feel good, she said. Because I was very attentive.

But Greaseball kept turning up. I tried to get him to stop, but he felt he had a claim on her.

'You sneaked around behind my back, Tone. Is that the way to treat a friend?'

He annoyed me. I told him I wouldn't share her with him. We shared everything, but I wouldn't share her.

He huffed. 'Are you trying to tell me you're in love?'

'I'm in love, Greaseball.'

'And Linda? Is she in love?'

'I think so.'

I stayed off school. I lost interest. Often I walked Linda to the station in the morning and went back home to lie on the bed. To read, to sleep. At lunchtimes I went to meet Linda. Everything was about Linda. She was now my big obsession. When I went to college I'd often arrive late. A teacher stopped me one time and said, 'John, you're going off the boil.'

He said he was concerned that I was losing interest. He told me not to lose my chance.

I didn't care. I was better than all of them. I had genius. I didn't need to go to all the classes like the rest of them. I was an artist; they were just playing around. They were stupid students, and bad artists trying to teach something that couldn't be taught.

Linda went back to Edinburgh for a week. I was heartbroken. For a week I was lost, walking round London unable to go to college. Unable to think about anything but Linda. I went out drinking with Graham but it wasn't the same.

Graham told me, 'You've lost your *joie de vivre*, mate.'

'No, I'm in love.'

'That can fuck it up. Dump her, mate – she's destroying you.'

Later that night I left Graham and felt angry. He didn't understand about Linda. Linda was everything to me.

But school wasn't good. I had gone from being a favourite to being ignored. When I tried to put my hand to work it didn't happen. Nothing held me.

I moved into a room in Earl's Court. Linda was back from Edinburgh and she wasn't as affectionate as she'd been. I knew she was tiring of me. She sometimes said that she needed to be on her own. I always tried to protest, but she wouldn't listen.

When I wasn't with her I would just wander.

But she was better whenever I hadn't seen her for a night.

'I love you but we have to stop being obsessed with each other.'

But I was the obsessed one; she just put up with my obsession.

One night we walked through Chelsea and I told her I had a confession to make. I told her that I wasn't Jonathan De La Rue. I told her the truth about my family.

She looked puzzled. 'Are you playing games?'

She didn't believe me. I had to prove it.

We took a bus along the King's Road towards Fulham. Occasionally she looked at me in her quizzical way.

Outside Broxholme House she stood looking at the block of flats.

'There? But you said you had a family in Fulham who worked on your father's estate.'

'This is the estate.'

We walked up to the third floor and I knocked on the door of the flat. Linda looked as though she was in a dream. My mother came out. I hadn't visited her for a while and she looked happy to see me. I told her that Linda was my girlfriend and she ushered us both inside.

They were all sitting in the front room on the long sofa. My father looked happy. They were very welcoming to Linda. My mother made some tea and Linda sat among my brothers. She was very friendly with them, but I knew she was shocked. We stayed for about an hour and later, as we made our way back to Earl's Court, Linda couldn't help but laugh.

'Jonathan, you are such a con man. I can't believe it.'

'Sorry, Linda, I just lie.'

'You're not a black sheep.'

'No, none of that.'

'What an eye-opener.'

She seemed to see the funny side of it all.

She was still laughing at me when we got into bed that night. 'And you even had "De La Rue" put on the doorbell.'

22

Spring. I went into school nervously. Even though I no longer enjoyed college, I wanted to stay on. People were gathered in the hall, looking at the notice board. Some were celebrating while others looked sad. I was shaking as I approached the board. I looked for my name on the list of those people who would be continuing their courses. My name wasn't there. I looked again and again, then I left the school in a trance. I was lost. I had given up and they had given up on me. I had wasted all my chances. I was nineteen and on the scrap heap. I would never be the artist I wanted to be. I rang Linda at work: I started crying.

'What's the matter, Jonathan?'

'I didn't get in. I'm out. That's the end of me.'

'Oh Jonathan, Jonathan.'

A few days later I met a teacher on the stairs.

'Sorry, John, but you did give up.'

'I had problems.'

'Problems or not, we can only have people who work.'

The other students ignored me. What had started well for me ended badly. I was lazy – I knew that – but I was the best of all of them. The very, very best.

I had to get a job. Linda's wages didn't last. We moved into another room and I still owed rent to my previous landlord. I left suddenly, while the landlord was out.

The new room was big, at the top of a house off Kensington High Street. Linda got an evening job, working in a Swiss restaurant. I got a job in a hamburger restaurant, the Golden Egg, on the King's Road. It was run by a German woman who was very tough.

'You have to work hard, boy.'

I took orders from people who didn't even notice me. I liked the work, though. I knew I was down, defeated by being kicked out of art school. But I had to get through somehow. Maybe I would apply to another school, though I would not get good references from Chelsea.

'Serve those boys.'

I served the boys. I ran around. I cleaned. I worked as hard as I could to try and forget two things – the school and the fact that Linda was tiring of me.

'Come on, boy, keep moving!'

The German woman kept on. I worked. I cleaned. I tried to forget about everything. About art. And about Linda.

'Jonathan, don't you want to see other girls?'

We sat on the bed in our new big room.

'Never. I love you.'

She looked at me as if she had something to say. I knew I was swamping her.

'We never do anything except work and sit in this room.'

I never saw anyone. Brian was locked up and so was Greaseball – they had got time with Mick the Mouth for a robbery at an estate agent's. I didn't want to see my family. All I wanted to do was be with Linda.

'I don't want to see other boys, but I like the idea of having friends.'

It was not going well. Money wasn't the problem. Something wasn't going well between us.

I had an argument with the German manageress. I got pissed off with her pushing me and I told her to stick her job up her arse. I wandered the streets looking for work. I bought a paper and looked at the small ads. I scanned the pages; I had to get some kind of job. And then I saw what I thought would be the ideal job for me. I went home, put on my best clothes and went for an interview at *London by Night*.

The office was in a dirty street in Soho. I found the number and climbed the ugly grim stairs to the top floor. I walked into the dirty little room and almost walked straight back out. A big old man sat behind a desk. He was bald and had a stupid smile.

'Don't be put off by the appearance, young man. We're going places. This is the best magazine London's ever had.'

He stood up, came round the table and shook my hand. His name was Mr Blinkinsop.

The office was tidy but everything looked worn – the carpets were frayed, the walls were grubby and stained.

'This is only the beginning.'

'You have to start somewhere.'

London by Night was an entertainments magazine published weekly. People were needed to sell advertising.

'Seven pounds ten shillings a week plus loads of commission.'

'That sounds good.'

'Have you sold before, young man?'

'No, but I'm sure I can.'

The door opened and a girl with a bitter face came in. She was about my age and tall with dark hair. She turned up her nose at the office.

'Bit rough-looking.'

Blinkinsop stepped forward to shake her hand but she ignored him. Then she looked at me and sat down. Blinkinsop went back behind his desk and made the introductions. The girl said her name was Miss Daly.

'Well Miss Daly and Mr Bird. Welcome to *London by Night*, London's greatest magazine.'

The girl put her legs up on another chair. Her skirt was short. The old man ogled. He got out two copies of the magazine and gave us one each. The girl smiled at me.

'Looks a pile of crap to me.'

It was. It was badly printed on cheap newsprint.

'Well it's only in the development stages. We're upgrading it all the time.'

He cleared his throat. He explained how he was building a sales team. What he said was not impressive. Nor was he.

I signed up. The girl did too, reluctantly. We would start the next day.

We left the dirty little office together. As we walked down the stairs she complained: 'This is going to be a shit little job.'

'I know. But I don't have a choice. I've got to do something and seven pounds ten shillings is something.'

'It's slave wages.'

Out in the street she said, 'Marie.'

'John.'

'Fancy a coffee, John?'

I didn't have any money, just my bus fare. But she said she'd pay. We walked down Old Compton Street and she talked all the time, telling me about losing her last job. And sharing a room with a nasty girl. She had a beautiful wide face.

At a cafe we sat and drank coffee. I told her about art school and about falling out with the German woman.

'Got a girlfriend, John?'

'Yes.'

'Pity. We could have had some fun.' Then she laughed.

For the next two weeks I pounded the streets of Bayswater and Kensington. I was getting nowhere with the magazine. Every restaurant owner I showed it to said it looked poor. Despite my protests that it was being improved I sold nothing besides a few small ads. Things were not looking good. And Blinkinsop started moaning.

'I know you're trying but you'll have to try harder.'

I went to a Greek restaurant in Queensway. The owner was friendly, until he saw the magazine. He said he didn't like it.

'Not even a small ad?'

'No good, but – ' He appeared to be considering something. 'But if you did a review I might consider it.'

He wanted me to come back. He'd feed me well, he said. Then if I wrote a review of his restaurant he might take an ad.

An idea came to me: I might not get ads, but I must get a load of free meals. Linda was pleased when I told her we were eating out that night. She was sick of baked beans and toast. But when I met her at Notting Hill she was nervous.

'We don't look grown-up enough for doing reviews.'

'Don't worry, darling, this could be very useful to us.'

The owner was very good to us. He fed us, gave us bottles of wine. Soon we were drunk. Linda relaxed; she loved it. The owner came up at the end of the evening and asked when he'd get his review.

I tried to pretend I wasn't drunk. 'In a few weeks. I'll let you know.' I smiled.

'Now, don't let me down.'

'I promise.'

I staggered out of the restaurant. Linda was drunk, but not as drunk as me. We got home and I was sick in the sink, the room spinning.

I developed a system. I'd ring up restaurants and tell the owners I wanted to write a review. Some restaurants didn't go for it, but a number accepted. So even if I didn't get any ads from them I still got some meals.

We were going out two or three nights a week to restaurants. I lied to everyone, told them they'd get their reviews in a matter of weeks. The Octopus in Knightsbridge was the poshest we went to. We were treated so well there we went back again. They didn't seem to mind the arrangement, and when we left they gave us a bottle of their finest wine.

But Linda didn't like it that I got drunk every night. She said I would become an alcoholic. I would stagger round the streets, shouting and screaming at everyone. At home I would drop on to the bed, insensible.

My scheme lasted a month. One Friday I went into the office to pick up my wages and found the door bolted. Maria arrived and we kicked the door. We went away and came back. A notice had been hung on the door, saying that the owner had ceased trading; *London by Night* was no longer.

Linda was sick in the morning.

'I hope I'm not pregnant.'

'I hope not too.'

She went to the doctor. The doctor got her to give him a sample of her urine. A few days later we went back to see him. He took out some papers from a file and told us that the tests were positive.

Linda let out a little gasp. I was confused: 'Positive she's pregnant or positive she's not?'

He smiled. 'What do you think?'

'I don't know. You tell me.'

He leant forward. 'Positive. She's pregnant.'

Linda gasped again. She thought it was terrible. I said nothing, but I was glad. At least we would be together. It was as though the future had become about Linda and me. She couldn't run off and leave me now.

We had been talking about parting. I knew Linda was really tiring of me. I knew that I stuck to her, clung to her. She wanted to live again. We were like a married couple and Linda didn't want that. But now she was finally stuck with me.

She cried as we walked back to our room. She didn't want to tell her mother. She felt ashamed.

'I'm sorry, Linda. Really sorry.'

I knew she was feeling that this was the worst thing that could have happened to her.

She was seventeen and I was nineteen. We would have to get married. She rang her mother. I went home and spoke to my father in the kitchen. A few months before, Pat had made his girlfriend pregnant. And now this. I smiled and he laughed.

'God, I've got a cock-happy lot.'

He couldn't stop laughing, even when my mother came in. When I told her I was going to be a father she snarled.

'You dirty little fecker. The fecking poor girl. The poor, poor, girl.'

Linda's parents came down to London. Her father was furious. He didn't like the idea of his Protestant daughter moving into a Catholic family. He said I'd taken advantage of his poor girl.

Linda's mother annoyed him. She said, 'It takes two, Harry.'

He fumed. Linda sat looking depressed on the bed in our room. We were to be married in a Catholic church in Kensington High Street. Linda had to receive Catholic lessons. She had to agree to bring up our child as a Catholic. The wedding took place on a bright August day in 1965. It was decided that we would go up to Edinburgh to live with Linda's parents until the child was born. I had to hide my excitement. Linda was mine; we had settled down. And I loved Edinburgh. I felt as though I was being born again. And even Linda's father disliking me didn't matter – he would just have to put up with me. I was happier than I had been in a long while. I had a family and it would all be for the best. A few days after the wedding, we arrived in Edinburgh.

The Moore's Modern Methods printing plant stood on Cowgate and rose up to the George IV Bridge. Each morning I started at eight-thirty, making my way up the numerous floors, picking up orders and papers. I was called an assistant clerk, though my hand-writing was bad. I had to enter the orders in a big book. I was based in an office with two girls and two men. Tom and Tam and Sheila and Shirley. Tom thought he was tough; he joked at my expense.

Linda did temporary work at various offices. We lived at her parents' house on the edge of town. It was strange for both of us.

'You English people are snobs. You've destroyed the world.'

This was Tom. Tam was quiet. But Tom tried to push everyone around.

I told Tom, 'My mother's Irish; I'm not just English.'

'You're English. Don't hide it.'

Every now and then Tom said something about the English. He was red-faced and red-haired.

'I'm proud of being Scottish. Are you proud of being English?'

'I'm proud of being me.'

'Ach, away with you. When we get independence there'll be no fucking English left in Scotland.'

Tam sometimes got annoyed, told Tom to leave me alone. And for a while Tom would stop, return to his work, mumbling under his breath.

It was raining. I went out to meet Linda for lunch and got drenched. We sat in a cafe in the Old Town. She asked me about work.

'There's a bloke there I'm gonna have to whack sometime.'

'Oh no, don't get into trouble.'

We were getting on well. Linda had accepted that soon she would be a mother. But she was worried – my mother had written to me; we had hired Linda's wedding dress and my wedding suit and hadn't returned them. My mother's letter said that the debt collectors were after us.

'What if they trace us up here?'

'They won't. My mother'll say nothing.'

The rain came down in torrents. I walked back through Princes Street Gardens. It was a beautiful city. The weather didn't bother me; I liked the cold. It was crisp if it wasn't raining. As I walked I felt good that Linda and I were together. And there was nothing that could separate us. I met Tam walking back to work. He told me to pay no attention to Tom; Tom was a hothead but meant no harm.

At work Mr Holly, the manager, looked at the big ledger I wrote in. My handwriting needed improvement. He told me to try to make it neater. I tried. It meant writing slower, but by the end of the afternoon I had improved.

The office was very old-fashioned. It was like something from a Dickens novel. Everyone wrote away in longhand with fountain pens into big books. The girls were particularly neat.

Tam asked me to go for a drink on Friday night at a pub near the castle.

'We play darts. How's your darts?'

'Fucking terrible.'

So on Friday night we left work, Tom, Tam and me, and went to the pub. Tam was excited – he loved darts. My first dart struck the board, bounced off and ended up stuck in Tom's shoe. Tam and Tom were beside themselves. Tom nearly choked with laughter.

'God, you're the worst darts player I've ever seen.'

I spent most of the night watching them. I could have told them that I avoided all proletarian pursuits. Tom got drunk and insisted on an arm-wrestle. If I lost he would try and bully me more at work. If I won he would be so embarrassed he would have to try some other feat of manhood. But he persisted, so we sat at a table and Tam was referee. We were all drunk now. We grabbed hands. He had big arms but no power. I pushed his arm over.

Tam screamed in delight. 'See, Tom, I told you he was no girl!'

Tom was upset. Should I let him win with the other arm? He put up his other arm, said it was his strongest. And again I won. Tam roared with delight. But I knew now that Tom would want to have a boxing match, or wrestle. That was the kind of bloke he was. I was in no mood to play silly games. I wasn't drinking much, or smoking. I wasn't staying up late. I was a serious person.

I was right, though. We left the pub and Tom wanted to have a boxing match. He threw a few punches close to my head. He was dead drunk now. I didn't want to play this stupid man's game. Tam held him back. As they walked off Tom shouted back at me: 'I'll have you, Birdie, you just see.'

I got back home late. I went to bed kind of happy that I'd humiliated the bully Tom. But I knew there would be other times when I would have to prove my manhood to him. I realised that he was like all the boys I'd known from Fulham: he had to keep proving how big he was.

Linda was beautiful. Even now that she'd become big with child. Her thick blonde hair shone; her skin glowed. I would look at her and realise how lucky I had been. But I knew she could not be happy, married at seventeen, a mother at eighteen. There were other things she wanted to do with her life. But, while I knew that she could not be entirely happy, I had never been happier. Her father was still difficult with me because I came from a Catholic family. But at least Linda wasn't in London on the game. Things could have been worse.

At work Tom was in a constant bad mood. He never had a girlfriend, and now he was wanting to have a go at me because I had a Scottish wife.

'What you English doing, stealing our good-looking girls?'

Tam and the girls looked up. He kept on at me. At first I said little, just told him he was talking rubbish. The others were silent. But I couldn't keep it in; after a few minutes it blurted out almost by itself.

'Well, whatever I did to get Linda, she wouldn't go for a fat shit like you.'

Tom leapt out of his chair and rushed over to me. Tam jumped up and grabbed hold of Tom. The girls slammed their books in disgust at my language. I looked at Tom fuming, told Tam to let him go. I knew Tom wouldn't do anything.

I had been polite for too long. I had really tried. But this bully was too much to stomach. Tom's face was fierce but he didn't frighten me. I could shut him up.

Later Tom suggested that we should go down to the gym and sort things out.

I laughed. 'Tom, I've nothing to sort out. You're a bully; you bully as much as you can get away with. I've met your type in the nick.'

This was my way of telling him to leave me alone. I had let him know I was no shrinking violet. He took the point.

We became friends. We went out drinking, without the darts. Tom didn't try to throw his weight around. That was the end of it. I didn't have to wrestle or fight with Tom. Knowing he might lose was enough for Tom. He wasn't bad, he just had to prove himself. Probably because he had been bullied at school.

After Christmas Mr Holly called me into his office to talk to me again about my handwriting. It was never going to improve enough. And I wasn't enjoying sitting at a desk all the time anyway. So I started looking in the papers for another job. I handed in my notice at the print works and got a job in a bakery on Princes Street. The money was good, better than at Moore's Modern Methods. I started work at six each morning. It was good getting up at five with the cold and with virtually no one around. And with everyone you did meet wishing you a good morning.

My job was to put fancy cakes into trays for delivery lorries. I had to wear a hairnet. The girls called me Robbie Burns because of my thick curly hair and my sideburns. But the work was even more boring than at Moore's Modern Methods, so I looked around again.

Merchiston Castle was a public school near where we lived. They were looking for a gardening assistant. I got the job. Mr Davidson was very friendly, but also a hard worker.

'Work hard, lad, and one day you may have my job.'

He smoked a pipe. He liked to talk about the news. He always had an opinion. I listened to him. He talked about politics on my first day, said we had to give the Labour government a chance. When I told him I didn't vote he looked at me with surprise.

'So you don't care if those Tory bastards get in?'

The Labour Prime Minister, Harold Wilson, had a small majority.

'I don't vote because I'm too young, Mr Davidson.'

He smiled when I said that. 'Oh. For a moment I thought you didn't realise that we had to keep that scum out.'

'No, Mr Davidson. I'd always vote Labour.'

I knew I had to say what he wanted to hear.

I loaded coal into the sick-rooms boiler. I tore up dead plants in the cabbage field. I put trellis back against the walls in the garden. At the end of my first day Mr Davidson congratulated me for my hard work.

'The old fellow I work with is thorough but slow. You're thorough but quick. It's good to have a young pair of hands around.'

It was good. It was like being back at Park House but without the authority. Mr Davidson left me to my own devices. He was an older, slower man. Whatever his job was, it wasn't working in the gardens.

I went to the art school two nights in the week. I joined the drawing class. Mr McKay was a good teacher. One night he watched me drawing.

'You know, lad, you do the most difficult things with ease. And the easiest things you find difficult.'

I had been drawing a model. He pointed out what he meant but I didn't really understand him. Although I still saw myself as an artist I felt empty about it all. I couldn't see myself getting into a proper art school again. I enjoyed the evening class but I felt I was turning into a Sunday painter. I painted in the loft at Linda's mother's house. I painted abstractions based on Matisse's work; I was obsessed by his work. But I knew I would have to get back into art school or I'd become just a part-timer, someone who painted as a hobby.

Linda's mother stood above the bed. 'Linda's had the baby. It's a baby girl.'

She'd woken me at seven in the morning to tell me the news.

Emily Jane was dark-haired and looked like me. When Linda's parents left, Linda turned and looked at me.

'Have we done the right thing, Jonathan?'

'Well, we've done it.'

'I'm worried. How are we going to live?'

'We'll manage. I promise.'

I walked up into the Royal Park. I felt good. We would manage. Now I had Emily Jane *and* Linda. I'd manage and we'd manage.

23

'Have you a criminal record?'

'No. Why?'

'Because of all this stuff – there's cigarettes and drink here. They check with the police.'

It was a big warehouse. I had been there a week and no one had told me about the police check. I'd have to get it done, because they were worried about employing the wrong people to pack, stack and load. The job was good. I was left alone in the vast warehouse. I had things to pack and unpack, trolleys to pull. I didn't need to be watched over.

'There's stuff being nicked all the time. Managers nick stuff.'

Steve lived on the council estate opposite. He was only twenty but he had three kids. He had tattoos and looked as though he liked a fight.

'Shall we have a drink tonight, John?'

Steve liked me. He had a kind of passion for me, was always looking for me at lunch and tea break.

It was Thursday. We had just got paid. I had survived a week without filling in the security form. I was safe until I had to do that. Linda and I had come back to London from Edinburgh on a high. We moved to Richmond. Then I had to get a job. It was difficult – I had no skills. Apart from my mouth, but a mouth was not enough. So I'd ended up at the cash and carry, aware that I was heading for the scrapheap of life. Twenty-one years of age and all art gone.

Steve's brothers were in prison, but he'd never been nicked for anything. I could trust him.

'I won't pass the police check.'

'You won't? You've done bird?'

'I've been in trouble.'

We met after work. Steve knew everyone in the pub. He introduced me to his mates. A gang of us sat around. I thought that had the working classes always been as friendly as this, I might have not wanted to get out so fast.

Steve told me to take the form for the police check and keep losing it. It had taken them two months to get his back from him. But, however long it took, I'd still have to do it.

Soon we were all drunk. I sat looking at Steve and his mates and wished, for a moment, that I belonged. Like he belonged. He belonged in a council estate in south London. He seemed content. He had the widest of smiles. He had his kids, his wife and his mates. And I was blown around all over the place, lost. I didn't know anything about the future. Steve had his future; he was already living it.

During my fourth week at the warehouse they made me fill in the form. Or tried to. I refused.

'I'm leaving. For a fucking job like this I'm not having you looking over me.'

The foreman looked surprised. 'But you've got nothing to hide.'

'That's not the point. I'm not dancing for any little Hitlers.'

He fired me. He said at least I could get social security.

'It's a pity. You're a good worker.'

He fired me for bad time-keeping. I went down the dole office and signed on. The woman who interviewed me was very rude. She asked me why my time-keeping was bad.

'I have a young daughter and my wife's not well. I have to get up for her in the night.'

'Is your wife under the doctor?'

'Not yet. She's depressed or something.'

I lied. The woman knew I was lying. I was a piece of social shit. But what could she do?

To avoid getting put forward for bad jobs, I signed on the executive register. I had no qualifications, but I told them I had been a draughtsman. They knew nothing about draughtsmen – and there were no jobs going for draughtsmen.

I left the dole office and went to the cafe at the station. I had started writing a novel called *The Aspirin Saga*. It was about a man who had arrived in London from Scotland. He was handsome. People liked him – particularly girls. He was a writer and he was gradually becoming accepted. He had many friends and lovers. He lived in poverty but he was on the move. Slowly he was being recognised.

I sat in the cafe and wrote in a small notebook. My writing was so small that only I could read it. It was the best thing. I could carry my book around in my pocket all the time and stop to write whenever I felt like it. I didn't need anybody.

We were always running out of money. We'd run out of electricity and Linda would be beside herself. I wrote cheques without having any money in the bank. People were always calling at the door and we'd have to hide from them. One day a man came round with his son. I had got some groceries from him and paid with a cheque I couldn't honour. He was angry when he came to our door.

'You owe me three pounds.'

'Sorry, mate, I'm broke.'

He was so angry he punched me in the face.

I laughed. 'Well, that gets rid of the debt then. Now fuck off, before I bite your nose off.'

I closed the door. He fucked off.

Linda's mother came down to stay for a week. She gave us some money. When she left, Linda and Emily went back to Edinburgh with her on the night train. I said goodbye at the station. Linda had a worried face.

'Jonathan, I don't know if I want to carry on like this. With all the trouble.'

I told her I'd get things straight – I'd get a good job, stop bouncing cheques. I promised her. But as the train pulled away she looked sad. I walked all the way back to Richmond. It took me until the early hours. I sat up all night writing the novel that would change my circumstances and make me rich and famous. The character in my novel was making it – why shouldn't I?

In the morning I was weary. I carried on writing, knowing that this book would be the thing that made me. Stanilas, the main character, was bright and creative. I could make it like Stanilas.

A week later the letter arrived. It said what I thought it would say: she wasn't coming back. She wished me luck. I wrote back, releasing her from me. *'You have to do what you need to do, darling. I shall always love you.'*

I got a heartfelt reply – she still loved me, but she couldn't take the life.

The day the letter came, I went to see a friend of mine who worked washing dishes in Harrods. Danny was a Chinese-Jamaican I had met at art school. He was a kind, friendly good-looking bloke. He looked at my sorrowful face.

'I've lost everything. I'm such a fucking slob. I could have done it; I could have made a home for her.'

'John, you've got to make your own life. You're an artist. You're a writer.'

He didn't listen to my self-pity. He was right not to – I could have gone on about stuff all day.

He told me he had a great plan for a business. He had seen a member of the Monkees pop group arriving at an airport. 'D'you know what all those people wear?'

'Clothes?'

'Beads. Exotic beads.'

I hadn't noticed. I hadn't noticed much about flower power. It was boring.

Danny thought he could get his aunt to make the beads and we could sell them. I wanted to know if there'd really be money in it.

'Course there is. D'ya want to help?'

'Help' meant watching Danny and his girlfriend, Chrissie,

organise everything. Go out, get the orders, get the beads made up. My job was delivery.

The industry was great. Danny's West Indian family ran a workshop. Danny designed the beads and his family made them. I felt slightly useless. My input was limited: watching, carrying and delivering. But Danny seemed to like having me around.

Danny and I were in the Six Bells when we met a bloke called Ross. He was in his fifties. He was balding and grey, and wore an old-fashioned suit with a yellow waistcoat.

Ross was drunk. We took a drink from him when he offered, thinking that he was just another one of the queers who haunted the King's Road. He invited us to a party. He was just being friendly. We went off with him to the party and saw that Ross was known by all the young girls. They kissed him and fussed over him. We were pleased and surprised; we decided that Ross was worth knowing.

I met a group of four American college boys who'd come over to live the Swinging London scene for a while. They were hot for girls. George did all the talking for the others.

'You have a finger on the Swinging London pulse, John?'

'I don't know. I can't see the difference to any other time.'

'Spoken like a true Londoner.'

I didn't know any more about Swinging London than they did. The parties and personalities passed me by.

I took them to the Cafe des Artistes near Earl's Court. It was crowded. George and his friends were generous. I hadn't eaten for a few days, and in the dark club we had dinner. I was halfway through a plate of spaghetti and was talking to George when I turned round and saw a big bearded man eating my food.

'What the fuck are you doing?'

'Sorry, friend, I thought you'd finished.'

He handed back my cutlery, but I didn't want it.

'No – fuck you – I'm not eating it now!'

'Oh, that's grand.' And he carried on eating.

I was amazed by his cheek. I watched him wolf the food down. Once he'd finished that, he picked up my beer and started drinking it.

'Is there anything else?'

'No, don't spoil me.'

He wiped his mouth on the cuff of his shirt. 'Jim. Charmed.'

We shook hands. I couldn't help laughing. 'You are out of this world. I've never seen that done except in a Charlie Chaplin film.'

He smiled. 'Well, when you're down on your luck. So, who are the Yanks?'

He indicated with his head.

'Some blokes I met at a party.'

Conspiratorially he drew near to me. 'Have they got any money?'

'Yes, but you ain't getting any.'

He pulled away. 'For the love of God, what would I want with their money?'

Jim was Irish. I introduced him to a girl I knew. He got on to the dance floor and started cavorting. He was wild, pushing people out of the way and then apologising. He was manic.

The club closed and Jim tagged along. George drove us back to the flat that he and the others were renting in Fulham. We started to drink. They liked Jim, but I kept an eye on him. I didn't want him scrounging or causing trouble. He told us wild stories about Dublin, his home town. He was a cross between a dog and a bear. Big, hairy and very unclean.

In the early hours, Jim wanted to fight somebody. He was getting awkward, calling people names. I stood up and threw a few punches at Jim and then I jumped on him, bit his face. He was big but he wasn't strong. Everyone clapped and he apologised; shook my hand; we were all friends together again.

When I left, Jim came with me. He told me I was an animal.

'Well, you're just a vegetable.'

Jim didn't have a home. He said he was going to sleep in the park. As we walked down towards Fulham Broadway, I wondered whether I could risk taking this madman back to my flat.

'If you come back with me, Jim, I'll fucking murder you if you cross me.'

'That sounds like a fine arrangement.'

We shook on it. He was big on handshaking.

It was a hot Friday. I walked down the King's Road weighed down by forty strings of beads hanging round my neck. People looked at me and smiled. Probably thinking I was the ultimate hippy, overdoing it with the beads.

I was almost at Sloane Square when I heard a car horn. I ignored it; I didn't know anyone with a car. More beeping. I turned and saw George and the gang waving at me from an open-topped car.

'John, what the fuck are you doing?'

'Making a delivery.'

They said they were going to a love-in.

'What's a love-in?'

It was a pop festival at Woburn Abbey. They wanted me to go with them. I was supposed to be delivering the beads to Harrods. But I figured I could always deliver on Monday.

We drove out of London. George and the others were still having problems with Swinging London. It was passing them by. No girls in sight, just four blokes looking. It took us an hour to drive into the grounds at Woburn Abbey, the place was so crowded. When we'd parked up we went walking. The place was thick with girls.

'If you don't score here, George, you won't score anywhere.'

I had no money, so I started selling the beads. By Saturday I had sold them all, at a shilling a string. It was a three-day festival and we slept out under the car. I met girls and listened to the Small Faces, high on the endless supply of grass. But George's group didn't like it. They kept complaining. No one was interested in them and their clean American looks. I didn't like it much either. It was boring, just fields of people trying hard to swing. After a day and a half I wanted to leave. I wondered what I could say to Danny about the beads. Perhaps I'd tell him they'd been stolen.

George called me aside. His friends were restless. He said they reckoned I didn't know the scene; I was out of it.

'I never told you I did.'

'But you took our drink and food. And what do we get?'

'You get me.'

'And getting you isn't getting girls.'

We left early. They dropped me in Chelsea, right where they'd picked me up. I was sorry that I hadn't given them what they had wanted. London was full of people looking for a good time. But everywhere was awash with fakes and frauds. London was no more swinging than it ever had been. And George was right: I wasn't a part of it. I didn't know anyone who was meeting Terence Stamp or Michael Caine, or who was dating Julie Christie. Whoever these people were, I didn't meet them.

A week or two later, I was walking with Jim through Fulham when I saw Danny ahead of us. I ran into a bed shop and pretended to be browsing. Danny walked in.

'It's all right, John.'

I told him I could explain everything – I said I'd got lost – but he didn't seem to care.

'Look, John, I know you're an arsehole. But don't hide.'

The bead business eventually dried up. It may have been down to me; I never asked.

There were about ten of us in my flat. Jim was trying to screw a girlfriend of mine. He was trying to tantalise her but she wasn't tantalised. Whatever we were taking, it affected me. I smashed all the windows in the flat and then collapsed on the floor.

I woke at about midday. The landlord was up a ladder fixing the windows. I looked at him and fell back to sleep. I woke up hours later. Only Jim and I were left on the floor. Anna was sitting watching TV. The place was a wreck.

Anna told me that my landlord was very upset. We had to clean up. I kicked Jim, trying to wake him. I kept kicking him until he got up.

The landlord arrived. He said there was a young couple round the corner who were interested in taking the flat; they'd give me seventy pounds.

I hadn't thought about leaving. 'I owe you so much rent. But if things improve – '

'Forget about the rent. It would be best if you left. You can keep what money you get.'

He said no more, just turned and walked away. I felt so sorry for him. He was a nice bloke and I had done him over. I called after him, said I'd sort something out.

He waved. 'Just leave – that's all I want.'

What could I do? I needed to get out. I was drinking too much and taking too many drugs. I was not going anywhere. I hadn't been writing for a while. *The Aspirin Saga* was on the back burner.

Jim and I went to Earl's Court. We did our usual trick of getting down on the lines to cross to the opposite platform. It put the fear of God into people. We could have stumbled at any time.

We went to a restaurant on the King's Road and had a meal. Afterwards I complained that I had lost my wallet. I looked for it all over the floor. I was told to leave.

We did that a few times that week. On Thursday I met Ross. Ross worked as an inspector for a cleaning company. He had a little grey van. Jim and I joined him for the inspection, gave out new brooms and cleaning material. We made a strange threesome.

On Friday we met Ross again and offered to treat him to a meal.

'But you haven't got any money.'

I was on social security, collecting money for Linda, Emily and me. I would usually spend the money on a wild night out. That week I owed most of it to my brother. Ross was right: I had no money.

'Don't you worry, Ross my old friend. Jim has got the key.'

We went to a restaurant in Knightsbridge. We ordered bottles of wine and had a meal. I told Ross to bring his van round to the front of the restaurant.

When he'd gone, Jim called for the bill. It was his turn to say he'd lost his wallet. But he was drunk and he exaggerated everything. He had put his rough old overcoat in the cloakroom. When it was returned he started to complain.

'Hey, hey, I had money in this coat – where the fuck's it gone?'

The waiter looked worried. He called the manager.

Jim could hardly speak, he was so drunk. 'I had money in this fucking coat and one of you cunts has nicked it. Where's my fucking money?'

He argued for about fifteen minutes. He even demanded that the police should be called. And then we got up to leave. They didn't try to stop us. Jim was shouting at everyone about how we had been robbed. The waiters stood round looking at us. The other customers looked frightened.

Outside we walked towards Ross's van; it sped off before we reached it.

I could see why. A group of policemen were coming towards us. Jim immediately went up to them, started shouting about his stolen money. But the police weren't interested. They pushed us back into the restaurant. The manager wanted us charged.

Jim went wild, bucking and fighting with the police. I started. Soon the restaurant was full of policemen trying to control us. Within a few minutes they had us on the floor. Then we were thrown in the back of a police van and taken away.

We were charged with incurring a debt through fraud. I gave them a false name; I knew I'd be sent down if they found out my real name. And then they wanted to take our fingerprints.

If we refused we'd be stuck in the cells for days, maybe a week. If we gave them our prints, we'd be in court the following morning.

I'd told them that I'd never been in trouble. That my name was John Auchinleck – Auchinleck was the family name of James Boswell, the author of *The Life of Samuel Johnson*. With the fingerprints they would know that I was John Anthony Bird.

When they took my fingerprints I pretended that I'd never had it done before. I reasoned that I would be in and out of court before they could get the results.

We pleaded guilty in court and were fined six pounds each. We asked for time to pay. I was relieved when I walked out – until I saw the policeman who'd charged us. He had a smile on his face. He knew exactly who I was, that I had a record as long as my arm.

I stood looking at him, wondering if I could make a run for it.

'If you don't pay the fine I'm going to sling the book at you. Understand?'

'I understand.'

'Now piss off.'

That was it. I left quickly, before he could change his mind.

Jim asked me, 'What was that all about?'

'Mistaken identity.' I hadn't told him about my past. 'I'm leaving, Jim. I'm thinking of going to Paris.'

Jim looked sad. He said he'd always wanted to go there. So I told him he could come with me, and then he was happy.

I would sell the lease on my flat to the couple that the landlord wanted to have in the flat. Take the money and leave. I had nothing to keep me in London. Jim had a problem, though: he couldn't get his passport unless he went back to Dublin.

I thought about it and found a solution.

'All you need for a passport is a birth certificate. I'll have to get my brother's. You'll go to France as Patrick Finbarr Bird.'

He jumped in the air.

I went round to my parents' house later that day. I knocked a few times, then I pulled the key through the letterbox as I had done as a child. In the kitchen on a high shelf next to some writing paper was a tin box. It contained a few foreign coins, all our birth certificates and some decorative spoons from the last coronation. I took out Pat's birth certificate, and mine, put the box back and left.

It was simple. We went to the post office and filled out forms, handed over the birth certificates. We were given one-year passports. That was good enough.

I moved my stuff into Pat's place and signed away the lease on my flat. The landlord was pleased and relieved, but he said he was sorry to see me go. He understood that things had become difficult when Linda left.

'It could break any man.'

We shook hands. He said, 'I hope you find what you're looking for.'

'And I hope you get the tenants you want.'

I went to pick up my last social-security payment before leaving for France. When he saw my name on the book the man giving out the money looked up at me.

'Oh, Mr Bird. Could you just come into the office for a few moments – just a routine interview.'

I could see two men through the glass door. I knew there would be problems. I was still claiming for Linda and Emily, and they were living in Scotland. I told the man I needed to pop out for a minute first. He tried to stop me but I didn't listen; I turned and walked out, and then ran.

Back at my brother's place, Jim was hardly awake.

'We're getting out of here. Now.'

'What the fuck's going on?'

'Social-security problems. We're going to Paris tonight.'

I packed a bag and went to buy a ticket at Victoria Station. It was Thursday. We had planned to leave at the weekend, maybe Sunday. But now I had a feeling of unease. I could see myself getting nicked – and I knew it could be serious this time.

PART THREE
Mr Ordinary

24

Jim spoke French with his heavy Irish accent. The hotel woman was impressed with his French, but not with his general dirt. But it was the kind of hotel that would take almost anyone.

We wandered off down to the Latin quarter. We soon got drunk. We met a group of winos. One played a harmonica. Jim and I danced a kind of foolish jig. A crowd gathered and they started throwing money at us. The winos were grateful, and we kept up the dancing. Then Jim started arguing with a girl. The girl started shouting. She was with a group of boys and girls and Jim started insulting them all.

The girl carried on shouting. The boys tried to pull her back.

'English fool.'

'Hey, I'm Irish.'

Jim was building up for a fight. It went on like this for a few minutes.

Jim wanted to fight the boys. Police walked past. I pulled Jim away, told him not to make a fool of himself.

'Fuck 'em, the French shits.'

The group moved off. The girl called back to us, said we should be ashamed of ourselves. I had to hold Jim down.

'John, the cow called me English.'

We went off to eat. We sat near the door in the cafe and when the waiter wasn't looking we ran off. We kept laughing at the stupid French. Jim was by now really drunk, and he threw insults at people in the street.

Paris looked like history. Every day we walked for miles along the riverbank. We walked around museums and up little streets to Montmartre. It was a big setting for a history novel.

Jim went out stealing bottles of whiskey. He was good at it, hitting the little shops that seemed to be everywhere. We got suspicious looks but we weren't challenged. We were drunk most of the time; we'd sit for hours on end in our hotel room singing and arguing.

I sat on benches and wrote. Jim got restless but I told him to be quiet. I was writing a new book. A modern book. A mix of poetry and rant, story and conversations. I called it *Mechanik Virgin Paris Days*. I was writing it under the pseudonym Jacob Breakfast; the name had come from nowhere and seemed to fit the work.

'Jim, will you stop moaning. I have to write – I've come here to write – so shut up.'

He was like a sulky kid. He began to bore me.

One night on the Champs-Élysées we met a one-legged Indian man selling the *London Evening Standard*. I bought a copy and started talking to him. He was a revolutionary and was very insulting.

'You English people have destroyed the world. Your empire has killed millions of people and exploited the poor. You should be ashamed of your nation.'

I listened to him. He was called Lionel and he was from Goa in southern India. I just listened, didn't even try to defend the British Empire. Jim wanted to smack him in the mouth for calling him an Englishman, but we carried on talking with him – with him doing most of the talking.

He had an Egyptian friend. I told him about my Egyptian aunt, Alma. He was very pleased. Lionel said we could sell the *Evening Standard* and stay in France for as long as we wanted.

We met a few times. I was intrigued by Lionel's anger about British imperialism.

The following week we were walking towards the Opéra when we saw the girl we had argued with in the Latin quarter come out of a language school. She was with another girl. I walked over to her.

'*Bonjour, mademoiselle.*'

She smiled. We introduced ourselves and shook hands. We didn't argue.

The girl's name was Katya. The other girl was her sister, Daria. We went for coffee. Jim and I looked at each other, happy that we had found some girls to talk to. They were blonde and good-looking, tall and elegant. Katya was eighteen and Daria was seventeen. Katya was the talker. She talked about revolution and the need for the people to rise up against capitalism. I listened. I knew nothing about capitalism, or about revolution.

'The Third World is full of exploitation. How do you feel about that?'

Daria just sat smiling at Jim and me. She didn't seem to pay much heed to the revolution or the Third World.

The conversation turned to the Rolling Stones and the Beatles. Had we heard *Sergeant Pepper*? What did we think of it? Jim and I had no opinions; it had kind of passed us by. But Daria warmed up and said that she liked the Rolling Stones.

I was lying on the bed in the hotel. There was a knock on the door. The concierge stood puffing, having climbed the many flights of stairs.

She told me that Jim had been arrested for stealing whiskey from a shop. I feigned disbelief. She didn't look me in the eye as she leant against the door frame. But she told me that the police were on their way to the hotel; they wanted to talk to me.

I must have looked frightened.

'You can of course go before they come.'

'I can.'

I had ten minutes to get out. I packed quickly. I left the room strewn with whiskey bottles. That was Jim's payment to me – he had to supply the whiskey. I ran down the stairs, thanked the concierge and disappeared. I ran out into the night and went down many different streets. I had money and I had my stuff. And I had lost Jim. Maybe that wasn't a bad thing.

I walked down to the Champs-Élysées and looked out for Lionel. When I saw him he had a smug smile, as if he knew everything.

'My British exploiter. How are you?'

He shook my hand. It was strange, the way he combined politeness with insults.

I told him about Jim getting nicked for shoplifting, and about having nowhere to stay. He screwed up his face, made a strange kind of huffing face.

'You'll have to come home with me. You can sleep on my living room floor. I won't charge you much.'

He had a determined face. It sounded like a good idea. He also said he'd take me to the office at rue La Boétie so that I could start selling the *Evening Standard* and the *Herald Tribune*.

Lionel's one-bedroom flat at Barbès-Rochechouart, near Montmartre, was small and dark. He gave me the mattress on the living-room floor and told me the rules.

'You cannot bring girls back here to fuck them; I will not have that. They may visit you in the daytime but they cannot stay at night. No rude business when I am around.'

He sat rubbing his stump. He started to talk about Che Guevara and the great revolution of Fidel Castro. I listened. It was Obsession Number One. He said he would turn me into a comrade and turn me against my imperialist family. I couldn't see how my family could be classed as imperialists, but he didn't seem to want to hear any denials.

Katya came round to visit me at Lionel's flat. She walked in gingerly and looked around, as though visiting a museum. I watched her.

'This is how the workers live.'

'I know. I have been in a poor place before.'

Lionel wasn't around. I couldn't imagine what he would have made of Katya. In her fine clothing, with her clean looks.

We went out. We walked in the direction of Pigalle. Katya talked about her sister. She said I must keep away from Daria.

'She is very young in the mind. She is not like me; I have always had to lead her.'

As we walked she held my arm. I had become her boyfriend.

'Daria is sexually simple. I do not know the correct English word. It is that she is not wise.'

I didn't understand what she meant. I had met Daria with Katya, but I had never really talked to her. Katya told me that Daria had been talking about me; perhaps she was interested in me.

'I am bourgeois but that does not mean that I am not for the revolution.'

We were headed towards l'Étoile and her house.

'I agree.'

I didn't agree. I didn't disagree. I just didn't know what 'bourgeois' was. She had to explain – the bourgeoisie was the capitalist middle class. The people Lionel thought I came from. Could the bourgeois people be revolutionaries? Lionel talked a lot about it. Katya talked a lot about it. Lionel and I went to a meeting at the Mutualité meeting hall. Bourgeois this, bourgeois that. I didn't speak French, and regardless of that their ideas meant nothing to me.

Selling the *Evening Standard* was easy. Lionel went up towards l'Étoile, I walked down towards place de la Concorde and we would meet somewhere in the middle. Sometimes he would sell one side of the street while I was on the other. We would meet throughout the evening for coffees. Go for dinner in the self-service restaurant opposite the lido. Lionel was a good seller, but he tried to talk to too many people. He spoke to any African that came along. He was always shaking someone's hand. Because of his talking I sold more papers than him. He complained that people bought from me because I was white.

'Only the racist bastards buy from you.'

'Bollocks. You talk too much.'

He had a puzzled look. 'Bollocks? What's this, bollocks?'

'Crap. It means crap.'

Lionel had a university education. He spoke English in a posh way. He knew many words that I had never heard of. I didn't think he could be a worker – workers didn't go to university or have all those words. I asked him if he was bourgeois.

'How dare you even ask me that question. It is an insult to be asked that by a white man.' He cursed me and walked off, dragging his false leg behind him.

I sold papers to some English-speaking French people, but mainly I sold to the many English and Americans in Paris. I charmed people for their money; I told them I was a struggling writer. I got tips. I was even taken for drinks one evening. A well-dressed couple took me to a hotel bar and told me how they sympathised with the poor who struggled to improve themselves.

One night I was selling when I saw Jim ambling towards me. When he saw me a smile appeared on his face. His head was shorn of his long dirty locks. He still wore the old coat that I'd given him months before. With his hair cut short he looked like a lunatic. They'd done it in the French prison. They'd cut his hair, taken him to court and told him to leave the country.

He showed me the index figure on his right hand. It was wrapped in a bandage.

'And they broke my fucking finger.'

I took him to a self-service and fed him. I gave him some money.

'Johnny, I've had enough of this fucking French life. Fuck 'em. I'm off back.'

After the meal he just wandered off. He looked lost. He didn't want to hang on. As I watched him go I felt sorry for this man who was like a child.

Katya came to see me. I told her what had happened to Jim. She said she was appalled but not surprised: 'The police are fascists.'

I started to talk to Lionel about Marx. We lay on the sofa in his living room. He told me about revolution in history. And about how unjust the world was. I told him I had been a Catholic, that that was about helping the poor. He exploded as he always did.

'Religion is the opium of the people.'

'Lionel, why is your life all about slogans?'

He jumped up and shouted at me. 'I'll never get through to you with your bourgeois attacks.'

The discussion was over. I realised then that Lionel wanted me to agree with him. He was not much different from the Catholic Church. To say you believed was enough; they then left you alone.

I worked on *Mechanik Virgin Paris Days*. I got up early most days, went out to the library. I sat in cafes. I wasn't enjoying being with Lionel and his anger at life. I would often meet Katya from school at lunchtime. Until one day she said something that seemed strange.

'John, I am sorry but I need a revolutionary boyfriend. I need someone whose ideas are the same as mine.'

Paris was weird.

'But you're just a kid.'

She got angry. 'I am a revolutionary. And I know I am going to be more of one. And you are a drifter; you have no ideology.'

Another difficult word.

'Fuck me, Katya, I just want to be your boyfriend, not your teacher.'

This was about sex. It wasn't about Che Guevara and Fidel Castro. I was getting pissed off with all these strange people going on about revolution and the bourgeoisie. I didn't care about all that. It was like a fashion that swept Paris. And I didn't need to be fashionable.

'Then I must find another boyfriend.'

'Then fuck you. And fuck the bourgeoisie.'

She smiled. She had been talking to the wrong people. Her head was full of shit about revolution. She'd fit it in between her English-language class and her piano lessons, and her dancing classes on Saturday mornings.

We parted. That night I told Lionel that if he went on about the revolution a minute more I would leave the flat. I told him not to lecture me. He knew I was seriously angry, so he left me alone.

I met a Dutch bloke whose girlfriend was a stripper in Pigalle.

Instead of going out with Katya and her friends that Saturday night
I went with the Dutch bloke to see his girlfriend perform.

'What do you think of her?'

'She's beautiful.'

'And she's sexy. Would you like a girl like that?'

'We would all like a girl like that.'

The theatre was full of men in suits. They shouted at the girls; it
was sick. I was bored by the dances and the nudity. I had drawn too
many naked women to get turned on by shit like this. But I said the
right thing.

I told the Dutch bloke about Katya dumping me because I didn't
go on about revolution. He said I should talk to her about revolution.

'What does your girlfriend like to talk about?'

He smiled. 'She likes to talk about sex.'

Later we drank at a bar, waiting for his girlfriend to join us.

'My girlfriend wants to do a three-way.'

I looked carefully at the Dutch man. 'Two women?'

'No, two guys.' He laughed.

When she arrived she was laughing and smiling. I left them soon
afterwards and walked back home. I had a feeling that he'd been
priming me to make up the threesome; that's what his friendship
had been about. I wasn't going to go down that perverted road.

But he was right about Katya. All I had to do was say the right
things. Then I would have a good-looking bourgeois girlfriend. It
was better than nothing. I had to go along with her revolutionary
rubbish or miss out on her affections.

She came by on Monday night as I sold on the Champs-Élysées.
She looked downcast. I put my arm around her.

'Darling, let's go and have a coffee and talk about revolution.'

She looked hard at me. 'Why are you saying this?'

We sat in a cafe and I told her about my new conversion. I'd led
a very sheltered life; I needed to know more about politics, and the
poor of the world. Could we talk about it?'

She smiled and we sat. I was half-sincere. For an hour she held my hand while she told me about her ideas for bringing revolution to Europe. I listened carefully. Occasionally she kissed me. I told her I was almost converted. But we would have to work on it. Later I walked her home and we kissed on the steps outside her family's big apartment. I didn't sell all my papers until after midnight. But it had been a good evening. I felt better. At least I would not be losing my bourgeois revolutionary girl.

A week later, I lay on the mattress on the floor while Lionel sat on the sofa rubbing the stump of his half-leg. We had not been talking. He looked exhausted.

'It must be difficult walking with only a leg and a half.'

'*Très difficile.*'

'How did you lose it?'

He seemed reluctant to talk. He began slowly. He described his life. How as a boy he'd been involved in a car accident – he'd been run over. He told me about his poor but educated family. And about how the Indians had taken over Goa. It had been a Portuguese colony until it was made part of India by Nehru. I listened carefully, asked odd questions. He talked for a long time. When he had finished I told him, 'Lionel, if you talked to me about your ideas and didn't lecture me I might agree with you. But you have to stop telling me off.'

In the morning we went for coffee in an Algerian cafe and he finally started to talk to me as though I wasn't an idiot.

One morning I picked up the papers at the office. There was a lot of shouting going on, people holding up the paper.

'The Americans have killed Guevara!'

I read the front-page story – Guevara had been killed in Bolivia. I saw Lionel in the street. He looked stunned.

'We cannot play games.'

That's all he said. Later his eyes were red and inflamed. He had probably been crying about Che Guevara's death. A few days afterwards I saw the photo that became famous. Of Che laid out like Christ, with a bare chest. And happy army officers standing

271

beside him without a care. It looked bad, inhuman. Like the soldiers
were taunting the dead body of the hero.

At the Mutualité meeting hall that night a great crowd of revolutionaries gathered. I stood beside Lionel and some of his African
and Algerian friends. The mood was sad until the political leader
started shouting his speech. And then all raised their hands, me
included. We would begin the revolution here and now.

Afterwards Lionel and I sat in the Algerian cafe at Barbès. I told
him that I felt I was being converted. He looked at me as if he was
wanting to read my mind.

He said, 'Revolution is a serious business.'

I had the same feeling I had when I took God seriously. When I
read or heard something about Christ that moved me. Che had
looked like Christ, laid out on that bed. Like Christ when he'd been
taken down from the cross.

I got tired. Revolution was the big thing. But I was doing the same
things every day – selling the paper, talking to Lionel and then being
with Katya. She was beautiful, sexy. And yet she mixed revolution
with clothes and pop music. We had an argument. I told her I
thought she treated revolution like a fashion. She almost hit me.
We were lying on my mattress in the flat. She screamed at me and
stormed out.

I was missing England. The French language wasn't coming to
me. I was getting bored. One day when Lionel was out I left him a
note to say goodbye. I left a bucketful of shirts soaking in his kitchen.
I rang Katya and went to the Gare du Nord to get a ticket. I knew
that I would have problems with the police in London, but I didn't
want to stay in Paris.

At the station Katya came running towards me. She was crying.

'Please, don't go.'

We walked around. We had coffee. She carried on crying. And
then I told her the truth; I told her that I'd lied about being interested
in revolution – I'd just been after her body.

'But now, Katya, now I'm serious. I'm a revolutionary. I believe in it.'

It didn't seem to matter anyway. She said she didn't care. She wanted me to stay. Nothing I said seemed to make her less unhappy.

I got on the train and looked out the window at Katya. She looked sad, but I knew it was just a kid's thing; it was growing up. She had to try her heart out on people. She had to lose it, and then find it again.

I travelled overnight to Victoria. The sea was rough and I sat on the deck listening to a girl play Leonard Cohen songs. In London I went around to my mother's place. She opened the door to me and scowled.

'So, the fecking prodigal comes back.'

She didn't even let me in the house. The police were looking for me; I couldn't stay there. She hadn't seen me for months and she closed the door on me. I didn't feel angry, though. I knew that she considered me a bad lot. That she thought there'd be trouble wherever I went.

I went to my brother Pat's place near Fulham Broadway. He had a council flat with his wife and two daughters. He wasn't in, so I sat in a cafe and waited. I wrote some more of *Mechanik Virgin*. When I walked back over to Pat's he was there.

He smiled at me. 'Brother.'

We hugged. I asked if I could stay the night.

'You can stay forever. The wife is driving me fucking mad.'

I lay on his big sofa. We talked about the police. Pat talked about family life. Nothing changed in working-class Fulham.

25

Linda's parents now lived in North Berwick, near Edinburgh. I had hitched all through the night to get there. It was now about nine in the morning. I looked up at the windows; I didn't want to meet Linda's father. Eventually I knocked at the door. Linda opened it. Her face betrayed her surprise – her fear, almost.

'Jonathan. The police have been up, and the bank and creditors.'

She was on her own. Emily was out with Linda's mum. We went into the kitchen and she watched me as I walked around. She said I couldn't stay. Her parents would tell the police where I was.

I didn't care. I had come to see Linda and Emily. But it looked as though that wasn't possible.

She rushed into another room and came back with some money.

'Here, take this.'

It was tempting. Perhaps five pounds. I took it from her hands.

'You can have the money if you'll go. I don't want you upsetting things.'

I left. I had hardly said anything and now I was back out again. But at least I had some money. At least I had that.

The bus into Edinburgh went along the coast, stopping at small villages. People smiled and looked at each other. Old ladies in sensible coats and hats and thick-soled shoes. Men dressed as though they were going on to the moors to shoot – tweed hats and tweed jackets with leather patches on the elbows. I watched them and realised that I didn't belong to these people. I was an outsider. With my long hair and unshaven face, my ragged-looking clothes. Occasionally someone looked at me. But that was all.

In Edinburgh I made for Paddy's Bar on Rose Street. I was tired, fed up. Linda didn't want to know me. Emily was kept from me. I longed for an ordinary working life but it wasn't happening. One day the police would catch me and I would be locked up.

I got a drink and I sat in the corner watching the bar, and writing. After a while I noticed a man with a black eye-patch watching me. He came over and sat down, asked me what was engrossing me so much. He was about my age and had a posh accent. He put out his hand and I shook it.

'Patrick, by the way. Nice to meet you.'

I told him about *Mechanik Virgin Paris Days*. He looked at my notebook, at the tiny writing in it. He said it was impressive. We talked on, had a few pints together. It got late and I was supposed to be hitching back to London. Patrick said I could stay over at his place; he lived with a few people, all drama students like he was.

It was tempting, what with being so tired. But I felt I had to say it: 'I'm not queer, by the way.'

He laughed. 'That's good. Nor am I – I'm just friendly.'

I was relieved. When the pub closed we walked back to his place, down by the Dean Village. It was like a boiler room. One of his flatmates was sitting smoking. When Patrick told him I was staying the night the man stood up, looking angry.

'I don't like the look of him – he looks like a thief – and you've got no right bringing strangers back.'

They argued. I picked up my small bag and was about to leave when the man stopped me. I could stay, but if I stole anything Patrick would be in trouble.

I slept on the floor, wrapped in a blanket, and woke early; no one else was up. I left the flat quietly, and walked up the hill towards Princes Street. I'd been going to head straight to London but changed my mind. I'd remembered that a friend of Danny's was now at art school in Edinburgh. Christine had been a big friend of Danny's; I liked her, though she'd never seemed that struck by me. I made my way to the college on Lauriston Place and found her in one of the studios. When I walked in she almost jumped with joy.

'John! I can't believe it. What are you doing here?'

We went for a tea in the canteen. I was surprised that she seemed so pleased to see me. Her face fell when I told her I was just passing through. She said I should stay for a few days at her flat. There was nothing pulling me back to London. Maybe I could go and see Emily sometime. At least if I kept out of trouble in Edinburgh I wouldn't meet up with the police.

Later she took me to her flat. It was a big old place with shabby furniture. I'd be sleeping on the sofa in the living room.

The following morning Christine was excited. Her boyfriend, Ray, had just arrived; he'd come up for Christmas. Ray sat smoking in the kitchen. He was an older man, with thick black hair and a long beard. He wore a cap that made him look like a rabbi. They called him 'Ray the Priest'. He was weird, but he was friendly. We soon got talking.

There were other people in the flat. They were friendly enough, too. The only rule was that I couldn't eat their food. My money soon ran out and I lived on toast. But there was always some party to go to. One night Christine introduced me to her posh friend Vicky. We became friends, and I stayed at her flat while her flatmate was in Africa for the holidays. Vicky had money; she gave me money and fed me. I was happy again.

Paddy's Bar was the place to be. We went there every day; it became our living room. We sat there at lunchtimes and at night. It was like some big family. There were drug dealers and petty thieves. I met people, made new friends. I met one bloke who knew Linda. He handled stolen goods, and one night I broke an antique-shop window and stole some clocks for him.

Edinburgh was becoming an exciting place.

It was Saturday lunchtime and Paddy's Bar was full. It was a few days before Christmas and I was drunk. I was playing around with one of Christine's friends, Lynne. A group of big men came in wearing scarves and sheepskin coats. They looked like a rugby crowd and didn't fit into the atmosphere of Paddy's. They stood at the bar smirking, looking at us. One of them was staring at me and muttering to a friend. I went over.

'All right?'

'All right.'

He was still smirking. It looked as though there was going to be a fight. We stood looking at each other.

Then we smiled.

'So, what's your name?'

'Gordon.'

Gordon had a nose as big as mine. It was good to meet someone with a nose.

'John.'

We shook hands. I asked him what he did. I laughed when he said he was a poet.

'A poet? I'm a poet.'

Now he laughed, too, and we shook hands again.

Soon he was buying me a drink and we were talking about poetry. I read him a piece of *Mechanik Virgin Paris Days*. He laughed and encouraged me. He didn't have any poetry on him; he said he'd bring some with him the next time we met. We parted as friends with a plan to meet in Paddy's after Christmas. He was so unlike anyone else I had met. He was like a farmer, big and healthy-looking. I was surprised at how friendly he was.

I spent New Year 1968 in the house of a one-legged girl. There was a mad mob of people at the High Street gathering; I followed some of them to a party and met Elspeth. She had lost her leg suddenly a few years before – I never really knew how. Back at her house her family were pleased to meet me. Later Elspeth and I sat and discussed the meaning of life. We lay in her brother's bedroom and I knew I had to do something other than drift. I kissed her violently and she laughed.

'I haven't had many kisses since I lost my leg.'

I told her about Lionel. That within six months I had met two one-legged people. We both laughed at the coincidence.

A day or two later I met Gordon at Paddy's. We talked about revolution but Gordon was dismissive.

'That's all middle-class bollocks.'

I protested: 'You're just a fucking reactionary arsehole.'

'Maybe I am. But I haven't got my head up my arse.'

I loved arguing with him. He wasn't polite. He called me a stupid cunt, told me I should get rid of all the ideology and I might add up to something. I read him a bit more of *Mechanik* and he said, 'Stick to poetry. Even bad poetry is less harmful than bad ideology.'

Like Paris, Edinburgh was full of people talking about revolution. It was the politics of the left everywhere. So Gordon was refreshing even though I didn't agree with him. By March I'd decided that I wanted to get into politics; I wanted to be useful. I'd been back to London briefly, to go to a big anti-Vietnam demonstration in Grosvenor Square. Now I wanted to get back there permanently.

I told Gordon, 'I'm just a drifter. I want to change the world.'

'Start by changing your underpants.'

But he was leaving Edinburgh for Littlehampton anyway; we would keep in contact. I soon left Edinburgh. I gave Gordon my brother Pat's address and he bought me a drink for the road.

'Four shillings an hour.'

'Do you get free food?'

'You get staff reduction.'

Four shillings an hour meant two pounds for a ten-hour day. Ten pounds a week. The same as I'd been earning when I was nineteen. I was now twenty-two. But washing up and clearing tables at the South Kensington Restaurant was about the only job I could get without proof of identity. And with the social security still looking for me, it was better than nothing.

I started at seven each morning. Pat would wake me at five-thirty with a cup of tea and a slice of toast. I always arrived on time. The job wasn't too bad; I could give Pat five pounds per week, which made him happy. And living in Pat's front room on the sofa wasn't the worst place I could be. Though it did mean being back in Fulham with the constant threat of arrest.

One Saturday I went with Pat down to North End Road market. Some people were selling a left-wing paper outside Woolworth's. I stopped and spoke to them, told them I had been at the anti-Vietnam demonstration. The man talking to me laughed.

'That's just adventurism. We're a serious group; we're not playing at being revolutionaries.'

The Socialist Labour League had a twice-weekly paper. They held meetings every Wednesday night. I gave them my name and walked off with Pat. Pat thought it was all rubbish; he said they were just shit-stirrers. The poor needed money, not revolution.

The following Wednesday I went to the meeting, in a small room over a pub. The organiser was a bloke called Terry. Terry had glasses and looked like a schoolboy. I wasn't impressed. But when the meeting began it started to make sense. I listened, asked a few questions. Everyone was young. There were no girls worth thinking about, but I liked the seriousness of the people. Afterwards I told Terry that I wanted to join the Socialist Labour League.

'You can't just join. We *ask* you to join, once you've worked with us. We're serious.'

We spent most of our evenings at meetings and selling papers on the streets. I was good at selling papers, though I still had a sketchy understanding of revolutionary politics. The SLL told you to read. They didn't want you to join for emotional reasons.

One Sunday we went to St Pancras Town Hall for a big meeting. The place was full. There were many speakers, before a small, round Irishman had his turn. He started off very quietly – you could barely hear him. Then he got louder. Before long this little man was bellowing, red-faced and aggressive. At the end of the speech he got a big round of applause.

Terry was sat beside me. He said, 'So, what about that?'

I was stunned. 'I didn't quite understand what he said. But God, he can speak.'

I was told I had to leave my washing-up job and get a job in engineering. If I was going to be a revolutionary I had to get a real job – among the working classes, not among the leftovers of the underclass.

I saw Brian a few times. We still had that love-hate thing going. I did cocaine with him sometimes, even while I was selling the paper and trying to join the SLL.

Brian lived at Shepherd's Bush and I would soon be moving there too. One bus ride away was the AEC factory, where buses and trucks were made.

Brian and I signed up for the engineering training course at AEC and were soon working with thousands of others in the vast factory. The SLL were pleased with me. From being a dish-washer on the edge of society I had moved into the very heartland of the class struggle. It was fascinating.

Gordon had written to me many times, always carrying on with the counter-revolutionary insults. Then one day I got a letter from him that was unlike the others. In it he said he had met a great woman; he wanted her to meet me. She was living in Littlehampton and her family ran cafes down there. Would I like to come and stay for a few days?

I arranged to meet him. I took a day off work and didn't tell the SLL.

'So, this is your new kingdom?'

He met me at the station in the little seaside town. It looked south-coast grim. We walked the short distance to his damp little flat, where Anita, his girlfriend, would meet us. He was still writing and thinking about his next move. He thought I'd like Anita; she was very committed.

'Committed to what?'

'To radical stuff.'

'But is she a true revolutionary?'

'How would I fucking know?'

We weren't in the flat long before Anita arrived. She was dark-haired and very beautiful. She was a radical, but she wasn't into revolutionary parties. Very soon she was telling me what was wrong with European revolutionaries.

'They just talk. They don't do. It's all about debate and not action. The revolution will start in the Third World. Europe's full of a load of fat-arsed lefties sitting around talking.'

'The Socialist Labour League is about building working-class consciousness – revolutionary consciousness.'

'Crap. That's all words. What about the revolutionaries of South America? The revolution isn't going to start here. It's going to start among those who have nothing to lose.'

She was like a whirlwind. She didn't draw breath. I became annoyed with her, told her she was just some crazy romantic – just like all those radical students who soon wore themselves out. She said that everything was theory for me; it wasn't about getting out there and getting my hands dirty.

Gordon watched, laughing and smiling at the way we went at each other. We ignored, talked over and interrupted each other. Gordon said we were as bad as each other. No wonder all us lefties never achieved anything – we could never agree.

Night came and we went to a pub. After that they took me to the station. I was drunk. I asked a railway worker when the next train to London was coming. He told me to look on the notice board.

I grabbed hold of him. 'Look here, mate, you're a fucking public employee.'

He ran off. Anita and Gordon laughed. Anita wanted to know if that was how I treated the working classes.

I was told off the next night when I met up with the SLL. I shouldn't have skipped away for the day. I protested that I had to have some kind of life outside the group, but the SLL members were insistent: 'You only have one life, comrade. And that is the struggle.'

After three months I was tiring of this revolutionary zeal; I needed time off. But they didn't accept that anyone could have any life other than that dedicated to the cause.

I had a problem: I never seemed to meet revolutionary workers. I came from the working classes and they seemed to be very unheroic, very un-revolutionary. They appeared to be interested only in their creature comforts. I was getting pissed off with what was beginning to sound like a revolutionary religion.

Terry and I were arguing. I wasn't happy with the discipline. The months slipped by. I was committed for a while. Then it felt like being back at school. It was all about control and I didn't know if I could take it. As winter approached I decided I was going to leave.

One cold morning I got a train to Littlehampton and found Anita and Gordon. We walked along the beach. Anita quizzed me about the revolutionary struggle. I told her I was leaving.

'I'm fucking tired. I don't like the discipline.'

She laughed at me. She had no sympathy for me. Political differences were one thing but giving up because I was tired only proved my lack of commitment.

She was right. All the activity and the control just weren't for me. I didn't need them. I was best off getting out.

Back in London I went drinking in the West End. I ended up in Covent Garden, drinking in the all-night pubs. This was more my thing, better than working in a factory and trying to incite revolution in the working classes.

Christmas Eve. I was staying at my mother's.

'For feck's sake, go out. And don't expect too much tomorrow.'

I had lost my room in Shepherd's Bush – I couldn't pay the rent because I wasn't working. Pat and his family had been evicted from their council flat for non-payment of rent. They were now living with his wife's parents.

I wandered up to Earl's Court and met a bloke I knew from Edinburgh. Later we gatecrashed a party. I went out for a walk with a girl and came back to find the door locked. It was a glass door so I kicked it in. I ran upstairs to the party drunk and stupid. I had left my coat behind.

'Fuck you, you load of cunts.'

Everyone stood looking at me as if I was a madman. I left and walked down the road, felt blood running into my shoe. A trail of blood behind me. At the hospital they said I was very lucky that the blood loss hadn't killed me. I fainted in casualty.

I got home to my mother's at six o'clock in the morning and she cursed me for waking her up. It was a bad Christmas; my parents didn't want me around.

'You should be with your wife.' My mother said this as she put turkey on my plate.

'But she doesn't want him.' My father said this with a smile.

My brother Richard worked in a hotel in Kensington High Street. After Christmas I got a job there: all-night washing up for the hotel's twenty-four-hour restaurant. In a way I was happy. At least I had something to do and I got all the food I wanted. During the daytime I slept at my mother's, frightened that I'd be discovered by the police. But at least I'd escaped all that revolutionary discipline; I couldn't stand any more of that.

26

It was early January 1969, coming up to my twenty-third birthday. As I walked through Hyde Park I wished it wasn't Sunday. I wished it was Monday so I could go to my parents' place. Weekdays no one was home and I could lie in the living room and rest. Or get into one of my brothers' beds. Peter's was the best. He was the youngest and his bed smelt good.

I had asked for a room at the hotel where I worked. They had said they would put me on the list. Usually they gave rooms to chambermaids and waitresses and not to people who washed up on the night-shift. Of course, they said, if I trained as a waiter it would be better. But I didn't fancy being a waiter. Already I was old. I had lost my youth.

The park was alive with people running, playing football, walking. I joined the walkers. I walked briskly. I got to the Serpentine and sat on a bench. I looked out over the water, watching the ducks and the reeling gulls. I took out my notebook and found the page where I'd written about a city with walls and green fields beyond. It was a medieval city that I was trying to imagine and write a story about.

It was cold, so I moved on. I walked the length of the Serpentine and headed across the park towards Kensington, past the Round Pond and the Victoria statue. It was good to walk through this landscape I'd known since I was a child. It made me feel better about my parents and the bitter days back then. I wished that I had a room of my own and didn't have to return to their house. And the moans and misery that they still lived in. I needed to get a small room of my own.

Eventually I reached the King's Road and walked down to the

World's End. Ahead of me I saw Danny and I called out to him. I hadn't seen him in almost a year. He was happy to see me. There was none of the anger I thought he should feel towards me about the bead business of two summers before. He shook my hand and we chatted easily, catching up as though I had never done him a wrong.

There was a spare room at Danny's aunt's house, he said. His Aunt Mabel lived in the World's End. I knew the house; it would be perfect. Like actually having a home, not just a room. Danny and I walked there. The room was small but I wouldn't have cared if it was a phone box. Danny lived on the floor below.

We dug out an old bed from the back-yard shed. We got some blankets and sheets. There were no curtains so we put a painting by Danny in the window so that no one could look in. It looked bleak but I would soon stick up postcards and newspaper cuttings.

'Two pounds a week. And no messing with the rent.'

I gave him the first week's money up front. 'Danny, you're a life-saver.'

Entry to the club was free on Monday nights. Chrisa had invited me. She was with her boyfriend. A girl who wanted to meet me again was supposed to join us, but she didn't turn up. I was drunk and danced around noisily. The bouncers kept trying to lure me towards the door, but I stayed on the dance floor. I took my shirt off and whirled it round my head.

Chrisa's boyfriend had invited a group of very young girls he had met at the Tate. I went and sat with them, asked each one of them for a dance. A tall blonde volunteered. I danced stupidly. Chrisa didn't enjoy my performance; she went off with her boyfriend.

For the rest of the night I danced with the blonde girl, Tessa. She put up with my foolish dancing. The club's staff wouldn't allow me any more drink so I sobered up as the night wore on. When it was time to leave I stuck with Tessa while her friends dispersed. She was going home and raised no objections to me going with her. We took a cab to her flat off the King's Road. It was a basement flat. Her schoolfriend's father lived above; he was the golf correspondent for *The Times*. I told her stories about my boyhood. She listened intently.

And at some point she told me she was sixteen.

'God above!'

I lied. Told her that I was twenty-one coming on twenty-two.

In the morning she gave me an orange shirt and I left my dirty one behind. She gave me some money because I was broke. As I left the flat I promised I would come and see her. She gave me her phone number. It was strange – I had never known a girl with a phone.

I walked down Oakley Street towards the King's Road and thought that she was too young for me. Much too young.

I couldn't get Tessa out of my mind. She was too young. But she was fresh and lovely, like a newborn horse with her long legs. A few days went by and I called her.

She sounded happy to hear from me and we arranged to meet that night in the pub opposite her flat.

When I got back from the phone box Danny was hanging around. We talked about going out with sixteen-year-olds. I was embarrassed. How could I meet a sixteen-year-old in a pub? She could pass as seventeen, maybe even eighteen. But I was convinced that I looked thirty, even though I'd only just turned twenty-three. I looked weathered and beaten around.

I arrived at the pub a few minutes late and she was sat there by herself. She smiled as I came in. Nervously I sat beside her. But she seemed not to mind. And at least I had grown out of telling people I was the black sheep of a millionaire family. And that I had gone to some obscure public school hidden in some remote county.

But then she told me, 'You said your name was Jacob Breakfast the other night. I thought a Jacob was going to ring.'

I got us some drinks and then I told her that I felt a bit awkward knocking about with someone of her age.

'I feel so much older. You're still at school and I've been halfway round the world.'

'Really? Where?'

'Well, Paris and Edinburgh.'

'That doesn't sound like halfway round the world.' She'd been to Europe. To France, Spain, Italy, Germany, Austria . . . She convinced me that I was less travelled than I'd thought.

I showed her my latest notebook. I had moved on from the story about the walled city. I was writing a comic story, 'The History of the Mouth Organ'. I read her part of it. She was certainly a good listener. I read her a few poems. She told me more about herself and her family. She'd been at boarding school in Bristol but had revolted; she'd insisted upon continuing her studies in London. Hence the flat below her schoolfriend's family home while the friend was still at the boarding school. At sixteen, Tessa had got her way and now lived like a bachelor girl.

Her father was a baronet. She said he was very 'old school'. Sir Robert and Lady Ricketts lived modestly in Gloucestershire. She had a younger brother, an elder brother and an elder sister. And they were all friends.

'Tessa Ricketts? What a weird name.'

'At least I've only got one name – you can't even remember who you are.'

I stayed with her a few nights. I conquered my embarrassment. But I tried to hide whenever I saw someone I knew. Tessa was slightly concerned that I was embarrassed to be seen with her. I tried to reassure her that I wasn't; I just wished she was a few years older.

But really I knew that if she'd been a few years older she'd also have been a few years wiser. And I couldn't see a wise girl wanting to be with me.

I got a new job, at a factory in North Acton where Vaseline and baby products were made. I drove a truck clearing the lines of broken glass and boxes. The factory was full of women. The pay was good and the girls and women spent most of the time being sexually rude. I loved it. I worked hard; I never had any time off and got into the swing of labour. Each lunchtime I would work on my writing. Stories and poems, and pieces of dialogue in the hope that I might write a play.

I was also saving money. Tessa was going to Spain for a few weeks in the summer. I was going to join her and we were going to do a tour of Italy and Switzerland and then go into Germany. She was now seventeen. I had proposed to her in Trafalgar Square one evening. I was drunk and she took me seriously. I was surprised. But now we were inseparable. She was getting on with her studies in Latin and Greek language and history. She had decided to read ancient history at university. She put up with me even though I sometimes got drunk and abusive.

I was paranoid. I was convinced that I was going to be arrested. We'd be walking down the King's Road and I would get a feeling that I was about to be lifted by the police. I had bad dreams; I couldn't sleep. I knew that at some stage I would have to face the police and get the whole thing out of the way. But now, with Tessa with me, the prospect of a jail sentence frightened me. What if she didn't wait for me? What if she met someone else? My life would be shattered. I would be drifting and purposeless again. Lonely and separate.

Brian came to France with me – we were to go down to Spain and meet Tessa there. We stayed in Paris for a few days. We argued. Brian kept on about how I used people.

'You even use Tessa. You're just a fucking opportunist.'

We argued constantly. We headed south, got as far as Versailles on a bus. Then we hitched. We got one lift and then spent the next fourteen hours walking. We cursed the meanness of the French drivers. At four in the morning, after a few fights, we arrived at the gates into Chartres. We fell asleep on the green in front of the cathedral.

I woke to the noise of Brian arguing with an old man. The man had a stick; he was shouting at Brian and trying to hit him with it. We had disturbed his sense of civic pride by sleeping at the doors of the cathedral.

We walked round, tried once again to hitch a lift. We were getting nowhere. Brian had had enough: 'I'm going back to Paris. This is just crap.'

We stayed the night in a hostel with some American girls who allowed us to sleep on their floor. I took the train to Spain the next day. Brian and I parted friends – I loved the old fool, and sometimes he loved me.

By nightfall I'd arrived in Deva in the Spanish Basque Country. I called at Tessa's hotel. I was five days early but she was pleased to see me. I got a room with an old woman who fed me for hardly any money at all. At the end of the week we took the train to Italy.

In Florence we booked into a room but we were running out of money. Tessa wrote to her mother and asked her to help. I wrote to a few people, and within a few days Brian sent us five pounds. I begged from English, German or American tourists. The Germans were the most generous. They wanted to know all about our hardships and sometimes they'd take us for coffee or buy us slices of pizza.

Whatever money we got I spent immediately. Tessa's mother sent some cash and said that she had also given some to Julia, Tessa's best friend from school. Julia was coming with friends to Lucca, about ninety kilometres from Florence. Hitching from Florence to Lucca was easy. Having a tall blonde with me was the best passport.

Lucca, three o'clock in the morning. It was cold and it started to rain. We stood in the rain on the hill above the walled city. Tessa was angry with me. My wild spending had got us into this situation.

'This isn't a holiday.'

I promised her I wouldn't be so wild with the money.

A man let us shelter in the garage of his house. The rain kept on. We slept for a while and then went down into the town. I was in a mad mood. Tiredness didn't affect me the way it affected Tessa. She told me to shut up as I gabbled on. We found a bar. Tessa had a coffee and I had a grappa. It made me drunk, but it shut me up.

We walked to the other side of the little walled town. There were fields, green and neatly ordered. I tried to tell Tessa about the story I had been writing when I met her. About the medieval city.

'I imagined this all six months ago, Tess.'

But she wasn't listening. She was dog-tired and cold. In the field there were bales of hay. I made a little house of bales by some trees and a stream. From there I could see the city walls in the distance. I was excited that I had arrived in the pages of my story. Tessa got into the little house of bales and fell asleep.

We had days to wait before Julia arrived. We hung around the streets. I begged, and did well, but we never got enough money for a hotel room. At least we ate, though, and we had our hay-bale shelter.

At times Tessa laughed. 'I would never have thought that we'd end up like this.'

'It's all my fault.'

'I know.'

Julia arrived and we were happy again. We were joyous as we continued our journey. We headed south, towards Naples, and stopped in Rome for a day. We were better with the money but still not good enough.

We were away for five weeks and things got worse. We were broke. We went to Switzerland and then to Germany. A man took us to his home and left us there to sleep. He gave us the money to get on the boat when we got to Ostende.

Back in England, Tessa went to stay with her mother; she was exhausted. I met Brian in the pub and and told him about my adventures. He said I was boasting. He was pissed off with me.

The London publisher Hodder & Stoughton ran a competition. They offered five hundred pounds for the best new novel. I had got a job as a road-sweeper for Kensington and Chelsea and in my spare time, I worked hard on the novel. Tessa's sister Sara got a friend to pay for the manuscript to be typed up and bound. I told everyone I was going to win the prize. I was convinced that *Oven Ready* was an apocalyptic book.

I delivered the manuscript on time. A polite man took me into his office when I handed it in. I had to give him an idea of what the story was about. I explained: a man of twenty-three was going to shoot someone from the window in his room – some kind of political figure. And each chapter reflected upon the life of this young man. It was pure autobiography with some gross exaggerations.

The publisher listened carefully. 'Well, it sounds better than some of the crap I've been reading so far.'

It was 70,000 words, and looked good as a bound manuscript. He shook my hand and wished me luck.

Two days later it was returned without so much as a compliments slip. I was sick. And embarrassed. Especially as I had told everyone I knew that I was about to become a great and published author.

It was 1970 and I felt old at twenty-four years of age. The business with the police weighed heavily on me. Tessa and I moved to Bristol. I got a job laying concrete paths and rebuilding walls. It was good money. The plan was for Tessa to improve her Latin in preparation for university the following year. We got a flat at the top of a house in a nice part of the town. Ross moved down there too and he was good company. He lived in a house round the corner from us. Mrs Langran, the old landlady, said that Ross was a gentleman. I told her that he was a lord. She was very impressed. So Ross temporarily became Lord Ross Kelly, his true family name. I called him 'milord' and opened doors for him.

We met a woman who wanted someone to run her shop, selling antiques and bric-à-brac. We were to pay her a small rent and got a percentage on what we sold. We sold her things and never told her. It worked for three months until she realised we were screwing her. We called it 'The Micawber Gallery Bookshop', though there were no books for sale.

One afternoon I had a visitor at the flat: Terry, from my days with the Socialist Labour League. I was surprised – I hadn't seen him for two years and I thought he must be after money for the cause. But he said that wasn't why he was there.

I had always respected Terry. He'd seemed like the brightest, the least religious of the SLL members. He told me he'd left the group. He felt that it was full of yes-men, that the leader had lost his way. The SLL had become self-serving and was no longer concerned with the struggle to lead the working classes to revolutionary consciousness. I listened. This was all over my head. I didn't know why he was talking to me; I had no reputation in the movement. If anything I'd been seen as a self-promoter – one leading SLL comrade had actually said that 'John Bird loves himself'. So why was this wise person wasting his time on me?

Soon I understood. He was just looking for a friend; at that time, he needed friends more than anything. He had a young wife, who had stayed with the party. He was out on his own, floating, trying to make sense of the revolutionary needs of the time.

He said that the debate needed to be developed. He told me he'd always thought that I was a cheeky bloke with potential. He had tried to keep me in the party. He had excused my 'petit-bourgeois individualism'.

When he left me in Bristol that day, we said we would keep in touch.

One Sunday I went to an open-air market. I walked around looking at all the bric-à-brac, the assortment of useless stuff. I picked through some books and came across a Victorian miscellany. I looked at the decaying book and the illustrations inside. Among them was a drawing by George Cruikshank, *The Temptation of St Anthony*. It was a beautiful black-and-white line drawing, small but full of detail.

The stall owner wanted twelve shillings for the book, but he said

I could pay him the following week. I had no real idea why I wanted the book. I just knew that I was strongly attracted to it, if only for the Cruikshank illustration. I agreed to pay the man later and took the book home.

Later I looked at the illustration and knew what I wanted to do. I wanted to reproduce it as a poster. It was such a great drawing I could imagine it printed many times bigger.

I told Tessa that I wanted to start publishing posters. I showed her the illustration. I was desperate to get into some kind of publishing; I wanted to be a publisher. I would start with posters and move on to books, maybe even magazines.

She was irritated. 'We haven't got the money.'

'This could make us some money.'

'Do walls and paths instead. Please.'

Tessa's friend Julia came to stay. She lent me ten pounds to publish the Cruikshank as a poster. Within a few months I'd published many different posters. In the summer Tessa bought a van and we travelled round selling them. We made money. I had begun my journey to the world of publishing. But now I wanted also to be a printer; I wanted to print books and magazines as well as posters.

I never went back to pay the man in the open-air market for the book. I thought about it but never made it down to see him. That was probably the last time he told anyone they could pay him later.

Tessa decided to enrol at Sheffield University. We looked around the town. It was full of old streets and factories. An estate agent offered us a house in Attercliffe, a run-down working-class area. It was thirty shillings a week; two bedrooms, a living room and a kitchen. It was one of a number of old houses built for a mine that had long since been closed down. In September we moved in. The neighbours were like caricatures of northerners. Friendly but nosey. They wanted to know everything about us.

Tessa was in two minds about the place. 'Birdy, do you think we're going to like it here?'

'How the fuck do I know?'

I certainly felt better being out of London, away from police who might recognise me. And I hadn't liked Bristol. It was full of hippies. I felt uncomfortable among them, with their constant talking about tarot cards and your planets.

Sheffield was 150-odd miles from London and it was a different world. We were southerners; we weren't used to this sort of run-down industrial landscape. The people seemed rooted in the past. And with our toilet at the bottom of the garden it felt like we were living in pre-war Britain. In all the London slums I'd lived in, I'd never known an outside toilet. Just at my grandmother's farm in Ireland, where you went up the field to shit.

I met up with the local branch of the Socialist Labour League. They were a moralistic and desperate lot. Their main system of control was guilt. If you didn't agree to do all that they asked of you, you were a counter-revolutionary. An enemy of the working class. I did what I felt I could do, but it was never enough.

'Why can't you come and sell papers tomorrow night?'

'I have work to do.'

'There are comrades sacrificing their families – '

And so on. They were humourless and I didn't know how long I could suffer their torments and their blackmail.

Terry came to stay. We had long and interesting discussions. But he had all the answers and he knew all the questions. I was dazzled by his knowledge, his grasp of everything from film to philosophy to art.

'Birdy, you know we have to develop a perspective that is different from the party and its increasing isolation.'

'Yes.' That was all I could say; I had no real suggestions. But then Terry started talking about critical analysis of art and art history. I knew something about that and I got into the idea. We talked about starting a revolutionary art magazine. I wanted to call it *The Red Wedge* after a revolutionary painting by the Soviet painter El Lizzitsky.

⋆

'I don't know if I can stand this place.'

Tessa was being straight: Sheffield depressed her. It depressed me, too. There were no bookshops, no coffee bars. The people were better than Londoners but there was little to do. To me, it was a landscape of deprivation. I began to understand how lucky I had been to be born into poverty on the edge of plenty. And that however poor you were you could take a bus journey out of it.

The Miners' Strike began and the SLL went out on to the picket lines selling the *Workers' Press*. We did not win many converts to the party but we became involved in fundraising. Yet the terrible moralising and nagging that went with the party branch once again took the edge off things for me. Branch members defined themselves by the failures of others; everyone tried to look good at everyone else's expense.

'Tess, I think we should get out of this place.'

We got out. We packed up our stuff and moved back south. It was the end of 1972. We both felt that we were returning to the real world, to civilisation. I was twenty-six. I knew what I wanted to be. I wanted to be the best printer in the world. As well as the best writer. And thinker. Though I could never see myself as being the best revolutionary.

27

The flat had high ceilings. It had two balconies and was on the first floor, overlooking a roundabout at Little Venice, just behind Paddington Station. I felt I was coming home. I was also going to talk to the social security about my 1967 wrongdoings.

Tessa, Terry and I walked round the flat. The kitchen was small but there were two big rooms. Terry would have one and Tessa and I the other. We could carry on with our revolutionary studies. We could work to change the Socialist Labour League from the inside at its West London branches.

'But can we get the two grand deposit?'

Terry asked this very practical question. We needed the key money for the flat. It was 1973 and key money had been made illegal. Instead you paid an exaggerated price for the fixtures and fittings. Those being in this case a few lightbulbs, a window blind and some worn-out coconut matting along with the kitchen appliances, which had seen better days. But there was no alternative: if we didn't pay up, we wouldn't get the flat.

Tessa phoned her mother to see if she'd help us. Terry and I stood anxiously outside the phone box. There was a lot of shouting then Tessa came out. No luck. Terry went off unhappily. We had lost the chance of the flat and all the work we could do from it.

I made a suggestion: 'What if I tell her that if she doesn't give us the money we'll go off on our own and get married?'

Tessa was coming up to twenty-one; I had just turned twenty-seven. We were going to be together anyway, so why not?

'I don't know what it'll do, but let's give it a try.'

It seemed like an irrational response to her refusal to give us the deposit, but I couldn't think of anything else. And – amazingly – it worked. I could hardly believe it. That Lady Ricketts would approve of a marriage between her daughter and a lowborn person like me!

When I told Terry he pointed out that it was lucky I'd got my divorce through. He was right, but I had almost forgotten that I had once been married and had a child.

So I was back where I had started. I was happy to be a few minutes' walk from Notting Hill. I walked around as if this was a homecoming. I visited various aunts and uncles. Ted had just died, but I saw Alma and she was pleased to hear that I would be a neighbour again.

I was taken on by a print factory near Paddington Station. I knew nothing about printing, but I was still determined to become one. I lied my way into the job, and was sussed by the foreman, Pete, within hours of being there. He could tell that I knew nothing about print.

'You're a bit rusty.'

'Yes. Ever since the road accident – '

He laughed, said, 'Well, we better try to refamiliarise you. You never entirely forget it; it's a bit like riding a bike.'

We both knew that he was being generous.

Pete covered for me while I picked things up; he did all my work for me and blamed machine breakdowns for the delays on jobs.

The manager didn't notice until Pete had a few days off work. Then the manager realised I was incapable of running a job and got rid of me.

I had learnt enough to get another job, in a small print shop at the English Folk Dance and Song Society. I was the sole printer; I had my own room and a small press. After two weeks spent training I could run the small, limited machine with confidence.

Tessa and I married at Fulham Town Hall on 11 March 1973. Beforehand I got drunk in the pub opposite, I was so fearful of the ceremony. My family met the Ricketts family for the first time. It went well enough. The only hitch came after the reception, which was held in a restaurant on the New King's Road. A number of us went back to my parents' house. I later decided to go back to the reception venue to see if I could get some whiskey. I was with my little brother Peter. As we passed by the Lord Palmerston pub the door swung shut behind someone leaving. I pushed the glass door; it had locked behind the person leaving. I pushed so hard that the glass of the door smashed. I stood there feeling foolish when Tony Mancini came running out of the pub with a group of men. I was hauled into the pub. The police came. I was drunk and stupid, and couldn't answer when I was asked how I had broken the glass in the door.

'But, Tony, I used to walk your Alsatian for you.'

I was let go. Out in the street a crowd of our guests had gathered. I looked at them and started to cry. I felt like a stupid child.

My mother went to her doctor for one of her regular check-ups. She had had health problems. The doctor weighed her and told her she had to go straight into hospital. That night we all gathered and looked at my mother as she sat in bed. She couldn't see what all the fuss was about.

'For the love of God – apart from being tired, I'm perfect.'

Doctors reassured us that it was only routine; they just needed to run some tests.

I asked the obvious question: 'So why rush her in from her doctor's?'

'Weightloss – sudden weightloss – is always worrying. But it's not always a worrying sign.'

I couldn't understand this play with words. I had spoken to the doctors out of my father's and brothers' earshot. I wanted to know the worst. But all they'd say was that we'd have to be patient.

My father wanted to know what they'd said.

'Oh, the usual. Routine. They have to do tests.'

'Did you ask why they whipped her in so quick?'

'They don't like weightloss. But he doesn't think we have anything to worry about.'

My father looked reassured. Though I knew I had slightly amended the doctor's comments for him.

For weeks the doctors avoided our questions. They were always rushing off somewhere else. They told my mother nothing. One Friday in anger I demanded that a doctor speak to me first thing on the following Monday morning. I needed some answers. I was mad all that weekend. I went selling our paper, the *Workers' Press*; I canvassed for members around housing estates. Anything to take my mind off Monday.

By Monday I had calmed down. I felt that I'd probably let my imagination run away with me. I cycled down to the hospital and went up to the ward. My mother was in the bed nearest the doctor's office. She was thin and discoloured-looking. I gave her a kiss, said I'd get things straightened out.

'Well some fecker has to,' she said. 'I'm going crazy here.'

In the doctor's office I told him he'd pissed around too long, he had to tell us what the problem was. The doctor had a folder on the desk in front of him. He touched it as he spoke. He told me my mother had cancer of the liver.

I paused for a moment. I wasn't prepared for this.

'Does that mean that you'll have to operate?'

He turned the folder automatically. They couldn't operate, and the cancer had spread to other parts of her body. This was happening too fast for me to take in. The doctor had to explain: My mother was going to die.

I stood up. 'What? *What?*' I hadn't even considered the possibility. I had blindly walked in. I hadn't rehearsed the possible outcomes, gone through all that he might say to me that morning.

I tried to gather my thoughts. I realised that my mother was in a bed on the other side of the door. I spoke in a whisper, asked when he thought she would die.

He looked at the folder. He didn't look at me. I wanted him to but he kept looking down at the folder. 'It could be six weeks, it could be a year.'

'And which do you think it will be?'

'Six weeks.'

I paced around his office. So that was what all the delay was about – they didn't want to tell us.

He looked at me now. 'We had to investigate. We had to be totally sure.'

I sat down. This was terrible. What would I tell her? What would I tell my father? The doctor said all this was up to me. But he said that he wouldn't recommend telling my mother. I knew I couldn't tell either of them. My father had a bad heart. And I couldn't have her knowing.

We went through everything again. He explained once more that there was nothing they could do, that it was too far gone. I had to pull myself together. A nurse brought me a cup of tea – she just appeared, as though it had been planned. Everyone in the ward knew; everyone except my mother.

I went to her. She had tears in her eyes when she asked me what he'd said. Her face was full of panic.

'Nothing, Mum. Don't worry.'

'But you were in there such a long time.'

I laughed. 'Mum, you know me. I asked the same questions three times, took him round the houses. In the end he told me to piss off.'

She calmed down, relieved. 'You would tell me if it was bad news? You would, wouldn't you?'

'For fuck's sake, Mum you'd be the first I'd tell.'

She took my hand. 'So what is it?'

I'd forgotten to ask the doctor for some benign explanation to give her. So I told her it was liver inflammation; they had to put her on all sorts of stuff to clean her out.

I pulled away from her. Said I had to go. I had to go to work. She smiled at me, glad I'd reassured her.

I kissed her and made to leave. I stopped at the door, said, 'I might not make it tonight, Mum. I'm pissed off with all this hospital stuff.'

'And your poor mother stuck in a fecking bed.'

She laughed. I could see that she was relieved.

I had to see my father afterwards. He was working on maintenance at Selfridges in Oxford Street. Foolishly I had agreed to meet him to give him what I'd believed would be good news. I called Tessa at work. She was temping until her course at the University of London began in the autumn.

'What did they say?'

'That she's dying of cancer. For the love of God, she's got six weeks.'

Silence. Then she said to come and meet her before I saw my father. We went to the Wallace Collection, off Oxford Street. I cried. Tessa was lost. She didn't know how to handle this turn of events.

'I can't cry because I have to see the old man in a few minutes.'

We walked round. Tessa had never been to the Wallace Collection before. I showed her the beautiful Rubens with the rainbow. We looked at *The Laughing Cavalier*. So many times I had gone to galleries to learn. Now I was there to forget.

When I met my father I smiled at him.

'Well, son?'

'Some shit about jaundice. Liver inflammation. They have to dose her up with stuff. Don't worry, Dad.'

He was relieved. He shook my hand. 'Thanks for doing that, son.'

'No problem, Dad. Except my poxy boss will be moaning his arse off.'

He smiled again. 'Well fuck him. Your mum's worth more than any arsehole job.' He shook my hand once more. He never shook hands. He was pleased. I was not pleased. I'd lied to him, lulled him into a false security. But there was little else I could do.

Six weeks almost to the day, we sat round the bed in the small room they had put her in to die. At nine o'clock, with the Catholic priest in the room with us, she died surrounded by her husband and some of her sons. Peter was too young and had been sent home; Eddy was in Feltham Boys' Prison. When she died my father turned to us. 'I don't want any of you cunts crying. Understand?'

We said yes. So we didn't cry. She lay there shrivelled like a prune. Dark and without breath. And the priest anointed her earthly remains.

The SLL would become a huge party. The party would prepare for the inevitable revolutionary situation; it would be the vanguard of the working classes. We all toiled for the cause. Mass gatherings took place. We were all on a high – we could make this new reality; we would push ourselves in preparation for the revolutionary overthrow of the bourgeoisie. The Workers' Revolutionary Party would not be caught napping.

In preparation for the mass struggle I got a new job. I went to work at H. J. Heinz, the processed-food empire. Tessa's younger brother, John, had joined the WRP; he had left public school and thrown his lot in with the working classes. He joined me at Heinz. Brian had also joined the party, had laid aside his indifference to revolution. He too came to work in the canning department of the US conglomerate. Other WRP members joined us there. Soon six of us were among the factory workforce.

But the rest of the workforce were indifferent to the struggle. We tried to sell the *Workers' Press* but found few buyers. I felt I was wasting my time and after four months I decided to leave Heinz. I wanted to get back into printing and factory work didn't suit me. Leaving a factory caused me problems in the WRP but Terry sorted them out.

He was now our West London leader. He had the most experience. He dominated the at times slow and uncreative thinking of the branch members. He and his ex-wife Maureen would spend hours talking about the health of the party. Terry did not have a strong belief in its leadership. Doubts were soon cast about our so-called separatist nature.

Our district was better organised than others. But this was not seen as a plus; we were simply viewed with further suspicion by the central office.

I got a job with an educational publisher. I worked in the print shop and improved my skills. I loved printing and it was a good liberal business to work for. They gave me time off to draw and write. They allowed me to work a four-day week. It was perfect.

Towards the end of the year Terry and I decided to publish our own political and cultural magazine. It would soon be the bicentenary of the painter Turner's birth. We talked about launching the magazine with a special Turner issue. I contacted the Royal Academy, where the main Turner exhibition was going to be held. They encouraged me. I was allowed to go there and write up material as the exhibition was being hung. The Academy even offered to sell the magazine.

I read all I could about Turner. Terry researched the political aspects of Turner and his time. At last we had something to get our teeth into. And at last I would be the publisher of a magazine. It was to be called *Art Perspectives*. The production would be simple and the end product would be inexpensive.

Terry was struck by the power of what we were doing. I was pleased to have something tangible in my hand; something that I had helped to create.

I was in awe when I saw the first copies of *Art Perspectives*. On the cover was a red line-print of a Turner painting, upon which the title stood out in black. I took the first batch to the Royal Academy. Our magazine was displayed alongside their official catalogue. Soon they called for more stock. We sold hundreds of copies at thirty-five pence each. I distributed to bookshops throughout London, and made trips to Oxford and Cambridge. I went down to Brighton. The magazine barely covered the costs, but it was to me a great achievement.

My own writing, describing the Royal Academy's exhibition, was acceptable. But it was obviously the work of an amateur. It was Terry's background piece that really sang. I read and reread our pieces a dozen times.

Tessa called me at work one day. She seemed agitated. She wanted to meet me straight from work.

'What's the problem? Bad news?'

'No. Not at all. I just want to meet you.'

She had been ill and I was concerned that she might have some news relating to her sickness. But when I met her later Tessa was smiling.

'I'm pregnant. It's due next August.'

I nearly fainted. Tessa was twenty-two; I was twenty-eight, I would be a father again at twenty-nine.

We celebrated, but I kept thinking about my mother. I was sad that she would not see her new grandchild. That night when I went to bed I was happy and sad at one and the same time. In the middle of the night I went into the bathroom and splashed water over my face. I looked in the mirror, and my mother appeared standing behind me. But it was not a lovable mother. It was a mother with her hands held up behind me; her hands had become claws. I fainted and hit the ground with a thump. Tessa found me on the floor. I was delirious.

We worked on a new issue of *Art Perspectives* for which I wrote an article about Michelangelo. The second production was of a higher standard than the first. I had by this time left my job at the educational publishers and bought a print machine. I tried to become a self-employed printer. I got a few jobs doing drop cards for mini-cab firms. I had a small print shop behind Paddington Station. I was set up. At last I was what I had wanted to be: a printer-publisher.

And, on 12 August 1975, Patrick Jack Bird was born. The night before I had dropped Tessa at the hospital and gone off to a party educational class. At eleven I went back to the hospital to find out how Tessa was doing. She had a short labour and Paddy was born at just after one in the morning.

Terry had been right: the Workers' Revolutionary Party viewed us with ever increasing suspicion. Were we a disaffected group? Were we planning to break away and form a more efficient version of the WRP? We seemed to be everywhere. We certainly seemed to be the most successful of the WRP branches. We sold the most papers; we raised the most money; we supplied skilled people to carry out the party's requirements. Our branches were big and active – and our youth branch was enormous. At the annual Young Socialist National Conference a quarter of delegates came from the West London area.

Gerry Healey, the leader, bit the bullet. He turned on the West London branches. An enquiry was held and all evidence suggested that we were on the road to separatism. Our success was not an insurance policy; rather, our efficiency served only to highlight the inefficiencies of others. Healey had the support of most of the yes-men surrounding him. Within a matter of weeks Terry and I were out of the party.

'What do we do now?'

Terry and I contemplated the future. It could have been bleak. But Terry insisted that we should not become anti-WRP. We would still help as and when we were needed. In spite of all that Healey represented, he did provide some revolutionary continuity.

Tessa became pregnant again. Terry was also about to become a father. We knew that we all had to settle down and also move on.

Eileen Diana was born early in the morning of 15 November 1977. I cried at the beauty of it all, as I had with Paddy. I took Paddy into the hospital to see his mother and his new sister. It was the best of feelings to see the both of them together.

A few weeks later we all moved into a big old house in Acton in West London. Tessa and I, our babies and Terry. It was perfect. There were many rooms, and stables out back that I would turn into a print shop. We had weathered the storm of leaving the WRP. We had not become a reactionary anti-party rump; we had kept our integrity.

28

The machine throbbed. You could hear it from the road. A steady noise, a rhythm like a man dancing. Terry stood in the print shop looking amazed.

'How does this happen? One month and you've earnt a thousand pounds?'

I told him precisely how: you simply did what people wanted you to do. Which in our case was printing and delivering on time. There was no great art to it. Terry couldn't believe that there was this kind of money to be made from printing. But I knew that if you provided a service, people would pay for it.

It was winter, early 1978. The print shop was up and running. We had put all our efforts into making a business. The workshop had been built inside the old stable in the yard. Against the wall we had built long, waist-high benches; on there we prepared the paper for the machine. Tom, Terry's former father-in-law, worked hard. He was a retired carpenter but had the energy of a younger man. I worked with him, labouring first to convert the stable and then to renovate the house.

'Johnny, you'll have to go and get some more screws and nails. We've run out of the fuckers.'

Tom was good at the job but he seemed incapable of guessing the right amount of materials. We kept running out of everything. I'd go down to hardware shops and woodyards but I seemed always to bring the wrong wood, or wood that wasn't in good enough condition.

'It's just shit – look at it. You can't work with this.' In his thick Irish accent he would curse me.

It was fun. Tom was skilled and could easily cut and lay out the wood. He was strong, though forever complaining. About the wood that he would never have bought, or the tools.

'Never buy Korean – never. I'd rather use my fucking hands than those shit tools.'

Then he would stop and remind me how his daughter had once bought him Korean tools. He'd told me that story a hundred times. It was a kind of running joke: Tom was surrounded by idiots. And I was one of them. Terry another. And as for his daughter, well, she didn't know one end of a chisel from the other.

Each lunchtime I had to take him round the corner to the Anchor pub so that he could see his friends. There he would tell them about the shit wood he was working with and the dreadful tools he was expected to use.

But now the workshop was finished and the machine throbbed. And Terry and I were convinced that we had a business that would prosper. Perhaps we would resume our publishing work again, but we had to make money first.

We'd abandoned our publishing efforts when *Art Perspectives* died the year before. Now money-making was our priority. We needed to secure our little community; there was no one to bail us out if things went wrong.

Margaret Thatcher was going on about reviving the enterprise culture. I was a part of that culture – the culture of small businessmen who did what the big firms couldn't do. She was leading the Tory party and the Labour government were messing things up. She was campaigning, extolling the virtues of the 'little man'. Even though the election was more than a year away.

We laughed at the irony of it all. Here I was, in a shed at the bottom of the garden, so to speak, doing what Mrs Thatcher wanted everyone to do. Forgetting about class and returning to an earlier form of entrepreneurship. My little print-shop enterprise was exactly the sort of thing that the Conservatives were offering to the electorate. The little man, irrespective of class or race, could make his way in the world. And I was proving it.

Out of the blue I was reacquainted with Pete, the foreman from the printing works by Paddington Station. He was looking for work and I was sitting on a pile of stuff. He came on board.

We soon decided that most of our customers were ignorant. We were polite to their faces but between ourselves we joked at their stupidity. This was my first real business venture and it seemed so easy. It was good that the world was full of ignorant people who needed our service.

But Pete and I hadn't realised the canniness of the average middle-class customer. Once we'd given them the completed jobs they were the ones laughing. They disputed prices, they took forever to pay and they politely asked for reductions, as if they were friends. We were often the fools. We took their incessant questioning as a sign that they were interested. But largely they were conning us.

'It's so kind of you to put yourself out.'

The breathless woman stood in the print shop, smiling and praising us. She sought our advice, listened to us intently. She leant forward, pressing herself against Pete and me in turn. It was a kind of seduction. She ran a theatre company. Later she brought another attractive woman along and they both cooed at us. Made us feel special.

'We've got an Arts Council grant, so you don't have to worry about payment.'

'I'm not worried.'

We delivered the job personally. And then we waited for the money. Eventually on the telephone I got hold of one of the women, who said that the company had run out of money and I had to join the queue for payment. I called her a middle-class tosser and she hung up on me.

I dialled again. It went straight on to a machine and a message: 'You either pay us the money or I ring the Arts Council and tell them you misused the money. I want the cheque tomorrow.'

I felt angry at my own stupidity.

A day later the woman came round, not so breathless and

flattering now. She had the cheque, though. She said that the production had cost too much.

'You commissioned us; you pay.'

She slammed the yard door as she left.

Most of the jobs paid. The thing we had to learn was never to treat customers as friends; they would run you ragged if you did. We also learnt not to get done by other people in the same business. A bloke who ran a local instant-print shop offered us complex work he couldn't manage. I didn't mind when we'd done the job and I saw him wrapping it for the customer as though he'd done the work. But when I saw that he was charging the customer double what he'd paid us, I knew this sort of arrangement would get us nowhere.

We worked round the clock. Pete often slept wrapped in a blanket on the floor beside the machine. His hands were always black with printing ink. He was exhausted by the amount of work that came through the door.

He started to complain:

'It's too much work. I can't keep up with it.'

And one day in the summer he didn't turn up for work. I rang him, chased him, but never caught up with him. I never saw him again. He'd gone as quickly as he'd come.

I'd picked up many new skills but there were still jobs I couldn't do. I was exhausted. I got another printer, Alex, and even offloaded work to other printers. But we never seemed to get on top of everything; it was all a bit much. The work was getting more complex. I longed for the kind of simple jobs we'd got to start with, the ones we could knock out in a few hours. Now we were expected to help with design and even editorial matters. It seemed as though we were being pushed into everything.

Alex was more carefree than I was. He would work but he wouldn't accept my evangelical commitment to print.

'John, it's only a fucking job.'

But I had ambitions. I wanted to return to publishing. I negotiated with Oxford University Press to do a reprint of an out-of-print book.

Alex and I printed a thousand copies and sold them to bookshops and by mail order. The book proved popular and we made money. But it was tortuous doing everything ourselves.

Eileen, Terry's partner, came to work for me. She started off disinterested and indolent but her attitude changed within a matter of weeks. She learnt fast; she was thorough. I got a contract to oversee a monthly magazine, printed by a bigger company. Soon Eileen was running the job herself. She was making money for us.

I ran the print shop for two years, during which time I was cured of the desire to become the best of all commercial printers. Publishing work became the goal. We had done well out of the Oxford University Press book. From now on I would try to get work that we could control; I was tired of being blown around in chaos.

I was living with Tessa and the children but I'd begun to feel like I was marooned on an island. An island full of deadlines and panicking customers. Mrs Thatcher could keep her enterprise culture; I wasn't going to be solving the problems of others by creating my own.

I hung around after the lecture was finished. I'd read a book on Turner that the lecturer had written and I wanted to meet him. He smiled at the people who waited for him.

I introduced myself and I told him about the Turner issue of *Art Perspectives*.

Now I wanted to go a step further – to produce a magazine devoted to Turner. A magazine about Turner and his times, covering social, political and artistic matters. About Turner as the pivotal point of British art.

I'd expected the lecturer, Eric, to be like the other art historians I'd met: aloof and full of his own importance. But Eric was different. He listened politely and we chatted about other things. He said he lived out in the middle of nowhere.

'So do I. Where's your nowhere?'

'Acton.'

I laughed, told him that was my nowhere too. He was pleased that we shared the same wilderness.

We met up the next day and talked more about my ideas for the Turner magazine. He seemed interested. Later he called to tell me that people at the Tate were keen to put the gallery's name to a Turner magazine because of plans to house the Turner collection there. This was an exciting development.

Eric had meetings with the Tate. He belonged among the gallery people. He had a reputation and was working on another Turner book. When I met them I was hardly included in the discussions, but didn't mind. The Tate gave the go-ahead. But they wanted a magazine exclusively about Turner, rather than one about Turner's epoch. This new plan was of less interest to me; I wanted to do something more commercial. But Eric insisted: the Tate would not go with a more general project.

In record time we produced one of the highest-quality pieces of work that I had ever been involved in. The magazine was beautiful to look at. Its contents, though, were quite academic and lacked sparkle. I backed out after we'd produced two issues. The money was lousy and the idea wasn't broad enough to hold my interest. The Tate and I wanted different things. As far as I was concerned, they could keep their specialist magazine.

'I'm not enjoying this; I've gone off communal living.'

I said this to Tessa while we sat in a Covent Garden bar. She looked concerned.

'So what can we do?'

Our lives were entwined with Terry's. We had lived together for so long – seven years in each other's pockets. But initially we'd had a common political mission and that now seemed to have gone. Thatcher had triumphed at the recent elections and we were without political purpose. All the irritations in the house had taken on new meaning. We were just getting on with our lives.

I was thirty-four and not quite sure of what to do next. Life had become a series of holding operations. This year, 1980, seemed like the right time to put delusions about revolution behind us. I argued with Terry. I couldn't see where we were going. I wanted to do something practical. And if revolution had been removed from our horizon I might just as well focus on being a publisher/printer.

Tessa and I left our communal Acton house and set up on our own. I felt we were growing up, becoming ordinary. But that's what you did when you had two children: you did ordinary things.

I hadn't seen my daughter Emily for years. Tess and I went up to Scotland for a few days. I knew that Emily was staying with her grandparents and I was desperate to see her. I rang the house and Emily answered.

'Hello, Emily.'

'Who's that?'

'It's your father.'

There was silence, then she spoke.

'And how are you?'

Her tone was very matter-of-fact. She sounded grown-up, though she was only fourteen.

'I'm well, and how are you?'

'Great.'

'Can I come and see you?'

We met Emily the next day, on the beach at North Berwick. She looked at me shyly. She looked at me as the stranger I was. I felt awkward. I talked about how good she looked.

The day after that we took her into Edinburgh. We talked in the car. She didn't ask me where I had been. I couldn't have given her a rational explanation. I hadn't seen her since she was seven. Why had I stayed away?

She was very grown-up in a girlish sort of way. She talked about politics; about Margaret Thatcher, who had recently become Prime Minister. I was pleased with her interest in the world, but sad that I had missed an important part of her growing up. However, when Tess and I left to go back down south, I knew that Emily and I were back in each other's lives.

29

I was about to launch a new magazine in Manchester. Ross sat watching me as I prepared to leave.

'Birdy, can I come to Manchester with you? I know the town; I could be useful. And when you wanted to pop off for a pee I could stay on the stall.'

Ross was always talking about going for a 'pee'. Wherever he went he looked out for the nearest toilet. He was sixty-five now, looking like an old man. He was not hugely different from me. He could still sleep on the floor wrapped in a blanket. He could still eat leftovers. He could still go out and chat up young women. Nothing had changed except his need to pass water.

He still lived in Bristol and every time he took the bus to London he put a polythene bag around his penis and secured it with an elastic band.

He was very proud of his invention and had thought for a moment of patenting it.

I smiled at his desire to return to the city in which he had once edited a spiritualist newspaper. I said he could come with me.

'But no moaning.'

He gave me his weird smile, like a faun or a gargoyle on a cathedral roof. It was mischievous. I had to laugh at him.

Ross had come up to London to help me paint the back windows of our house. I scraped out bits of rotten wood. Ross was to fill the gaps and then paint over them. One day I went out the back and found him filling the gaps with toothpaste.

'For crying out loud, what are you doing?'

'I ran out of that poly stuff. This is perfectly adequate.'

He argued with me when I took away the toothpaste and gave him more filler. In the end I had to tell him that toothpaste was more expensive than Polyfilla, just to shut him up.

Now he was coming to Manchester with me for the launch of the *Art Book Review.*

Eric and I had gone into partnership with his friend Gerald. We would produce a quarterly book review. Gerald would put up the money, Eric would edit the magazine and I would be the publisher and printer. I would also design and distribute it, sell advertising and occasionally write articles. We were launching it at the Art History Book Fair in Manchester.

The magazine was beautiful. It was simply laid out, and had a glossy, coloured cover. I looked at the first issue and knew I was doing exactly what I wanted to do. I was producing the best art magazine in Britain. It had been my idea; I had come up with the concept and the name. I was happier than I had been for a long time.

Eric and I had had a few fights. He didn't understand the complexities of launching a new magazine. One time I grabbed him by the throat and he hit me with a bottle of Lucozade. It was a simple dust up, just came and went. Like me, he was impressed by the look of the first issue. Though we'd had many obvious teething problems.

'Where's the fucking contents page?' Eric held the magazine open. 'There's no contents page. How are people going to find their way around?'

'It's a journey of discovery.'

He laughed, said, 'Fuck it. We'll live with it.'

I'd forgotten about the contents page. We had a stirring editorial, but no contents page.

Ross and I drove to Manchester. He had worked there, in the early 1950s, as editor of the *Spiritualist News*. Ross had worked on many newspapers and he'd also been an actor. His stories were legion, and he always gave them an original spin.

'Apart from my adventures with Dylan Thomas and Kate McNamara in Cornwall, I think working on the *Spiritualist News* was the happiest time of my life.'

Ross claimed to have given Dylan and Kate the ten shillings for the licence to get married in a registry office in Penzance.

The book fair was being held at the university. We had a small stand, which we loaded with copies of the *Art Book Review*. Almost everyone who walked by looked at the magazine and asked for a free copy. There was much excitement. People asked about subscriptions and I told them about a special introductory offer. But most seemed to want to leave it until later to order.

I was pleased with the interest but disturbed by the lack of subscriptions. By the end of the day we had a handful of orders and had given away about a hundred copies of the magazine.

The following day more people attended the fair and we sold more subscriptions. Interest in the magazine seemed to be greater. Ross stayed at the stall while I went round to talk to other publishers about advertising. Everyone seemed impressed by the magazine. I got back to our stand to find Ross telling a young woman about his polythene-bag device. She smiled politely.

Despite our efforts, though, the *Art Book Review* never really took off. We released seven issues and then ceased production. The printing business wasn't for me. I continued to take on jobs but I subcontracted the work to other printers. And I'd had my fingers burnt in publishing. I thought long and hard around my thirty-seventh birthday. I finally decided to enrol as a mature student. Perhaps a few years spent in a place of learning would freshen me up. I was tired of business and I was tired of being the linchpin. I wanted to coast for a while.

I had been reading Walt Whitman. Ross had given me a book of extracts from *Leaves of Grass*. And then I read a biography of him. Whitman had been an inspiration to me in my youth, and I now felt pleased to discover that he too had wandered apparently lost for the first thirty-six years of his life. I thought we had a lot in common: he'd been a printer, a writer, a social commentator and an activist. Once again he became an inspiration.

Ealing College was a bike ride away from my house. If I was going to go anywhere it had to be convenient. I had a family and some business responsibilities. The humanities course suited my interests. English, music, geography and American studies. It would be like filling the gaps in my education. I could spend three years floating about and writing.

I was accepted for the course. Ealing had many mature students so I wouldn't be lost in a sea of youngsters. I spent the summer reading Whitman and awaiting the new turn my life was going to take.

Paddy didn't want to go to the beach.

'It's boring, Dad.'

We were in Cornwall for a week, Tess, Paddy, Diana and I. Paddy was eight and, like me, he didn't like sand and sun. He wanted to go roaming in nearby Truro. So I drove him into town; after we'd had tea, and rolled pennies on the shiny floor of the cathedral, we sat outside and read.

The weather became overcast as Paddy and I sat reading. Then suddenly Tess appeared with Diana. Tessa went off to phone London and I looked after the kids. Then I looked up from my book and she was runnning towards me with a fearful look on her face.

'Your dad's died.'

'What?'

'I've just been told. He died this morning. Your brother Pete was with him.'

I got up and walked around. Paddy and Diana held my hands, trying to show sympathy about something they didn't understand. I thought of the old man of sixty-five, just retired. I thought about our days in Notting Hill. I thought of how unhappy he had been since my mother had died, ten years before. I remembered him sitting with us by his dead wife. What else should I think? What should I do?

Weeks later, I woke up suddenly from a dream. My father was a young man again. He stood on the balcony outside our Fulham flat. He had that good smile of his, a knowing smile. I woke up crying, realising that I would never see this contradictory man again. He wore a white shirt with the sleeves rolled up, showing his powerful labourer's arms. I lay in bed glad, in a way, that I had begun to feel something. Up until then I had just felt empty.

At the funeral I had cracked jokes with my Uncle Tom. I had played the master of ceremonies with apparent lack of feeling. But now his image had come back to me and I was glad that I had felt like this about him. About this contradictory man.

Tessa dropped me on the first morning. She smiled at my agitation and said, 'Cheer up, freshman.' Then she drove away.

All the first-year students gathered to listen to a course organiser telling us of the advantages of an education at Ealing. He talked about all the extra studies and training that we could do – in languages and business studies, in theatre and music groups and in sport. I was surprised at the range of opportunity and at how well organised everything was. It would be hard work, and any ideas I'd had about cruising through now evaporated. We had to produce a dozen essays a term; we had to attend lectures and go to tutorials. This was not going to be a holiday. Those people who did not commit themselves fully could be removed from the course. Our studies would be rewarding, but we had to do the work.

Bernie was an artist and guitarist. He had a face like a kabuki mask, with thick black hair and beard. He had a permanent supply of comic comments. I met him the first day and knew we would be friends. He was a few years younger than me and he had the natural charm of a leader.

Caroline was tall and blonde and had worked in a bank. She was in her early twenties and didn't seem to mind going around with people who were older than her. We became a kind of threesome. It was a good experience. We would meet for coffee and share notes, study together sometimes. It was how I imagined university life at Oxford might be, but I had not expected it to happen at a suburban college. I took Spanish, English, history, geography and music for the first year. There was an art-history department but I had no desire to get involved. I wanted to put art history behind me.

The careful dissecting of poetry was an eye-opener. I began to realise that I knew little about literature, though I had always posed as well read. I took it all very seriously once I realised how ignorant I was. I found the history course most difficult, because I thought I knew as much as the lecturer.

I soon established that my priority should be to perfect my essay-writing. I struggled within the constraints dictated by the lecturers. They wanted cogency, not waffle. I realised that much of my writing offered the latter. We were constantly brought back to the first principles of presenting an argument: to provide thorough explanation of the points being made and to back up everything with example. I realised soon that my grasp of history was as awry as anything else. And that my arguments were never clearly explained.

My attitude would need to take a sharp turn in order for me to succeed. I would have to let go of many preconceptions about my intellectual superiority. I would have to recognise that I had arrived at thirty-seven with a smattering of opinions that would not stand up to scrutiny. I was a waffler.

Within a few weeks I had begun to lose some of my sense of self-importance. I was just another middle-aged man who thought he knew more than he knew. I had to become humble, and that was the difficult part. How was a former slum boy, ex-offender, ex-runaway, publisher and self-employed printer to learn that he had a lot to learn? And probably from people who hadn't experienced the sort of troubles I had lived through.

*

I had written a short play called *Dreams on a Dancehall Floor*. Writing plays seemed like the best way to write with a purpose. I thought I could write plays that would get shown. I had been going to the theatre and thought I could produce something as good as the hundreds of plays being performed in the little pub theatres of London. I heard about a playwright group at the Riverside Studios in Hammersmith.

I submitted *Dreams on a Dancehall Floor* and then went down to meet the group's co-ordinator. You were required to submit a piece before you could be considered for membership. It was a kind of audition for me.

The co-ordinator was a small man with a moustache. As he talked he played with his moustache. He told me that my play had been accepted; I could join the group. But he said he had some reservations about it.

'I think it shows you have a skill for writing. I just doubt the integrity of the play. It's a kind of small Brecht pastiche.'

'So I can join but you're not happy?'

'I'm happy for you to join. But I feel you could probably do better. This piece is "clever". That's all it is.'

I had written the play in a day. It was set in post-war Germany and was about a woman who claimed to her pro-Nazi boyfriend that she was pregnant with Hitler's child. The simplicity of the writing made me feel that it was a good play. And I didn't want this squat man telling me that I was just being clever. But then he told me that the group's purpose was to develop talent. That talent often came unfocused and the group was there to help focus it.

It was apparent that the group was largely made up of people who worked hard on their writing, though a number of actors and talkers also attended. These were committed writers who were desperate for informed comment. We would listen to a rehearsed reading by professional actors and then we would discuss the chosen play's strengths and weaknesses.

Eddie was Irish. He had a soft, almost inaudible voice and had long hair but a balding head. He ran a travelling theatre company that toured in an old Post Office van. He was a fierce advocate of his countless plays.

Sam was another Irishman. He had recently written a play about a painter who used to take Turner out on the river. I went to the bar with him and Eddie after my first session with the group. I got the impression that they didn't like each other. Eddie did all of the talking while Sam and I looked on.

Eddie asked us what we'd thought of the play. Sam said he thought it was all right and I agreed. Eddie wasn't having it.

'It was just another pile of middle-class crap.'

He then set about demolishing every aspect of the play. Sam and I looked at each other. Eddie reminded me of myself.

A few weeks later it was my play that was read for the group. I listened to the rehearsed reading and thought it was reasonable. It was generally well received. Only Eddie had a sour point to make. He saved it for in the bar afterwards.

'Couldn't see the point of it. But at least it's not just another piece of middle-class shit about someone who can't get a screw.'

He laughed, pleased with his damning praise. I decided that I kind of liked Eddie. I liked his anger. I felt that it saved me from assuming a similar role in the group. Eddie could be the one to snap at the heels of the middle classes.

It was the morning after the night of the big storm. October 1987. The phone rang and Paddy picked it up.

'It's Angie for you, Dad.'

Angie had recently married my brother Pat. I thought that perhaps a tree had fallen on their house or something. They lived on the edge of London and I imagined they would be badly hit by the storm.

'Angie, how's things? You had trees down?'

Silence. Then she said, 'No, Tony, it's Pat.'

Angie always called me Tony. Pat still called me Tony. He could never get used to the fact that for more than twenty years I had been called John.

'Pat?'

It wasn't the trees and the high winds.

'He died last night.'

I shouted. Pat. The boy who was two years older than me. The one who had so much trouble in his life. A broken family. Health problems. The one who I still could laugh with, as we had as children. The milkman, builder, stoker, cowboy plumber.

I sat in the bedroom, stunned. Pat had been ill for years. A heart attack, and then a stroke. But I never imagined that he would die. I could not see how.

A few weeks before I had taken the Underground to Uxbridge and then cycled the seven miles to Chorleywood, where he lived. He was bright, helpful. He complained of hearing problems and the inability to watch TV. But I had joked with him.

'Most people talk shit and the TV's crap.'

He'd laughed hysterically, said, 'You should be a fucking therapist.'

I always made him laugh. Since his stroke I had got him to laugh at himself. When he had been in a rehabilitation unit and wouldn't get out of bed I had gone down to see him.

'Get out of bed, you lazy sod. Get in that swimming pool.'

I had pulled him out of bed because I knew he had to do things. There was no fooling around. He could either work at rehabilitation or get thrown out of the unit.

'Costs thousands to keep arseholes like you in this place. And you want to lay in bed.'

I got him into the swimming pool. I got him moving. I shouted at him and told him not to feel sorry for himself. He laughed as he struggled with the water.

He responded. He got some kind of health. He was strong. He didn't sit around when he left hospital. Angie and Pat got married. It was beautiful to see him getting better, getting some life together.

They had a dog and he walked the dog for miles around the fields and parks of Chorleywood. He did his best.

Now he was dead.

There was a Catholic funeral. Though Pat was a lapsed Catholic, he would have appreciated the fact that it was a Catholic service. Pat never quite gave up on his faith; he was always reminding me, 'Once a Catholic always a Catholic'.

After the service he was to be buried in the lawn cemetery on the edge of the small country town. It was a bright but bleak day. The land around Chorleywood bore the signs of the heavy storm. As the burial began, a taxi pulled up. I turned to see my brother Richard getting out of the cab.

He walked straight over to me, ignoring the service. His face was angry.

'Throw the key away, cunt?'

'What?'

'Throw the key away. That's what you said.'

He was referring to a phone call I had received from a policeman a few months before. Richard was being held in a cell for stealing videos from a shop in Kingston. The policeman had asked me whether I'd put up the bail money. I'd said I wouldn't do it; I'd said they could lock the cell and throw the key away. Now, here he stood, angry about my lack of concern for him.

But there was more to it than that. Richard had hit the skids. I wasn't prepared to hold him up when he wasn't prepared to help himself.

'We're burying your brother, brother.'

It was as though he suddenly realised where he was. He said sorry. He looked around him, turned just in time to see Pat's coffin being lowered into the grave.

Later, at Pat and Angie's place, Richard asked me about my flippant comment.

'Look, mate, every time I meet you you're sorting your life out.

Am I going to listen to your bullshit? And throw five hundred quid away?'

'I would have turned up for court.'

'Like you did last time. And the time before.'

He knew I was right. I told him he needed help. I thought that the sooner he got sent down for a long stretch, the better. Then he would get some help. The money hadn't been the issue. I just wasn't going to be like other members of the family, propping him up all the time.

Pat was dead. That was a reality. Richard could be next, if he didn't get the help he needed.

A few nights later I stood looking at myself in the bathroom mirror. Suddenly my face turned into Pat's face. Patrick Finbarr Bird stood smiling at me – a slight smile, roguish, as it used to be. But, this time, unlike when my mother died and she appeared in the mirror, I felt no terror. I didn't fall down. I looked at Pat and smiled. He just looked and looked, without bitterness or pain. Poor Pat, I found myself saying. Poor stupid, dopey Pat. Pat, who had claimed that, like Jesus Christ, he sometimes sweated blood. Who had claimed that America was part of Europe – and my father had agreed with him, so I got a whack for contradicting them. Pat, who had put up an artificial ceiling in the office of one of my print customers. And it had fallen down in the middle of the night, costing me the print contract. Pat, who at twelve had thrown me against the wall of our front room and given me one of the many bumps I had on my nose.

I must have been outraged and angry about Pat's death. For the first time in years I found myself wandering drunk around the streets of Notting Hill, almost looking for fights. Walking to where we had lived and lived no more. Every Bird had been removed from Notting Hill and Portobello. The area had become posh; its little streets formed some new privileged zone. Only white liberals and poor blacks in council housing lived there now. None of the Irish, none of the scum I had come from. Notting Hill as I'd known it was a fiction. It had never existed.

I was invited to a party and arrived there at four in the morning. I was mad drunk. I smashed the top off a wine bottle and drank from the broken neck. The hostess who had wanted me to come, who had insisted for weeks, looked at me with different eyes. The wine ran down my white T-shirt. I was asked to leave. Two men grabbed me. I hit one with my head, knocking him down. The other ran away. Then I cried. From conviviality to aggression to self-pity in record time.

Later I slept on the doorstep of our house.

I had always been angry. The kids and Tessa saw that anger. I would punch walls, smash doors with my head. I would shout and rage at Tessa and Paddy. I would frighten my own. I was a bully. I knew that the thing I had hated most throughout my life was bullying. But now I realised that I was a bully. Something I'd thought I'd never be. Perhaps it was Pat's death that brought all this out, this recognition that I wasn't just some sweet-tempered person who had come up from under. Perhaps I was like my father after all. I did not punch but I terrorised with my bitterness; it amounted to the same thing. I used my tongue instead of my fists.

The bitterness did not pass. It was a recurring problem. And I was drinking more than I had ever drunk. It was 1988 and I seemed to be marking time. I was forty-two and going nowhere.

The Workers' Revolutionary Party factionalised and disintegrated further. Gerry Healey lost support among the leadership. There were charges levelled at him about certain members' young daughters. It was claimed by some that security services and the Special Branch had infiltrated the party to destroy it. The splits were bitter and Healey was thrown out.

Though I was no longer a WRP member, I had continued to go to party meetings. I viewed the organisation as increasingly useless. The imminent fall of capitalism remained the obsession. Every financial crisis or strike was going to cause the final break that would destroy the system. The sense of urgency was lost on me; I was glad that I wasn't involved.

One day I got a phone call from Maureen, Terry's ex-wife. A WRP member called Stewart had died.

Stewart had been in the Shepherd's Bush branch when I was a member and we'd worked closely together. He had been a photographer in his native Jamaica before coming to Britain in 1962. He'd joined the party in 1969 and, though he was educated and well read, became something of a party workhorse. He was not respected and was seen as some kind of low-life hack. But I liked him; he was good, interesting company.

He had remained loyal to the party long after I had strayed. I would still see him at meetings. He always called me a traitor, a petit bourgeois, but never in any way that I took seriously. Given the way he was treated, it was perhaps odd that Stewart stuck with the party. But it was his life; he would have been lonely and lost without it. It was only when he got a girlfriend, towards the end of his life, that anything made him feel at home in cold, heartless, racist Britain.

When I learnt that he was dead I wanted to go to his funeral because I had respected him and knew that he had suffered in an empty world.

Brian came with me. The funeral was being held in Wales, where Stewart had gone to live with his girlfriend. Maureen drove us there. On the way, we composed a valedictory speech for Maureen to give at the service. I told her a story that Stewart had told me on countless occasions.

When he'd first come to England he couldn't understand the English. He saw all these grubby-looking, badly dressed people with their bad teeth and bad complexions and thought they looked like they lived underground. Then one day he overheard a couple talking. This, Stewart said, was his first insight into the English mentality. The woman had said to the man, 'D'you love me, Alf?' The man answered, 'Course I love yer, Elsie.' Then the woman giggled and said, 'If you love me, Alf, knock us about a bit, knock us about.'

Maureen couldn't understand the significance.

'It doesn't have a significance. It's just a little human touch; Stewart thinking that English women liked to be knocked about a bit.'

A row was going on when we arrived outside the chapel where Stewart's funeral was to take place. The undertakers were arguing with two groups of people who were trying to grab Stewart's coffin. Stewart's girlfriend was stuck in the middle of it all. This was about politics. The two groups belonged to opposing sides of the WRP and were arguing about where Stewart's loyalty had fallen. Both groups claimed him as their comrade and both groups felt they should carry his coffin. It looked like a fight was about to break out.

This was not the place for a political debate. Both groups could carry the coffin: three comrades from each group on either side. Simple. I shouted loudly above the din and like well-behaved children they followed my instruction.

Driving home afterwards we discussed what had happened. Maureen thought it showed great disrespect. Brian thought it showed that the class struggle carried on regardless. I thought it showed that the party comprised a mass of leaderless fools.

30

'God, that's Gordon Roddick.'

'Who?'

'That one there. The one with the nose.'

'Is he a friend of yours, Dad?'

'He was.'

Paddy and I were watching the early-evening news. It was summer. Paddy was waiting for some tennis scores. I was passing time. Gordon Roddick, Chairman of The Body Shop. An international businessman, wealthy and successful. And an old friend from Edinburgh; the man I'd nearly fought in Paddy's Bar.

I rang Gordon the next day. A few weeks later I went down to see him. Now he was this big powerful businessman and I was someone who may or may not make it. Our chat was interrupted by other people. I left feeling annoyed.

Then I came home one evening and Tessa told me that Gordon had called. When I rang him back he launched into conversation as though we'd just been speaking. No recognition that we had only met once in twenty years. He said that a friend of his had written a book that needed a bit of tidying up. He thought I could do it. It seemed like an interesting idea and I had nothing much on. Rewriting someone else's work might help keep the wolf from the door.

I had just had my forty-fourth birthday and there had seemed little to celebrate. I'd been doing a few small printing jobs to make ends meet. I felt I was on the road to nowhere. Gone were the politics and the ideas about making a big impact on society. My own writing had floundered. I'd given up on the playwrights' group because I couldn't work with actors; they seemed so dumb. I was now trying to start up another magazine, but nothing solid was happening. Perhaps helping Gordon would change things for me.

I arranged to meet him. He met me at Arundel Station and we drove into the countryside. He asked me what I was up to. I told him about my magazine idea and mentioned a story I had written, *Dickens the Socially Mobile Cat*. Gordon laughed as I summed up this Victorian spoof about the dangers of social mobility.

We met with a friend of his in a local pub. I became relaxed. Gordon was easy to be with. His friend knew the writer of the book I was to work on and we discussed its contents. It was a pleasant enough evening. Gordon didn't want to talk business, he wasn't interested in talking about him and Anita and The Body Shop, their big international company.

I agreed to help rewrite the book. I would help with that and Gordon would pay me. I left for London at the crack of dawn, feeling good about the fact that Gordon had some time for me. Thinking that at least I wasn't just one of the many who had crawled out of the woodwork since he'd become successful.

In fact, of course, I was.

Working on the book was fun. It was a great story, about a failed plan to blow away the main character. I sent parts of the rewritten story to Gordon and he loved it.

We met again. I went down to Littlehampton and he had more time for me. I think he was happy to have me as a friend again. He told me that I hadn't changed – apart from my grey hair and thicker build. He said that he thought I was still as angry as he remembered me being when I was a revolutionary poet. I met Anita again and she hadn't changed in all those years.

Work on the book progressed. I rang Gordon and told him that I wanted to start a publishing company. I had a friend who knew about book publishing and I wanted Gordon to help me get a few books out.

'What do you want to publish first?'

'*Dickens the Socially Mobile Cat.*'

He thought for a moment, then said, 'OK. We'll do that.'

I put the phone down and told Tessa the good news: Gordon was interested in helping me to start up a publishing business. We were on the way.

I worked through most of the summer on the cat book. I got an illustrator and a distributor on board. Gordon gave me the money and we began production.

In June 1990 Gordon went to New York. He was walking through midtown Manhattan when he was approached by a man selling a street paper called *Street News*. Gordon bought a copy and talked to the guy. He had just come out of a penitentiary and didn't want to go back to his neighbourhood. He didn't want to go back to where he might get into trouble again. Gordon was impressed with the man's story. When he came back to England it was all he would talk about.

He got The Body Shop Foundation to research the viability of starting a street paper in London. At the time London was full of homeless people. Full of young people begging and sleeping in doorways. Gordon seemed to be obsessed by the idea of creating a London street paper for homeless people to sell. He told me one day that he'd put a bloke called Richard in touch with me; he wanted to pick my brains.

Richard was a nice bloke. We met for a drink and he asked me if I thought a street paper would work. I said I didn't think so. The distribution would be a strategic nightmare. Richard had spoken with almost everyone involved in working with the homeless. Then he produced his report for The Body Shop Foundation. Most of the homeless organisations thought that a street paper wouldn't work. Some said that homeless people couldn't be trusted to spend the money wisely.

As a result of the report's findings, Gordon put the idea on the back-burner. But he kept going on about it every time I met him.

For Christmas Tess, Paddy, Diana and I went with another family to Portugal. We spent Christmas Day on an Atlantic Ocean beach, then we travelled down to the south of the country. I found the holiday boring, as I did most holidays. I sat on the beach and imagined what 1991 would bring us. I was not too hopeful. I was having problems with the distribution of my cat book. I couldn't see Gordon's support continuing if the publishing business failed. The new year looked bleak from that beach in the Algarve.

In March I went to visit Gordon, just to socialise. Nigel, the author of the book I was rewriting, was with us. Gordon took Nigel, Anita and me to a restaurant. I wanted to talk to Gordon privately about further publishing, but he wasn't interested. He pushed aside my attempts to talk about other books we could try to publish. There was something else he wanted to talk about.

'I don't see why you don't do this street paper. You're just the person.'

Anita and Nigel were deep in conversation. The Gulf War had recently ended and they were discussing what would come next. I looked at Gordon and tried once again to focus his attention on my publishing ideas. My efforts went unnoticed. He said I should do the street paper.

'You've got all the credentials. You know about printing, magazines. You've been homeless, on the run. You're just the bloke.'

I thought he was crazy. What would I want to do with some charity idea? I hated charities. I had had my bellyful of do-gooders. The orphanage alone was enough to turn me against the idea of imposed charity.

'And who said anything about a charity?' He wanted me to conduct my own feasibility study, as a business. It was his big idea for the streets. I smiled at him. I would do it for money. We agreed some terms: he'd pay me to work on a report for six weeks, two days a week. The daily rate was half what I asked for.

Back at his house, Gordon carried on about the street paper. He said it would help keep people out of trouble. I still wasn't convinced that I was the right person to help him. But he seemed to think I was.

'If you're not good for this, then I don't know what you're good for.'

On the train home the next day, I thought about the feasibility study. Where would I start? I wrote down who I would talk to. First of all, homeless people. I'd see if they wanted to sell a paper on the streets. I would talk to the police and tell them what we were doing. I would talk to Richard at The Body Shop about his own report.

I spent the next week talking to homeless people. I talked to beggars and those who simply sat, defeated. The social climate was becoming difficult for Britain's homeless. Newspapers were going on about aggressive beggars. The government and the police were talking about removing homeless people from the streets.

One day I stopped a boy sitting near Hungerford Bridge. I persuaded him to come to a cafe with me and answer some questions. He'd looked at me suspiciously at first, thinking I was a policeman. But he agreed to speak to me. He was about twenty. He looked rough. He was white and thin-looking. His thick blond hair looked unwashed. He slouched as he sat sipping a Coke, leaning forward to sip it from the table as though he couldn't lift the glass.

I had already spoken to about twenty homeless people. I had no idea what a feasibility study contained, but I figured that this was as good as anything.

I explained the idea to the boy. It would be a street paper, sold by homeless people; they'd sell the paper and make money from doing so.

'We haven't quite worked out the details. I'm just going round getting homeless people's opinions.'

He suggested that I go down to Lincoln's Inn Fields. He said there were hundreds of homeless people down there. He slept on the Strand.

I asked him what he thought of the street-paper idea.

'Selling? Anything's better than begging.'

It was a good way of looking at it.

He had given me a slogan. I didn't have a name for the paper; I didn't know how it would work, *if* it would work. But now I had a slogan: 'Anything is better than begging'. Something to push in the faces of all those people who said that homeless people were lazy sods who *wanted* to beg.

Over the previous few days, some homeless people had told me to piss off. Some had said that I was just another do-gooder. But now this boy had told me something that would be useful. I could rally people together with his words.

He asked for another Coke. I got him a cheese and pickle sandwich too. His hands shook. I watched him eat, feeling like I should help him. 'So how did you become homeless?'

'I was in care. My mum dumped me. Then I got abused. I kept getting in trouble. I was in a hostel, then I started having problems.'

I wasn't a social worker so there was no point in asking him what he was on. He was taking something nasty – heroin, probably. I couldn't see the skin on his arms, but he reminded me of people I had known in Scotland; thin, emaciated, too young to look the way he did.

We sat for half an hour. He didn't smile. He didn't warm up. He just sat and talked and looked listless. Afterwards, outside the cafe a young girl came charging up to him.

'Where the fuck have you been?'

He pointed to me, said, 'Talking to this bloke.'

She looked terrible. Rough and dirty, unfed and angry. She looked me up and down. When I told her about the street paper she snarled and pulled the man away. She looked back at me.

'You look like a fucking queer to me.'

Then the boy turned back to me, asked if I could spare some money. I gave him a fiver and the girl looked angrier still. As I walked away I heard her scream at him, the way an angry mother might turn on a child.

I went to Scotland Yard and spoke to the police community-liaison officer. I had my fears about going, having always seen the police as the opposition. I felt strange, asking them to help. But the officer was interested when I told him that we could convert beggars to earners.

'A unique way of limiting begging.' He smiled at the thought.

He asked me how we'd control things. Homeless people, he said, were a law unto themselves. I hadn't thought about this one. So I answered off the top of my head.

'We'll give each of them a badge. With a photograph.'

We discussed the legality of selling on the street. I had a photocopy of the Pedlars Act of 1875, which said that the selling of publications on the street was legal. The policeman was impressed.

'Where did you get that from?'

'Someone in your office sent it to me.'

He smiled again. He must have thought me efficient. But I was learning as I went along.

Janet Newman and Mary Asprey were working with the Suzi Lamplugh Trust. Suzi's mother had set up the trust when her daughter went missing. Janet and Mary worked with young street-dwellers. They too were interested in the street-paper idea. They introduced me to young street people and we discussed the benefits of offering them a way to make money. Many of these young people were selling their bodies so they could buy food.

Richard recommended that I visit London Connection, next to St Martin-in-the-Fields, a programme and drop-in centre for young homeless people. Richard's contact there was Pete, a man with a lot of experience in dealing with homeless youths. Pete put me in touch with a friend of his, Andy, who worked for a large publishing house. He thought that Andy might help me with design of the magazine.

I spent hours talking with Andy, about the paper's design and content. It was still without a name but I thought that its byline could be: 'Coming up from the streets'. Andy had designed many magazines and knew a great deal. He helped me set in my mind what kind of publication this could be.

After a while, though, it became apparent that Pete from London Connection had his doubts about me. He wasn't sure that I should be the one doing this. I knew nothing about homelessness beyond my own experience of being homeless in my younger days. We talked but I could see that he wasn't convinced about my suitability for the job. He thought the project was a good idea, but not with me running it.

'Gordon, I think I can do this street paper.'

'What made you change your mind?'

'Well, I've talked to homeless people. I got the feeling that it would work.'

'So you now want to do it?'

'I do. I can't see a homeless organisation running it.'

'Well, give us the report and let's get on with it.'

I met with Richard the day before the meeting. Richard was full of ideas. He told me what to write; he knew how to present it. We laboured till midnight and in the morning I went down to Littlehampton for the meeting. The meeting was run by Gordon. There were a few dissenters among those present but the report was accepted. I was given the go-ahead. The Body Shop would put up the money, but the paper would be independent. I could use The Body Shop name to open doors, but once the paper was up and running I would be on my own.

After the meeting Gordon took me into his office.

'Well, you're off.'

'I hope so.'

He shook my hand.

I said, 'You've got a lot of belief in me.'

'I have. You're hungry. You're rather ruthless. You'll get it up and going. So get on with it.'

At home that night I sat with Tessa and a few of her friends. We talked about the street paper. Tessa was pleased that I now had a big project. I would get a wage, and I could put all the things I knew about publishing and printing to use. It made sense, in a strange way. Even the fact that I'd been homeless and a runaway began to make sense.

I had met Phil through a mutual friend. I called him a few days after The Body Shop meeting. We'd been talking about starting up a literary magazine and I thought he'd like to come on board with the street paper instead. I told him it was sponsored by The Body Shop.

'Really? It's not a peppermint-foot-lotion digest? "Great shampoos I have used."'

I went over to see him on a Saturday morning. We sat in his living room and talked the idea through. Phil had loads of ideas. I showed him copies of *Street News* from New York. He wasn't impressed.

'I hope this isn't our model.'

'No, far from it. This will be well produced.' The idea was to produce something that wouldn't be a pity-purchase. We wanted people to buy it because they wanted to read it, not because they felt sorry for the person selling it. It was not to be a homeless paper; it was to be a paper sold by homeless people. We needed to fill it with good journalism, arts news, all the big social ideas, and we wanted to include some homeless people's writings in the editorial. The better the paper was, the more copies would be sold. So it would become a good source of income to the homeless sellers.

I had come up with a new slogan. 'A magazine that the homeless are proud to sell and the public are pleased to buy.' But we still needed a title. Finally we settled on the *Big Issue*. Once we had decided on the name, we knew we had it. Having a title kind of gave the idea new meaning.

'So what do you want me to do?'

Phil was a guitarist. He performed in clubs and bars and with bands. He also ran the London Emergency Volunteers, a rescue and first-aid group. He had no experience in publishing and distribution. But he had a great ability to get on with things. He had energy and humour, both of which we would need a lot of. He was cool and apparently unflappable. We enjoyed each other's company. I had a feeling, even though I had not yet worked with him, that he would be reliable. I wanted him to be my deputy.

'Deputy editor and also all-round deputy. You do what I can't do. We share the work. I'm the boss but you're my Number Two.'

'When do we start?'

It was now early May 1991. I had one helper. We needed to produce a dummy of the *Big Issue*. We needed to get an office. It was decided that I would spend most of the next month getting the dummy issue together. Then, at the end of the month, Phil would join the staff and we would get an office in Richmond.

Andy devoted hours of his time to getting the dummy issue right. When we were happy with it I took it to The Body Shop and showed it to Gordon and Anita. I talked to them about Phil's proposed input and they seemed happy enough. Anita had got some of her staff working on ideas. I was introduced to her press department, who would help co-ordinate the launch. Things were moving. Gordon, the main man, was happy.

After looking at a number of small offices in Richmond, Phil and I chose one on the green. It was a small, basement office, separated from a lawyer's office above. The building's manager asked what our business was and how were we financed. She was pleased to hear about our relationship with The Body Shop. The building was situated between two pubs. I was happy about that – we could hold meetings in the pubs if there was not enough room to do so in the office.

Early September was our launch date. We had three months to get ready. I felt that an extended deadline would serve only to slow us down. I wanted everything to be pushed ahead as quickly as possible. In that three months we would finalise the design and contents of the paper. That would be the easy part. The difficult part would be getting the team together to work with the homeless. And getting the homeless to sign up.

The month of June was passing quickly. With each passing day we seemed to be no further forward than the day before. We spoke to homeless people and realised that the more we spoke to them the more they said, 'Come back when you've done it.'

We began to think that we had bitten off more than we could chew.

Gordon was the only one to seem confident. He talked breezily on the phone, asking how we were doing.

'We're doing all right.'

'You'll get there.'

'I hope. There're so many obstacles.'

'That's what you need. If you had no obstacles you wouldn't learn how to do it.'

'You are a fine logician.'

He laughed. I was scared. I put the phone down and looked at our naked little office, bereft of human activity. I went for a planning coffee with Phil.

The paperwork looked good. The feasibility report showed an effortless transition from idea to realisation. But these first few weeks seemed like murder. It was like wanting to start an engine and being unable to find the start button.

Phil went off on a tour of homeless organisations. He went to talk to people like Pete at the London Connection. We met a homeless poet called Sky who was full of ideas. He started to gather some writing from homeless people for us, using the London Connection. Pete may not have liked me but he was useful. And Andy kept helping us to refine the paper.

One day he pointed out what should have been obvious: 'It's not a paper. It may look like a paper, but it's a magazine. You have to stop thinking of it as a paper.'

The format was to be tabloid, printed on newsprint. I had this idea that it would be busy, like a newspaper. But Andy was saying something simple. He said that it should be like a magazine: less immediate, more thoughtful; a more leisurely read.

'And it has to last. Longer articles.'

Andy was demonstrative, throwing his arms around. I watched him as he stared off into space imagining this magazine that had yet to be published.

Phil had further discussions with the police. I talked to the business people, the advertisers who would support us, the friends of The Body Shop we could persuade to help us.

In late June a young woman from Sussex University came to see us. Alex knew about street papers and we sat and listened intently to what she had to say. I had tried to talk to the founder of *Street News* but we hadn't hit it off. Alex, though, had been to New York to interview him. She'd spent time with him, and told us that we definitely wouldn't get anything from him. As Alex talked I felt that her experiences could be invaluable to us.

She asked if she could be a volunteer – she was free until October. She seemed to think we could use her help.

She said, 'John, my dear friend, it is early July. In precisely two months and one week you will be launching the most important innovation since the invention of the ice cream on a stick . . .'

Things gradually began to happen. We had some writers. We had a designer working with Andy. We had two new assistants running the office: VJ and Sophie. But the phone wasn't ringing; it seemed no one was interested in what we were doing. Our little office still seemed lifeless. VJ and Sophie went out to do some market research, which meant asking the public what they thought of homeless people selling a street magazine. The results told us nothing.

Gordon asked me if Nigel, his writer friend, could be of any use.

I said yes, eventually. Nigel came down to see us. He would be our driver and general helper. He was overjoyed to be given the chance to work with us.

Phil was commissioning articles. I was doing the business. And slowly the machine started to turn. VJ and Sophie were now answering the phone. As word got out that in a matter of months we would be launching, the press began to call. I did a few interviews on the radio. People came to the office to find out what all the talk was about. Alex was doing most of the promotion. Now each day we seemed to achieve more.

But there was still the problem of distribution. We had decided to work out of the back of a van, in the West End. Nigel had the van, but we needed someone to help us to work directly with homeless people. I wasn't sure where to look. Then one day as I sat in the office the answer stood before me: my youngest brother.

He was a live wire, he was a hard worker and he was looking for a job. He'd come to the office to tell me what I should do. With his continuous talking and constant joking, I could see him doing the job. Peter was energetic almost to the point of madness.

'Look, Tony, I can do this fucking job standing on my head. I'll put all the papers from the printers in my garage. And I'll drop them around to the homeless.'

We bought another van so that a friend of Phil's could do another round. We would have a van somewhere in the West End at all times, touring the places where homeless people congregated. Now I felt positive. We had a team. We had a magazine. And we had about six weeks.

I was exhausted. We worked through the night to get everything ready. We were a team of obsessives. The woman who owned the building began to complain; our hours were too late and too long. The phone rang all the time now, and there was a constant stream of visitors to the office. We did all we could to keep sane, but in fact the chaos and the disorder drove us on.

We printed the first issue a week before the launch. We got

copies round to agencies. The Body Shop were set to distribute copies through their shops outside London and Phil had organised the first team of vendors. We were ready for 11 September; we had successfully achieved what we thought might have been impossible. The Body Shop PR team worked themselves into a frenzy.

And the morning of 11 September arrived.

At the radio station after the event, the interviewer Michael Parkinson praised the magazine. I went on about what we intended to do. How we were going to give homeless people an alternative to begging. We were not going to get rid of homelessness, but we were going to give homeless people another way of making money.

But the man with the dog had rattled me. Didn't he know that I was not some well-heeled member of the concerned classes? Would I have to put up with thousands of homeless people seeing me as a do-gooder? Or an exploiter, out to use them? How many battles would I have to fight because people saw me as some privileged person, lifted from the everyday and put on a plinth?

I wanted the man with the dog to know that I was irrepressible. That I couldn't be ground down. That I was never going to give in. And that that was what had got me to this position, out of dereliction.

But in the car driving back to the office I realised that it had taken more than an ability to bounce back, to seize opportunity. It had taken more than that. It had taken some luck. Had I not met Gordon back in the sixties, none of this would have happened. Without luck, I would still be poring over my notebooks, planning some great magazine that might never see the light of day.

Yes, some luck just about summed it all up.